SKYE

DEREK COOPER

Birlinn

This Edition published in 1995 by
Birlinn Ltd,
13 Roseneath Street,
Edinburgh EH9 1JH

© Derek Cooper, 1970, 1995

ISBN 1 874744 37 8

A CIP record of this book is available
from the British Library

Designed and typeset by The Image & Print Group Ltd
Typeset in Plantin, Centaur Swash & Avenir

Made and printed in Finland by WSOY

Contents

Illustrations

Illustrations in the text

Plates

Preface

What I set out to do in the 1960s when I began to compile this book was to anatomise the unique attraction of Skye's 430,000 acres of magic. No other off-shore island has excited such attention; it is as if Skye were possessed of a numinous quality denied to lesser places. Even a short exposure to this extraordinary island's charm can produce a state of euphoria which has been diagnosed as Skye-fever, a malaise which, if you are fortunate, is incurable. Wilfrid Gibson in one of his poems describes Skye as 'the witch'. A brooding witch you may think if you only see her in foul weather, but when in Gibson's words 'she unveils her beauty to the light' she becomes the most enchanting witch of the western seas.

Although the island has not changed physically in the last 35 years there are signs everywhere of what in material terms might be seen as progress. A bridge now connects Skye to the mainland; there are roll on-roll off car ferries at Uig and Armadale. Three decades of roadworks have straightened dangerous bends and speeded up traffic no end.

The island's capital, Portree, has acquired suburbs and an edge-of-town supermarket with automatic doors. When this book was first published there was nowhere to land an aircraft. A runway was built and for a time planes flew back and forth to Glasgow. The airstrip is still here but the air link has been withdrawn. There were not enough passengers to justify the expense.

In the 1980s aquaculture came to Skye and filled the sea lochs with salmon cages. Crofters now talk expertly of feeding regimes, stocking densities, growth rate analysis and the depredations of furunculosis. The oil industry in its boom days provided bulging pay packets for those prepared to go and work in the construction yards and on the North Sea platforms.

9

There is talk of a second bonanza yet to come in the stormier and deeper waters of the Minch. Industrial estates in various parts of the island reflect the entrepreneurial spirit of the age. The old Highlands and Islands Development Board has given way to a local organisation called Skye & Lochalsh Enterprise dedicated to creating business opportunities.

On the surface Skye has slipped effortlessly into the new scenario of consumerism. Tourism once a seasonal diversion in the crofting year has become in the upbeat language of the local enterprise company a 'linchpin' of the economy. 'Crafts' once an eccentric fringe activity is now formally recognised as a main industry. Every township has those who toil at pewter and silver jewellery, pottery, woven things, etchings, woodcraft, candles, the painting of stones and the silk-screening of T-shirts with Celtic motifs.

The rise and rise of Enterprise has been marked by a gradual erosion of the Sabbath. Sutherland's garage in Broadford piously shut on Sundays when this book was written now advertises '24 hour shopping 363 days of the year'. There are boat trips for visitors on Sundays and locals go windsurfing; the rasp of the corncrake has been replaced by the hoovering sound of the Flymo and the hornet whir of the strimmer.

'Widening tourism opportunities' is the goal of the Nineties. Vegetarian guesthouses, snackbars, new restaurants and cafés abound. More seems to have happened in the last thirty years in Skye than in the previous hundred. The pursuit of 'Heritage' is reflected in the profusion of old crofthouse museums filled with bygones and nostalgic remainders of poverty and deprivation. The Victorian fever hospital in Portree is now an arts centre. There's a fine interpretive centre, Dualchas an Eilein, which tells the island story in vivid audio-visual imagery. There have been other notable advances on the cultural front. At Dunvegan castle the Chief of the Clan Macleod, a professional bass baritone, presides over an annual music festival now in its fifteenth year.

The creation of Sabhal Mor Ostaig, a college committed to the Gaelic cause with its *sgriobhadair* or writer-in-residence, its annual *feis* or music festival, its seminars and post-graduate courses has placed Skye at the centre of the Gaelic renaissance and the move to establish a dynamic University of the Highlands & Islands.

The Gaelic rock band Runrig founded in Skye has shot into the charts. The island now has its own museums service, its first publishing house and a BBC studio. In Sleat the Clan Donald Trust set up in 1971 has revitalised the gardens and woodlands round Armadale castle and its achievements in architectural restoration and conservation over the last quarter of a century have earned it over a dozen national awards.

One of the most significant events in the postwar years was the emergence in 1972 of the campaigning, radical *West Highland Free Press*. With its offices in Skye the Wee Paper as it came to be known gave the whole west coast a new and abrasive forum for public debate. This award-winning weekly provoked discussion, fought battles on behalf of its readers and encouraged the adrenalin of controversy to flow as it hadn't done since the crofters' revolt in the 1880s. The paper unleashed a new spirit of optimism in the community and gave the Hebrides its own brash and irreverent *Private Eye*.

This outburst of political and social activity has been accompanied by a small but significant increase in the population. When I was a child in the 1920s there were 11,000 people in Skye. By 1970 the numbers had declined to around 7,000. The 1981 census revealed the first upward turn in a history of depopulation which had begun in the famine years of the 1840s. Today Skye has the fastest growing population in the Highlands and Islands, the island is now more alive and well than it has been for a long time.

When Hugh Andrew of Birlinn was thinking about reprinting this book we discussed the practicality of revising it and bringing it a bit more up to date. I persuaded him, I hope wisely, that we should leave it be as a portrait illustrating the resilience of Skye and its capacity to endure. Its beauty, as I wrote then, will be here long after we are gone and long after we are gone the magic will remain.

Derek Cooper
Portree, Skye
April 1995

Skye – A View

In the summer of 1969 for the first time I saw the Isle of Skye from the air. I had sailed to Skye often enough; during a wet winter in war-time I'd even sailed round it, but until that moment I had never looked down on it and perhaps never again will I have such a dramatic view. The Cuillins were crowned with a grey cauliflower of cloud, but from Beinn na Caillich north the whole Eastern seaboard lay basking in the afternoon sun. Within the space of a few minutes Loch Eynort, then the great bulk of Glamaig, Loch Sligachan, the houses of Portree, the twin Storr Lochs, shallow curved Staffin bay and the northern cliffs of Rudha Hunish unwound six miles below like some skilfully constructed cyclorama. The American craning for a view in the seat ahead of me turned back and said, 'My, that looks bare, is that some kind of desert isle?'

'No,' I said, 'that's Skye, the misty isle.'

'Skye? Some place. I wonder who'd want to live right out there in the middle of nowhere?'

'I wouldn't mind living there – I did live there once, about thirty years ago.' 'Ah well,' he said, looking at his elaborate watch, 'it's not far from London,' and he returned to his paperback as the waterlogged bogland of Lewis slid under the port wing and the Boeing headed north to the polar waste on its paradoxical flight west to California.

But to get to Skye from the south takes far longer than an hour normally. If you come from London by train it takes all night and you don't reach Mallaig or Kyle of Lochalsh, the jumping-off points for the island, until early afternoon on the following day. By car it's a 630-mile drive from London, so that arriving in Skye presents something of an achievement especially during the summer months when there may be a two-hour wait for the ferry at Kyle or Kylerhea. When the bridge comes and when the airstrip is built the journey will be much easier and the short sea trip to Skye will be no more than a romantic memory of the past, a vanished bottleneck.

Perhaps Skye itself is little more than a romantic memory of the past, an island worn down by two centuries of mismanagement and neglect. 'Skye,' a friend of mine insists, 'is a distressed area.' His thesis is that the whole of this north-western corner of Scotland was deliberately devastated in the eighteenth century and allowed to drift along in the nineteenth – a bleak and wild region far too distant to be of concern in Westminster.

Even though today Skye exhibits all the signs of an affluent consumer society, his thesis has some foundation in truth. After Culloden the declared policy of both Whigs and Tories was to break up the clan system, extirpate the Gaelic language and damp down the fires of rebellion. The old system where the land had belonged to the clan or family and the Chief's prosperity was the clan's prosperity had bestowed dignity on the individual clansman. In return for supporting his Chief he was fed and clothed and housed and got his share of what was going. What was going in those wild days was theft, and almost incessant internecine warfare – a violent aggressiveness the remnants of which can still be observed on Saturday nights in Glasgow. For centuries clan warfare disfigured the Highlands in a pageant of horrific butchery that makes Elizabethan revenge tragedy look like drawing-room farce. The archetypal Skye vendetta would involve eye-gouging, burning a church full of worshippers, the suffocation of the survivors by lighting a fire at the mouth of their cave of refuge, stabbing one's guests one by one after a banquet and finally a pitched battle fought until the last MacDonald was slain by the last MacLeod.

This period of savagery which began with the invasion of the Norsemen at the end of the eighth century lasted until the beginning of the seventeenth century when life became comparatively peaceful and the only excitement was a bit of mild rieving. Compared with the days when one clan was struggling to gain ascendancy over another it was a soft and idle time, even though the latent capacity for inflicting destruction still remained – perhaps its last and most dramatic manifestation was in the valley of Glencoe on the cold morning of 13 February 1692.

But after the Jacobite defeat at Culloden in 1746 the clan system began to wither and no vital alternative emerged to replace it. The Chiefs were degraded to the position of landlords, their kinsmen became tacksmen or gentlemen farmers and the clansmen became either landless cottars or tenants who could be ejected from what little land they had at a moment's notice. The Chiefs, with some notable exceptions, abrogated their responsibilities and either let their estates or left them in charge of factors who were seldom noted for their humanity. Those who clung to their lands became no more than rent collectors. A by-product of the breakdown of the clan system was the anglicization of those who formerly held power. They either aspired to, or were encouraged to aspire to, a Lowland or English education for their sons, who acquired an expensive knowledge of Latin and Greek and forgot their native Gaelic. The Highland laird with his Oxford accent and Wykehamist tie and the Pakistani brigadier with his Sandhurst manners and Guards drawl are both in their way interesting tributes to the capacity of the English for moulding the élite of a dependent territory into carbon copies of themselves.

When Dr. Samuel Johnson arrived in Skye the rot had already set in. Emigration had begun three decades before and the exodus which a succession of bad winters, poor harvests and cattle sickness had started, was intensified by the advent of the Highlander's blank-faced four-footed enemy – the devastating Cheviot sheep. The logic behind sheep-farming was economically irrefutable. Here you had a tough animal which could roam the hills in all weathers, growing its wool and fattening itself and, apart from lambing and shearing, requiring very little attention. It was not subject to diseases like murrain, which could wipe out a valuable herd of cattle overnight, and it could be reared in such large numbers that even decimation of a flock would not prove an irreversible disaster. An intelligent unpaid dog could do most of the legwork and a shepherd imported from the South could do the rest. The only slight snag to the efficient operation of Skye as one glorious and profitable sheep-farm was the indigenous population who seemed far too insistent on staying where they and their families had lived for generations – but once the people had been persuaded to surrender their congested lands to the sheep all would be well. Persuasion took many forms. First an appeal was made to the Skyeman's patriotism; if he really loved his native land, he was told, he would pack up his possessions and embark on one of the sailing transports which could be arranged to ship him conveniently from the nearest bay. Not only would this demonstrate his determination to make good but it would stiffen his moral fibre. It didn't really matter where he went – Canada, America, Australia, New Zealand – the great thing was that he should go, and go without any fuss. If persuasion failed then the factor might, more in sorrow than in anger, be forced to evict a tenant and perhaps set the roof of his hut on fire as a practical hint that however tough it was going to be overseas at least he would be harassed by savages and not by his own kith and kin.

It is from these days, and particularly from the nineteenth century when emigration both forced and voluntary reached its peak, that the great Gaelic poetry of longing-for-home stemmed. As whole families marched down to the transports in the bays of Skye an almost unspeakable sadness was born. Convinced by specious reports of the Utopia that lay over the horizon and the slow realization that only poverty and destitution faced them in Skye they set sail with their Bibles, their bolls of meal and their bundles of clothing and left their glens to the sheep.

Some refused to go. The old and the dogged stayed despite the uncertainty, and those who hoped for better times stayed with them. A temporary respite in the evacuation had come at the turn of the nineteenth century when kelp started fetching high prices. Many landowners, anxious then for willing hands to collect seaweed, began to discourage emigration and encourage early marriages by offering young men land on which to build a home. The population decline had been temporarily arrested and by the time Victoria ascended the throne it reached its highest recorded peak. But by then Hebridean kelp was no longer wanted and the kelp collectors were wanted even less.

Efforts were made once again by landowners to free themselves of their unwanted tenants. Once again all the righteous reasons were advanced to convince the poor and the landless – the feckless and the shiftless as many philanthropists saw them – that it was their moral duty to leave with as little delay as possible. Had they been leaving squalor and ugliness behind them the going might have been easier. But the sun always seemed to be shining when the emigrant ships lay at anchor in the bay. Skye would never look so beautiful again.

The visible signs of the evictions – the Clearances as they were called – can be seen to this day. All over Skye are the traces of former habitation – here the foundations of a wall, a clump of hazel and a pile of rubble; over there the outlines of what was once a house. In some places one can stand high in a glen and look down on the remains of a whole township evacuated overseas a hundred and fifty years ago. The tumbled stones of a hearth down by the rocks mark where a family, denied land, built themselves a shelter on the edge of the sea. Not every ruin is the mark of emigration overseas: many people dispossessed of their homes got no further than Glasgow and ended their lives in a slum tenement.

The injustice and cruelty of the evictions continued until well within living memory. As I write there is still a man living in the village of Stein in Skye who remembers being evicted from his home as a child while his father was taken to Inverness to await trial as an agitator. For those who had been forced to leave, Skye became a focus of nostalgia and all the melancholy of the dispossessed. When the immigrant felt immortal longings creep upon him they were crystallized in a longing for Skye. Not the island too barren and rainwashed to support a large population but a Skye transfigured in his dreams into an enchanted isle of lost content.

The first generation passed their longing on to the second and the second down to the third. And so today you will still find Canadian MacLeods and New Zealand MacKinnons with their alien overseas accents looking for their roots in Glendale or Sleat. A Canadian I met recently had gone to great lengths to reclaim his past: 'We wrote a letter to your *Stornoway Gazette* and we had the pleasure of corresponding with some very helpful folks but we've drawn a blank here in Kilmuir. They left, my MacLean forebears, about 1860 I guess, but there just don't seem to be any records of who they were or what they did – coming back here is like knowing that this is where you belong; but then you come up against a blank wall and the past is — well, wiped out!'

Although Lord MacDonald has no trouble in tracing his ancestry back in an undisturbed line to Somerled Lord of the Isles and though the Macleods of Dunvegan have a family tree rooted in a thirteenth-century Leod, the majority of their clansmen who were forced overseas were severed as sharply from their ancestry as if cut off by an umbilical knife. But the nostalgia persists. The Australian from Orbost in Victoria will feel some kind of stirrings as he stands in Orbost, Skye, and the Canadian from Uigg in Nova Scotia will wonder as he looks out over Uig Bay in Skye what his great-great-grandmother must have felt as she left the island for ever. Skye continues to cast a spell and, like a lodestone in the Hebridean seas, she has the power to attract men back from all over the world.

A few years ago I was driving from Upper Ollach to Portree and under the shadow of Ben Lee, where the Braes crofters fought their small but decisive battle for land reform, I saw an old car with Minnesota number-plates parked at the side of the road. A few yards away a portly figure, cigar clamped in his lips, horn-rimmed glasses glinting in the rays of the dying sun, was stacking peats. 'Hi'! he said. The accent was richly American. Then in case I hadn't the gift of English he added in Gaelic: *'Ciamar a tha sibh?'* When he gathered I had no Gaelic he puffed out a dense smoke-screen from his cigar, loofahed his face with a bandana and said: 'These goddamed midges, they've got teeth like goddamed killer sharks.' It turned out that his great-grandparents had emigrated from Braes to Prince Edward Island and he had been brought up in a Gaelic-speaking household. Even after half a lifetime in Canada and the States he could still pass more than the time of day in Gaelic. When he retired he decided to return to Skye and settle where he felt his roots ought to be: 'We've spent a winter here, Mamie and I, but I get the feeling that Mamie's hankering for Minneapolis, so maybe we'll be going soon.'

The repatriate American-Canadian with his Gaelic carefully preserved like a talisman is today something of an oddity, but it's well to remember that once in Skye Gaelic was the only language of general communication – eighteenth-century travellers had as much chance of understanding the natives as they would have done in darkest Africa. There are no people left in the island now who don't speak English; but for many, particularly among the older generation, Gaelic is still their first language, a rich language full of words and phrases which have no direct equivalent in English and for which the language of the South is a poor substitute. Although the attempt to revive an interest in Gaelic is meeting with some success, most holiday-makers will not hear it spoken in Skye unless they overhear it – in the presence of the stranger, English is used as a matter of courtesy. Today Gaelic is in danger of becoming a cult language, but for a long time knowledge of Gaelic was regarded as a hindrance not a help. The language learnt at one's mother's knee had to be replaced as soon as possible by English, and many visitors went out of their way to report the comic effects achieved by a Celt having his first stab at English. *Punch,* which has a long tradition of laughing at people who try to get above themselves, was able to add an entirely new dimension to its repertoire of hilarity:

Old Gent: 'When is the steamer due here?'
Highland Pier master: 'Various. Sometimes sooner, some-times earlier, an' even sometimes before that too.'

And there was Donald and his comical friend Dougal slowly struggling to express themselves in the language of the folk who came to stay in the lodge:

Tugal: 'Dud ye'll ever see the *I-oo-na* any more before?'
Tonal: 'Surely I was.'
Tugal: 'Ay Ay! Maybe you was never on poard too, after this . . . ?'
Tonal: 'I dud!'

The Gaelic speaker wrestling with the intricacies of English led to what one might call the *Och Och* school of writing in which the utterances of the peasants were interpreted phoneti-cally to the point of tedium. Presidency of the *Och Och* school of reportage must go to Mary Donaldson, author of *Wanderings in the Western Highlands,* who was able to reproduce page after page of *Och Och* effortlessly — like this monologue from an old woman in Broadford:

Ochain, and if *Prionnsa Tearlach* chust wass lifing now! It wass he that was ta peautiful lad of ta yellow locks that wass aalways in ta Highland heart! There wass no tays like when he wass in ta Highlands, but it iss pack again he will pe coming to ta land he wass aalways loving. Yess, yess, he will pe coming pack, and it iss ta Highlanders that will pe rising again to pe giving him ta welcome of ta heart!

Ochain, what with radio and television Skye people have long since abandoned this eccentric mode of address – which is a pity because it must have given no end of pleasure to the visitors. The English have always had a patient contempt for those unable to master their language and have never been able to take either simple Paddy with his pig in the Irish bog or Tonal, the lovable illiterate Highland gillie without a certain amount of indulgent levity. Even today a feeling persists that somehow the quality of life in an island like Skye must be intellectually enervating and that unless one has proved oneself in the largely English-dominated outside world one is a bit of a failure. This myth is bolstered by the sad economic fact that Skye is unable to support the majority of young people she produces. Large numbers of boys and girls who leave Portree High School and graduate in universities and training colleges will never be able to work in their native island. An outstanding academic career is an almost automatic disqualification from finding suitable work in Skye and the most promising and potentially valuable representatives of each generation have had to emigrate to make the best use of their talents. Today, as in the past, Skye's main export is ability.

Nowadays Skye can afford to employ only two lawyers, two veterinary surgeons, two dentists, one chemist, one architect and one chartered accountant. If a young Skye girl becomes a nurse it will almost inevitably mean that her career will be on the mainland, and if she becomes a doctor she will have to compete with the men for one of the seven jobs on the island. Even when it comes to teaching there are only 77 posts available in Skye's 20 schools and for those who have a call to the ministry there are only 17 numbered among the chosen. There are of course large numbers of professions unrepresented in Skye and although I'm told one man does sit programming computers in a crofthouse somewhere in Sleat, he is a lucky exception.

As the young depart because they are ambitious and the old stay because they are set in their ways, Skye has perpetually an imbalanced population with a higher average age than the Lowlands or England. This population is still largely dependent on the land for some if not all its income. Crofting ranges from the family which may keep a few hens and grow a patch of potatoes to the dozen or so crofters who have secured enough land to enable them to become full-time farmers. The small croft, which a century ago might have provided a family with most of the essentials of life, is now very often no more than a piece of inherited ground on which stands the family house and from which the crofter goes out to find his real income. He may work on the road, drive a van, run a store, work in the post-office or derive a living in the summer by offering some form of service to the tourist. It is tourism that has changed life in Skye and brought a new and unexpected prosperity.

Tourism itself has changed its pattern several times since visitors first began to arrive in noticeable numbers. The early travellers came for specific purposes – to study the primitive customs and manners of the aborigines or the unique geology of the area. Others came to report on the island's potential as a fishing base or a source of settlers for the overseas territories. Curiosity brought Dr. Johnson as it brought Pennant and other eighteenth-century pilgrims. In the early nineteenth century Walter Scott published *Lord of the Isles* and turned Skye from a mere place into a shrine of romantic myth and legend. Skye of course was still a difficult island to get to. An uncomfortable journey by post-chaise was followed, unless one had letters of introduction to the quality, by an uncomfortable stay in the island's few and filthy inns. But the introduction of the 'swift' steamer ('swift' indicating that it permitted itself only a few scheduled stops and was therefore, to within a few hours, punctual) meant that passengers could embark in Glasgow and make their way comfortably over the sea to Skye – depending of course on the weather. When Queen Victoria and Prince Albert took their first cruise up the West Coast of Scotland it quickly became their first and *only* cruise. The weather was appalling and the Royal party turned back. Had that summer been a fair one, had the seas been calm and the sunsets fiery it is more than likely that Vicky, entranced with the bogus Gothic battlements of Dunvegan and Armadale, might have persuaded Albert that Skye would be a fine place in which to build a Highland seat. It would have been comparatively easy for Lyon King of Arms to trace a genealogy back to some notable Skye chieftain, perhaps even to Finn himself. The royal yacht would have been on hand to carry the Court on Progresses through the Islands, there could have been Fleet manoeuvres in the Minch, and in later years the Royal gillie stumping round Windsor might have been not glum John Brown but a MacDonald from Sleat. Perhaps the Isle of Skye and not the Isle of Wight might have been chosen for the final retirement.

But the Royal family beat a hasty retreat from Western waters and when they heard from the Court Physician that he had enjoyed a spectacular summer on Deeside while they had been exposed to the Hebridean blasts, Albert's mind was made up. They settled for Balmoral, and all thoughts of the West were abandoned. Even so the Royal family's choice of the Highlands as a suitable place for relaxation and recuperation conferred recognition on the whole area. Some wealthy brewers and the new industrial aristocracy built themselves shooting lodges for the annual slaughter on the moors, others came to be braced both spiritually and physically. Nowadays it is only Americans who can talk with a straight face about scenery being 'truly inspirational' but the Victorians derived unashamed satisfaction from the Highland landscape and the sublimity of its hills and mountains.

Skye, having the most awe-inspiring mountain range in Britain, became a particular focus of attention. At the height of the Victorian cult of tartan and heather the Cuillins swarmed with long-skirted women and tweed-clad men admiring the grandeur wrought by the Great Architect. By now the steam strain had pushed through to Strome Ferry, and instead of the long sea voyage from Glasgow, rail passengers were brought rapidly to the shores of Loch Carron where a swift steamer would bear them and their portmanteaux, their wicker picnic-baskets and Gladstone bags to Portree or Broadford. Despite the comparative difficulties of getting about the island the Victorians found plenty to amuse themselves. There were daily expeditions to the Quiraing and walks through the Cuillins, and when scrambling amid the hills palled there were ammonites to be collected, flowers to be pressed, birds to be watched. Between the conspicuous consumption of three-volume novels and the pursuit of sometimes conversation and sometimes salmon the time passed quickly.

There was a certain number of excursions to be undertaken, but in those days Dunvegan castle was not among them – it was either let to shooting tenants or in the possession of the family, who were not desperately keen to surrender their privacy for half-crowns.

Before the advent of the car, holiday-making in Skye was fairly lengthy – a month was not considered too long. For artists the continually changing cloudscapes, and the gratifying bourgeois demand for Highland Landscapes were an exciting challenge. William Daniell in the reign of George IV had not bothered much with clouds; he was more concerned with the accurate delineation of peaks and crags and the judicious if false embellishment of his views with plaid-draped shepherds and pastoral wenches. Turner was the first major artist to attempt a frontal assault on the mysteries of the inner Cuillins. His smoke-wreathed, tortured vision of Coruisk inspired so many imitators that before long a bearded Victorian landscape artist was perched on every accessible pinnacle, and down in the glens Royal Academicians with no head for heights were hard at work immortalizing the deer and the shaggy cattle.

For decades Skye was exclusively a middle and upper-class haunt, but holidays with pay and the advent of first the charabanc and then the mass-produced family car drove the wealthy away and opened the island to hikers and the motorist. The novelty of motoring has not yet worn off and driving through 'scenery' still seems to be an end in itself. 'We didn't realize Skye was so small,' a driver told me this summer as we sat in the queue at Kyleakin waiting to cross to the mainland, 'we came on Tuesday and in two days we've seen the whole island; now we're going to tour up to Ullapool.' No statistics are available but a survey of holiday-makers would more than likely confirm that the average time spent on Skye is three days. This figure wouldn't include the large number who leave their car in Kyle, cross over the ferry, have a cup of tea in Kyleakin, post a few cards 'frae the misty isle' and return happy to have been on Skye.

It is theoretically possible to see Skye from a moving car, if the windows aren't too steamed up, but it's not the best way. The roads have been so improved in the last twenty years that many motorists find themselves unable to resist the temptation to drive at top speed past everything worth a closer look. If you want to get some idea of what Skye roads were like before the internal combustion engine took over from the pony, pause on the new stretch of road which runs over the moors from Loch Ainort to Sconser – here three generations of roads can be seen at once. To the east is the old unmetalled earth track hardly wider than a cart and dating from the early days of the nineteenth century. It was so precipitous that many people in Skye still remember having to get out and walk behind a charabanc as it wheezed and strained up the steeper braes. This was replaced by a comparatively level but narrow coastal road with magnificent views of Scalpay and the south end of Raasay. Finally the new wide road, a beautifully engineered invitation to speed.

Many Skye roads are still only wide enough to take one car at a time but they are gradually being improved and soon no doubt it will be possible to 'do' Skye in a day. Even now it would take you only two or three hours to drive from Ardvasar in the south to the point where you can look out to the lonely Shiants and beyond that, nothing but deep rolling sea until the pack ice of the Arctic Ocean. But the real Skye is not to be seen from behind the wheel of a car.

And what is the real Skye? Some people find it on the top of a Cuillin pinnacle, others at the end of a fishing line or at the end of a hard day's walking. Certainly for scenic beauty Skye is spectacular. Like most islands the view from the sea is the most striking and the great cliffs of Trotternish or Dunvegan or Waterstein as they fall sheer into the clear green water are a majestic sight. But the particular charm of the island is created by a combination of land, sea and cloud. Visually Skye is dominated by the Cuillins, that huge mass of ancient rounded slopes and jagged peaks rising nearly two-thirds of a mile into frequently dramatic skies. In brisk weather the clouds conjure with them so that they are constantly disappearing and emerging; never for two minutes at a time is their profile the same. On sunny days the colouring on these hills is so complex that no painter has ever packed up his easel after a day in the Cuillins and gone away completely happy. Because they squat on Skye in such prominence and are viewable from all points of the compass there's an unfinished argument about where to go to see them at their most impressive. Are they best seen across Portree bay just before sunset when the extraordinary clarity of the light brings every fissure into relief and they seem only a few hundred yards and not nine miles away? Or is it from Tarskavaig across the choppy waters of Loch Slapin, or from Loch Harport, or Elgol or from Sligachan or some vantage point on the mainland – or is the climber on the summit of Bidean Druim nan Ramh or Sgurr a' Mhadaidh more likely to see them in full grandeur? They are the most photographed 'Inferior Mountains' in Britain but no photograph gives more than a diagram of their splendour.

My own feeling is that the Cuillins are seen at their finest across the water, and water plays such a large part in the creation of Skye's particular magic that it seems all the more sad that the sea is no longer the great highway it was in the past. To sit in one's car and be ferried back to the mainland at Kyleakin or Kylerhea is a prosaic way to leave Skye. What Auden called 'the bitter suction of goodbye' is reduced to a minimum, and before your ticket has been bought you're over the ramp, up the slip and off on the open road with hardly a backward glance. In the days when the steamer had the bulk of the passengers and cargo, leaving a place like Portree was an event. One got up in the dark and made one's way down the Quay Brae to the pier with its lights still burning in the vacuum between night and day. There were people to see one off and there was the whole eastern coast of Skye to sail down before one eventually berthed at Kyle. A clergyman, the Rev. J. F. Marshall, recalled those pre-war departures in a poem which ends:

> The daylight strengthens, and the sirens sound;
> The last rope splashes, and the engines churn;
> The quayside fades. O misty isle, it seems
> As if no time to leave thee could be found
> More fitting than the hour in which men turn
> From sleeping, and reluctant, lose their dreams.

Even if these days one has less opportunity to admire Skye from the sea, it still has a ubiquitous presence. Although it's only 50 miles as the crow flies from Rudha Hunish in the north to the Aird of Sleat, the deeply indented coastline is several hundred miles in length. It's not so much as if Skye were surrounded by water but constantly violated by it. No place is more than five miles from the water's edge and the sea lochs are often so large and irregular that even with the aid of a map it's sometimes difficult to make out exactly where one is. Lochs like Dunvegan and Bracadale are sprinkled with unexpected islands which add even more variety to the scene.

The land itself has a variety which would be hard to duplicate on the mainland. The crofts with their small acreages of hay, corn and arable crops form a brilliant summer jigsaw in the glens. The whitewashed houses set out like toyshop models on the hillside are patchworked by a kaleidoscope of greens, browns and brilliant yellows merging into the darker purple of the hills. The first thing that strikes a visitor is the way in which each part of the island has an individual identity. Sleat, Kilmuir, Waternish and Glendale are so different that they might be separate islands and if you look at the map you'll notice that the sea would have to edge in only a few miles here and there to make them into islands on their own.

Nowhere else in the whole of Britain is there so much contrast in one small area. There's moor, mountains, long winding valleys, fertile glens, fjords with steep sides and dark waters, sweeping bays, monstrously sculpted rocks and pinnacles, plunging water-falls and silent tarns where trout jump among the lilies. There is above all an incredible beauty of light. Far away from industrial smog the clear northern light has in the summer a luminous qual-ity. The sea really is postcard blue, the sunsets really are off the cover of a box of chocolates and even when the mist smokes over the hills there's an intensity of colour which one rarely finds in the south. In the long days of June there is no real darkness, only a period of twilight – an hour before and an hour after midnight – a bonus which is rudely snatched away in the winter.

Now that a holiday has come to mean risking third-degree burns on an overcrowded Mediterranean beach Skye is perhaps an unreliable, even a capricious place, to go for an overall tan. But, in 1968 when all over England an unending downpour of rain fell from porridge-coloured skies, the Hebrides basked in sunshine. In 1969 when it poured with rain on the Costa Brava, Skye was basking in an Easter heat-wave. Don't be put off by people who tell you that it's always raining in Skye. It can be so hot in May that the tar melts on the roads, so warm in November that men work in the fields in shirt sleeves.

Looking at the weather records the only predictability that emerges is unpredictability: in the last 50 years each of the 12 months has at some time been the wettest month of the year. Optimism is the right frame of mind to adopt; if it's raining when you wake up then it's bound to clear before noon and even if it's still raining in the afternoon it will be a fine evening and a dry tomorrow. My great-aunt, a Lewis woman by birth but Skye by adoption, had the right attitude to moisture: there was no rain only showers, and showers were only passing mist and in any case, the mist was warm and never harmed anyone.

Eilean a' Cheo, the Isle of Mist, was an unfortunate invention of the days when mist was regarded as attractively romantic. The Rev. J. A. MacCulloch, a Rector of St. Columba's Church, Portree, at the turn of the century, wrote a popular account of the island which was published under the title *The Misty Isle of Skye*, and the island has been stuck with the slur ever since; there's even a hotel in Dunvegan trading on this unfortunate misnomer – 'The Misty Isle' it calls itself, unmindful of the coach trade which wants to see scenery not mist. There is mist, of course, and it might, if you were unlucky, be possible to spend a holiday in Skye and never see the Cuillins fully revealed, but then what better excuse for coming again next year?

In any case Skye is not at its best in brilliant sunshine. It needs clouds and mist as Greece needs blue skies. Having been brought up in Britain, I like my weather to be noticeable. Although I enjoy the days when the island basks under the sun, the hay is dry the moment it's cut and old men fan themselves and grumble that unless it rains the salmon will never get a run up the rivers, I don't resent the rain, it's all part of the magic.

Another part of the magic is the remoteness and peace which is drawing more and more people every year away from the over-crowded south. The entire population of Skye would only fill one-quarter of the seats in London's White City Stadium, and even in the height of summer with perhaps an additional two or three thousand visitors in the island it remains relatively empty. Economic geography dictates that the Islands will remain empty. There have been visionary schemes in the past, but they never amounted to more than a rustling of blueprints. There was the British Fisheries Society's eighteenth-century scheme to set up a fishing station at Stein, there was Lord MacDonald's early nine-teenth-century dream for a vast town to be built at Kyleakin, there was a late nineteenth-century plan to build a railway through Skye; there have been other projects, but none of them has come to anything. The saddest example of this kind of misplaced zeal lies not in Skye but rusting on the shores of South Harris at Leverburgh, where a pile of bollards and a half-built pier mark the last resting place of Lord Leverhulme's hopes of bring-ing industry to the Outer Isles.

But optimism still exists in the highest quarters that emigra-tion will be arrested and what is now described as Counterdrift will occur. In January 1966 a White Paper prepared by the

Secretary of State for Scotland and subtitled 'A Plan for Expansion' suggested that Portree might expand from its then population of 1,800 to 5,500 by 1970. What these 3,700 extra bodies would do for a living or where they would come from was not specified. The breathtaking concept of Portree not only doubling but trebling in size caught my fancy and over the years I looked for signs that the Secretary of State's vision was about to come to pass. None was forthcoming. When at the end of 1969 I wrote to his office to ask how and when the miracle would be achieved, they could only admit that hope for a miracle was not the same as working one. 'In the event,' I was told, 'industry ran down further than had been anticipated and it has proved necessary to extend the time scale envisaged in the White Paper.' The epitaph for many an ambitious plan to reverse the tide of emigration in the Highlands and Islands could perhaps not be better expressed; 'In the event . . .'

I don't subscribe to the theory that Skye is going to double its population overnight or, if a bridge is built, be ruined by tourism. It is a paradoxical fact that the tourist, who some people feel is destroying the real values of life in Skye, is in reality largely responsible for keeping so many people on the island. Many a Skye housewife would have less money in the winter if it weren't for her summer bed-and-breakfasts; hoteliers and tradesmen and everyone involved in the service industries go heavier to the bank when the ferries are working overtime. But tourism is not welcomed unreservedly. The Free Churches see it as a potentially corrupting influence.

To this day no MacBrayne's transport moves on sea or land on the Sabbath and many people still respect the literal command to keep holy the Sabbath of the Lord their God. Shops are heavily shuttered, bed-and-breakfast signs removed or discreetly covered with a piece of sacking, restaurants owned by members of the Free Churches close early on Saturday and remain shut until Monday. In the old days when there was little communication with the outside world restrictions were even more severe. 'The power of the pulpit,' as the nineteenth century divine Dr. John Kennedy noted, 'was paramount and the people became to a great extent, plastic to its influence. The preachers could mould the opinions and habits of their hearers without any counter-acting influences to distort the impression which they desired to produce.'

Today the licensing laws have been relaxed so that anybody who wants to can drink on the Sabbath, the ferry at Kyle brings cars to and from the island on the Sabbath and television shines brightly seven nights a week. There are many who feel that the repressive aspects of Presbyterianism have an undesirable economic effect on the communities it seeks to dominate. Fraser Darling's *West Highland Survey* stated unequivocally that 'our observations lead us to the opinion that a very small and remote community would have greater chance of survival if it were Catholic than if it followed one of the stricter sects of Presbyterianism'.

The fight to keep the old Skye from changing is now very much a rearguard action fought by a vociferous minority. Casual readers of such papers as the *Oban Times* and the *Stornoway Gazette* might be surprised at the colourful language of reports from the Free Presbytery of Skye. 'Skye Tourist Industry in Alien Hands' ran a funereal-black headline in 1968 which not only attacked the Highlands and Islands Development Board for trying to encourage visitors but also contained attacks on the Church of Scotland and 'the Harlot of Rome'. Romanism, Communism, Ecumenicalism are all seen by the more extreme religious leaders as major threats to survival as are 'God-denying psychiatrists', 'cheap, unclean press, radio and television' and other unleashers of the floodgates of evil.

There are people who would like to see Sunday distinguished from other days of the week, not solely for religious reasons, but because they feel emotionally that there ought to be one day not dedicated to 'getting and spending', one day on which everyone stops rushing about. Tourists used to a Continental Sunday may find the islands a dull place to be on the Sabbath; very often the only sign of indigenous life is the morning and evening procession in sober clothes to the substantial number of churches that rift and division have made necessary. Portree is still a long way from Paris and many hope the distance and, more importantly, the difference will be preserved.

But Skye is no longer the place it was ten years ago and ten years from now will no longer be the place it is today. This need not give rise to either regret or alarm or even misplaced tears of nostalgia. The beauty will be there long after we are gone and long after we are gone the magic will remain.

Gazetteer

Skye place-names are almost entirely of Norse or Gaelic origin and where possible some suggestion of how they may have got their name is given. But even the best etymologists don't always agree. Does, for instance, Breakish derive its name from the Norse *brekka*, a slope, or the Icelandic *brekka*, a hollow among the hills, or from the large number of smallpox *(a' bhreac)* victims who once lived there? No one can say for certain, but as many of the place-names in this book commemorate a local tradition or myth they are given more for their interest than their accuracy. As Alexander Forbes put it (and his *Place-Names of Skye* is the most ambitious source book on the subject): 'The study of place-names . . . is the study of history: names which are an atmosphere of legendary melody spread over the land, older than the epics and histories, which clothe a race like an under-shirt, or *leine-crios*, words which are dear to the gods'.

An approximation to the pronunciation of these place-names is also attempted. Where the name is acceptably anglicized, the anglicization is given but it is worth remembering that on the lips of a Gaelic speaker a Gaelic name is given its full value. It is impossible to convey the exact quality of Gaelic vowels and consonants in English phonetic spelling, so the guide is intended primarily for the English speaker who wants to have a reasonable crack at getting as near as possible to the local pronunciation. The system used is fairly obvious. Each word is divided into syllables, and the stressed syllable indicated in capital letters

| ch | is as in 'church' | ile | is as in 'file' |
| <u>ch</u> underlined | is as in Scottish 'loch' | ine | is as in 'pine' |

31

g	is as in 'get'	ome	is as in 'home'
j	is as in 'jet'	ore	is as in 'gore'
ire	is as in 'fire'	oe	is as in 'toe'

The lower case 'u' is used occasionally in unstressed syllables to convey the indeterminate vowel sound normally heard in words like '*a*bout', 'ev*er*', 'tru*a*nt', 'dem*o*n'. A lower case 'a' or 'o' appearing as an isolated syllable also serves this purpose.

A

Abhainn (AH-vayn) – a river, closely related to the English word *Avon*. There are few rivers of any significance in Skye, *Abhainn Shniosoirt*, the river Snizort being the longest. Second longest is the river Varragill, which drains into Loch Portree.

Absentee landlords were not in a position to influence events in Skye, and it must have come as a profound shock to a man like Lord MacDonald when the outside world was made aware at the height of the Clearances just how ruthlessly and remorselessly his notorious factor Ballingall had abused the very considerable powers entrusted to him. Educated in English schools and at English universities the Highland lairds were products more of England than their native glens, and few of them had any sense of identity with their tenantry or any feeling of responsibility for them. Absenteeism, encouraged by the breakdown of the old clan system, reached its height in the nineteenth century. In the year 1882, for instance, 365,762 acres of Skye were owned by five absentee landlords, among them the two hereditary overlords of Skye, MacLeod of MacLeod and Lord MacDonald.

Agitators were anathema to the Highland gentry in the nineteenth century. Many sober and responsible people felt that their campaign to get a more generous return for their labours and some security of tenure was against the common interest. History has shown that it was due solely to the 'agitators' both inside and outside Skye that Westminster eventually began to produce the legislation that brought to the crofters the rights already enjoyed by the rest of the country. Even as late as 1920 Mary Donaldson, author of *Wanderings in the Western Highlands and Islands,* was still not quite sure that all this unrest was a good thing:

33

Every Highlander [she wrote] must have an intense sympathy with every class of Highland people, not least with those, chiefs and people alike, who had a hard and continuous struggle to live in their several spheres. But the alien agitator has no claim other than that of impudence to be heard on the subject with which he has generally scarcely even a bowing acceptance. He is often a Cockney tourist taking an initial conventional tour of Scotland, charged to make facts, more often fallacies at the best, fit in with the theories with which his employers have stocked him. As a townsman, he is by the mere force of his upbringing incapable of understanding problems presented by the exigencies of country life since he has as much in common with a Highlander as a Hottentot. The life of a crofter is exactly suited to the Highland temperament, and, when bad days have fallen upon Skye, in both Lord MacDonald and the MacLeod the crofters have found kindly and sympathetic friends, always ready with a helping hand.

Aird of Sleat has the distinction of being the site of Skye's most southerly fort – Dun Ban is on the slope of a conspicuous rock about 50 ft. from the seashore; it is connected with the land on the north-west side by a narrow rocky ridge. *Aird* simply means a projecting piece of land, not necessarily a cliff.

Air travel to Skye was possible in the 'thirties when you could leave Renfrew at half-past nine in a De Havilland Rapide and be in Glen Brittle by eleven. The service was withdrawn mainly because the road was so bad from Glen Brittle that the advantages of a flight were outweighed by the remoteness of the arrival point. In the 'sixties the Royal Engineers were prepared to build an airstrip at Ashaig, near Broadford, but a violent controversy blew up between the pro-Ashaig faction and opinion in the north, which thought a strip at Skeabost would be more convenient. As agreement couldn't be reached the army went off and built a strip on the mainland. It wasn't until the beginning of 1969 that eventual agreement was reached for a strip to be built, where the Kylerhea road joins the Kyleakin-Broadford road, at an estimated cost of £35,000. The runway is 2,600 ft. long.

Allt (AA-oolt) – a mountain burn with steep banks. *Alltan* is a small burn. Lealt in Staffin takes its name from a burn, one of whose banks is flat; it is in fact a half-burn or in Gaelic *leth-allt,* hence Lealt.

Am Baisteir (um-BAAST-y(a)) (3,070 ft.) – the peak of the executioner. At the Sligachan end of the main Cuillin ridge.

Annait or **Annaid** (AH-nett) – is a word of obscure Celtic origin applied to places which are sacred either through their pagan or Christian connections. They usually lie beside a stream or at the junction of two streams. A mile north of the Fairy Bridge on the Portree-Dunvegan road is an enclosure which takes the form of a narrow triangle 200 ft. long and 165 ft. across the base. A ruined stone wall can be seen and the remains of what may have been domed cells. There are also the foundations of what might have been a church – bodies of unbaptized children were buried in this spot until the end of the last century. It was Dr Johnson who first advanced the theory that this was a Christian place of worship and not the temple of the Goddess Anaitis as was thought by local learned men at the time of his visit. Dr. Douglas Simpson, the distinguished archaeologist, has described Annait as 'beyond doubt one of the most important primitive Christian sites in the Hebrides. Until the time shall come when it will be possible to carry out a systematic and careful excavation its immunity is being jealously guarded under the provisions of the Ancient Monuments Act'.

Architecture in Skye dates from around 500 B.C. when the first duns or hill forts were constructed. The remains of these forts are found on sea-facing promontories all over the island. There are remains of five castles in Skye: Knock, Dunscaith, Duntulm, Maoil and Dunringill and the substantial, but substantially nineteenth-century, Dunvegan Castle. As there has never been much money in Skye there has never been any grand architecture. The exception is Armadale Castle, erected in the Regency period, which merits a separate entry. The thatched houses, the remains of which can be seen throughout the island and many of which are still in use as barns or cattle byres, were built of rocks and stones and were fairly rough and ready. Two-storeyed houses were uncommon in Skye and were attempted only by the gentry. The remains of Monkstadt house are a good example of this style of building, and Talisker House and Ord House, still inhabited today, are fairly representative of the square sturdy houses of the late eighteenth and nineteenth century, white-washed and roofed with thick Ballachulish slates.

The mid-nineteenth century saw the era of Lodge-building in Scotland, ornate country houses with their libraries, billiard- and smoking-rooms, set amid the deer and grouse moors. In Skye the majority of these shooting lodges have been turned into hotels, the most elegant example being Skeabost. The discovery of corrugated iron by the people of Skye ushered in a new era of construction which is best passed over, but the remains of roofs and sheds are scattered like rusty memorials to this latter Iron Age. Contemporary building is every-man-for-himself. Stucco, pine, imitation stonework, manufactured cladding are set incongruously down without any obvious thought or premeditation. The new rash of prefabricated bungalows in Portree which will remain uncamouflaged by trees for far too many years to come is symptomatic of the very worst kind of non-planning. The public buildings put up in recent years by the Inverness County Council probably looked fine on the drawing-board in an architect's office in the Highland capi-tal, but they seem to be conceived with no consideration either for the traditional buildings among which they will be set or the landscape around them. It is sad that in an island where every prospect pleases, man's contribution should be so vile.

Ardtreck Point At the entrance to Loch Harport. There's a dun or fort here on the west shore of the peninsula about half a mile south of the point. The ruins lie on the top of a stack of rock rearing in a precipice 50 ft. above the shore. The walls are over 8 ft. thick, and the traces of a gallery can still be seen.

Armadale – Perhaps the dale where the forces collected; the ancestral home of the MacDonalds and the Skye terminal for the Mallaig car ferry. Armadale is pleasantly wooded, rich in rhododendron and fuchsias. In the grounds of Armadale Castle is an extraordinary profusion of exotic trees and shrubs. There has been a house on this site for several hundred years; the latest rebuilding was in 1870, but the main bulk of Armadale Castle was the work of the architect Gillespie. James Gillespie Graham, or Gillespie as he liked to be known professionally, was born about 1777 in Dunblane. He worked as a joiner and gradually raised himself in his profession until he came to be recognised as an architect and grew respected enough to enter the competition for the design of the present Houses of Parliament. Gillespie worked in the Gothic style and he already had Culdees Castle and Crawford priory behind him when he was commissioned by Lord MacDonald in 1815 to convert Armadale House into a more imposing residence suited to be the seat of a clan Chief. Two oil paintings of the castle commissioned by Lord MacDonald from William Daniell who was at the time making a series of drawings in Skye are still in existence. They found their way to the King's Road, Chelsea, a few years ago and are now in the possession of a south-west London caterer. Engravings of them appear in J. P. Neale's *Views of the Seats of Noblemen and Gentlemen.* The paintings show the completed castle from two aspects, and they must have been based on Gillespie's sketches because the castle as he planned it was never fully built. The principal omission was a large Windsor-type round tower; Gillespie only castellated the existing house and added a new suite of public rooms.

Alistair Rowan, the authority on Gillespie's work, in his unpublished thesis on the pseudo-castle-building phenomenon in the Georgian age, writes:

> If the design is compromised and a little disappointing outside, the interior of Armadale is by far the richest of Gillespie's castle-style houses. It provides a wealth of richly vaulted interiors and a superb entrance hall and staircase . . . The hall is divided from the stairwell by a lofty three-arched arcade, and by the use of a different form of vaulting on either side of the arches a subtle differentiation is made between the two spaces so created. This shows a care for interior design far superior to that of Nash. There is a strange satisfaction in the large Gothic window of the landing which unobtrusively repeats the proportions of the windows in the entrance porch; and even in the standard double-return stair Gillespie maintained a high quality of design by the addition of a slender arcade that gives an

almost effortless lightness to the whole design.

The castle was still lived in after the second world war, but it gradually fell into decay. The rain began to come through the roof, hooligans who made their way up the overgrown drives lobbed stones through the windows, ceilings fell and whole walls of rich Gothic plastering slid to the floors bringing down the huge Strath marble fireplaces with them. When in 1967 Lord MacDonald's factor took me round the castle it was obvious that it was only a matter of time before the fabric, weakened by weathering, would become a candidate for demolition. The interior was irreparably decayed, plaster had fallen on beds, furniture and books, vandals had emptied drawers of their contents and strewn them about; in one room a fire had even been lit in the middle of the floor.

Although several plans were advanced to save the Castle, including one to turn it into a hotel for wealthy Americans and another to make it a centre of Celtic revival, none of them was successful. On 23 October 1968 Lord MacDonald's famous ancestor, Somerled Lord of the Isles, looked down with a cracked and disapproving stained-glassed stare as the Edinburgh dealers bid for the remains of the castle's furnishings. The future was no longer in doubt; in April 1969 Lord MacDonald received permission from Inverness County Council to demolish his former seat.

Ascrib Islands Seven altogether, lie at the entrance to Loch Snizort; the largest is less than half a mile long and they are uninhabited. From these islands the stone is said to have been brought for the building of Caisteal Uisdein on the shores of Loch Snizort Beag.

Ashaig (ASH-ick) – Just before entering Upper Breakish coming from the direction of Kyleakin lies a former ferry and Christian sanctuary. There used to be a saying in this part of Skye praising Ashaig for its spring water, but it is even more famous for its use as a ferrying place by Saint Maolrubha. Tradition says that near where a small stream enters the sea the saint was in the habit of preaching. He kept his book of the Scriptures in a recess in the rocks and hung his church bell from the branches of a nearby ash. Ashaig is now the site of Skye's airstrip.

B

Bagpipes The most Scottish of instruments are completely non-Gaelic in origin. They were introduced into Britain by the Romans. The Highland bagpipe consists of an airtight leather bag from which radiate five pipes. The bag is placed under the left arm and the piper inflates it through the blowpipe. The chanter has eight holes and emits nine notes through a large drone and two smaller ones. Joseph MacDonald who compiled *A Compleat Theory of the Scots Highland Bagpipes* between 1760 and 1763 noted that

> whether of native or foreign invention it has been immemorially considered as our national instrument of music; used in wars, at tournaments, marriages, funerals and public exhibitions. In battle it animated the combatants for the most daring exertions. In seasons of peace the Pipers struck up the enlivening morning *Cuairts,* under the windows of their chieftains, and at mealtime their guests were regaled with favourite marches or *gatherings* complementary to their several clans.
>
> At funerals they played a variety of laments, composed in the elegiac strain, analogous to the *coranach* or dirge performed over the dead in the days of paganism.

The bagpipe is heard to best advantage in the open air and, as an American musicologist has said, it 'is more than merely a musical instrument: it is an embodied legendary epic'. There are no half measures with bagpipe music, you either like it intensely or dislike it intensely. If it all sounds the same then you are missing out on the fun. There are three kinds of bagpipe music. The most commonly heard is *ceol beag,* or 'little music', consisting largely of reels, strathspeys and marches – the staple repertoire of the Skye Pipe Band which plays frequently during the tourist season is *ceol beag*. *Ceol meadhonach* ('middle music') is mainly jolly jigs and airs, but the most respected of the three is *ceol mor,* big music, known as *piobaireachd* – which is Gaelic for pipe playing. The *piobaireachd* is the classic form of bagpipe music and consists of complex variations on a single theme. They are mainly martial laments and big set pieces and cannot be reproduced with fidelity on any other musical instrument. The greatest piping family of all time were the MacCrimmons, who began to be talked about in Skye at the end of the fifteenth century. There is a tradition that Alasdair MacLeod, Chief from 1480 to 1547, gave the MacCrimmons land at Boreraig where they later founded a famous piping college to which most of the Highland Chiefs sent their young pipers to be trained. The MacCrimmon line ran down from Finlay through Iain Odhar, Donald Mor, Patrick Mor, Patrick Og, Donald Ban, Malcolm Iain Dubh and Donald Dubh who died in 1825. By this time the great college had long ceased functioning, and the job of clan-piper was no longer a full time one. Apart from the MacCrimmons the Mackay family of Raasay were noted eighteenth-century pipers – John Mackay mastered about 250 *piobaireachds,* no small feat.

Two of the MacCrimmon pipes are still preserved in Dunvegan Castle, and it is recorded that on the homecoming of General Norman MacLeod of MacLeod from India, Captain Donald MacCrimmon, who had served in the American War of Independence, played for him on the castle battlements. (*See* **Boreraig**).

Bealach (BYAA-lu<u>ch</u>) – a hill-pass. A common descriptive place-name in Skye – nearly a hundred different *bealachs* are named. Two of the better known ones are Bealach Uige and Bealach a'Mhorabhain, both used as short cuts between Uig and Staffin before the road through the Quiraing was built.

Beann (BAYN-y(a)) – a ben – primary meaning is *horn* and so a peak or a hill or indeed a mountain. Alexander Robert Forbes of Sleat (author of *Place-Names of Skye*) wrote lyrically about the influence of mountains. They have, he said:

contributed much to the moulding of the human mind and the character of those who dwell among them; they inspire the mind and cause the most thoughtless to admire the glory of a Supreme Being. The afflicted and the persecuted alike flee to and take refuge in and among them, from the time of David the Psalmist down to Prince Charlie and his devoted adherents. Heroes' minds are formed and their bodies are braced by dwelling among hills and mountains, and it is they and such like, and not the dwellers of the plain, who play the most noble part in the progress of the world.

Noble and convenient sentiments for a Skyeman but not entirely vindicated by history. Forbes, of course, was only echoing the romantic notions entertained by nineteenth-century idealists about the moral benefits to be gained by lifting up one's eyes to the hills. As Ruskin said: 'Mountains seem to have been built for the human race as at once their schools and cathedrals, full of treasures of illuminated manuscripts for the scholar, kindly in simple lessons for the worker, quiet in pale cloisters for the thinker, glorious in holiness for the worshipper' – and provider of purple patches for the poet, he might have added.

Beehive Dwellings These are circular buildings made of stone. No one is quite sure what their purpose was, but certainly the dwellings in the middle of what was St. Columba's Loch at Monkstadt were used by monks or hermits as a place of contemplation and retreat. The best examples of beehive dwellings are at Lonfearn, four miles south of Staffin. Even though they may have been used subsequently by monks they date from an earlier period. The Lonfearn collection are referred to in Gaelic as *Tighean nan Druineach* – Druids' Houses.

Beinn Eadarra (BAYN-y(a) ET-ter-a) 4 miles due west of Culnacnoc in Trotternish, this hill rises 2,003 ft. between the Storr and the Quiraing. In the spring of 1945 a Flying Fortress on its way from Prestwick to Iceland crashed in midday mist on the summit. Two of its engines were hurled over the hilltop and the plane burst into flames with the loss of all on board. On the east side of the hill are several good fishing lochs.

Beinn na Caillich (BAYN-y(a) KAAL-yee<u>ch</u>) (2,400 ft.) The

Hill of the Old Woman overlooking Broadford has a large cairn on its summit. The old woman is reputedly Saucy Mary, who laid a chain between Kyle and Kyleakin to exact toll from passing ships, but tradition also says it may cover the remains of a Norwegian princess; some writers suggest it was erected as a memorial to a Skye chieftain. The mountain almost gave its name in May 1908 to one of six 4-4-0 engines built for the Highland Railway. But more by ignorance than design it was named Ben na Caillach - the hill of old nothing at all!

Beinn nan Dubh-Lochan (BAYN-nun-DOO LO<u>CH</u>-un) – the mount of the black lochs. (*See* **Talisker**.)

Bernisdale Bjorn's dale or glen. Seven miles north-west of Portree on the Edinbain road. A precision engraving works has been established in what was the old school.

Biasd Na Srogaig (BEE-USS na SKRO-ku<u>ch</u>) – If when wandering round Skye you see a large animal with long legs, bad on its feet and a bit shambling with one horn on its forehead then that's 'the beast of the lowering horn'. It was invented to keep children quiet, but with the coming of television to Skye it has virtually disappeared.

Biod an Athair (BEE-utt un AH-hair) – the sky peak. If you take the road from Dunvegan to Galtrigill, just south of Dunvegan Head, a walk of a mile or so uphill to the west will bring you to the summit of Biod an Athair. It's marked by a triangulation point and is 1,025 ft. above sea level. Here the cliffs, which are the highest in the inhabited Hebrides, fall spectacularly away, and the views across the Minch on a clear day are superb.

Bland is a good description of most factory food prepared for mass consumption – not too sweet, not too sour, not too much of anything in case any identifiable taste might upset the palete. But *Bland* was a common drink in medieval Skye. It was produced from beaten-up whey which was then preserved, if necessary, for months until it was highly fermented. It fulfilled all the functions which whisky performs today.

Blaven (BLAH-vun) (3,042 ft.) The meaning of this mountain's name is obscure – it could be the warm or sunny mount
from its red appearance, or perhaps the mount of the blast, or
even the Hill of Bloom. It is seen to best advantage on the road
to Elgol. Of Blaven (or Blaabheinn to give it its Gaelic name)
Alexander Smith, author of *A Summer in Skye* wrote:

> O wonderful mountain of Blaavin
> How oft since our parting hour
> You have roared with the wintry torrents,
> You have gloomed through the thunder-shower!
> But by this time the lichens are creeping,
> Grey-green o'er your rocks and your stones,
> And each hot afternoon is steeping
> Your bulk in its sultriest bronze.
> O sweet is the spring wind, Blaavin,
> When it loosens your torrents' flow,
> When with one little touch of a sunny hand
> It unclasps your cloak of snow.

There are 70 more lines in this vein; the Victorians believed
in bulk. Blaven was also apostrophized by Robert Buchanan and
Sheriff Nicolson, who claimed that he would like nothing better
than to be in Skye in the 'prime of summer-time':

> There in the bright summer days,
> Stretched on the sward I would be,
> And gaze to the west on Blaven's crest,
> Towering above the sea;
> And I'd watch the billowing mist
> Roll down his mighty side,
> While up from the shore would come evermore
> The music of the tide.

Boreraig (BORR-er-eck) – a Norse name meaning castle bay.
The MacCrimmons held Boreraig as a free township from the
MacLeods of Dunvegan and had their famous piping school here.
MacArthur, piper to the Highland Society of Edinburgh in the
seventeen-eighties was their last pupil. A rather ugly beehive cairn
paid for by Clan Societies and donations from all over the world
was unveiled in 1933. Its inscription reads: 'The Memorial Cairn

of the MacCrimmons of whom ten generations were the hereditary pipers of MacLeod and who were renowned as
Composers, Performers and Instructors of the classical music of
the bagpipe. Near to this post stood the MacCrimmons School
of Music, 1500-1800.'

There is an annual pilgrimage to the site of the old College
of Piping when the most distinguised piper present pays the
annual rent for the ground – 'a penny and a *piobbaireachd*' – to
the Martin family who now own the land. About half a mile
south-east of the township of Boreraig on the west side of Loch
Dunvegan is a circular broch about 35 ft. in diameter (inter-
nally) with walls 10 ft. thick.

Borline (BAWR-leen) – If you take the road from Carbost which
leads to Loch Eynort (it's only about 5 miles long) you will arrive
in Borline. Here in the lee of Beinn Bhuidhe na Creige are the
ruins of two churches. The larger one, probably eighteenth
century; the smaller (only about 26 ft. long and 16 ft. wide) of
earlier construction. A sixteenth-century font, which was found
in the churchyard, was removed to a museum in Edinburgh.

Bornaskitaig (BORN-a-SKEE-teck) – could mean the low
cape or again it could not. This crofting township 6 miles north
of Uig is said to have been the scene of the reckless gesture
which gave the MacDonald Clan its motto *Air muire's tir* or *per
mare per terras*. Donald, son of Reginald MacSomerled, engaged
in a contest with a rival clan for possession of a piece of
contested territory. Whoever put his hand on the shore first
would win the land. In the last few moments Donald's galley
was overtaken, but being a highly competitive man he cut off his
left hand and flung it triumphantly on to the shore. This story
of a race between two contending clans occurs in other countries and in other legends and its authenticity is highly suspect.

Here can still be seen the cave into which MacArthur the
piper marched to the words:

> Males now at breast will be fit for combat;
> Young suckling calves will be fully-grown cows;
> Young little kids will be rock-loving goats then,
>> Ere I return, ere I reach,
>> Ere I return from the Cave of Gold.

The Cave of Gold, *Uamh an Oir,* is marked on the Ordnance Survey map. The story, which is also told of the piper MacCrimmon, is that a banshee who lived in the cave gave the piper a silver chanter on condition that he would enter the cave in a day and a year. The piper, of course, never emerged from the cave, never found the pot of gold, and was never heard playing again. This story is also told of MacCoitir's Cave just beyond the Black Rock at Portree which, apart from swallowing a piper, is also said to run right through the island, emerging again in Loch Bracadale.

Borve There are two Borves in Skye – one in Skeabost, another in Snizort. The name means 'Little Fort'. The old Portree cattle market used to be held at Borve and thousands of head of cattle were bought and sold here and then driven down to Falkirk. Most of the neighbouring innkeepers set up tents at the fair so that no one should suffer from unneccessary dehydration.

-bost at the end of a name is a contraction of the Norse or Icelandic word *bolstadhr* – homestead, farm or steading. Thus Braebost is the *farm on the upper slope;* Colbost *the cold steading.*

Bracadale – meaning obscure: Norse – spotted dale. Gaelic –*breac,* a slope. Some think it means the dale of the stag. It lies at the head of Loch Eynort and was once known as Wester Fjord or Vestrafjord. In Loch Bracadale lie the small islands of Wiay, Oronsay, Harlosh and Tarner. It was in the parish of Bracadale that Communion was first dispensed in the Protestant manner at the beginning of the eighteenth century. Thomas Pennant who voyaged to the Hebrides in 1772 was very anxious that a town should be established on Loch Bracadale. 'This seems to me,' he said, 'the fittest place in the island for the forming of a Town. The harbour is unspeakably secure. It is the Milford Haven of these parts, it opens at its mouth to the best part of the sea.'

A later traveller, Lord Teignmouth, who found himself in Bracadale in 1827, looked around for evidence of Second Sight as the place had acquired a great reputation for this sort of thing:

The traveller naturally inquires in Bracadale for traces

of the second sight and may be disappointed when he is informed here, as in other parts of Scotland, in general terms, qualified not a little when investigated, that all the ancient superstitions of the country have vanished. Now this statement cannot be admitted. Serious, imaginative, indolent, solitary in the ordinary condition of their lot, though social in disposition, familiar with nature in all the changing aspects with which northern seasons invest it, and with dangers by flood or fell, the natives of these regions are peculiarly susceptible of religious impressions. And unhappily, during many ages, ignorant or instructed only in error, they blended with the pure faith which they had received from the missionaries of the gospel, all the absurd poetical fictions derived from the stock of which they sprang, from Scandinavian invaders, from monks, or from the innumerable horde of imposters, bards, minstrels, seers and dealers in second sight, who preyed upon their credulity. But the creed of centuries is not at once eradicated and it is impossible to converse familiarly with the natives without being convinced that they cling, in spite of education and intercourse with strangers, to the superstitious delusions and even practices of their forefathers.

Braes (BRAZE) – name of the whole district facing the island of Raasay and lying between Loch Sligachan and Tianavaig Bay. The village with its post-office is 6 miles south-east of Portree. It was here that the last battle was fought on British soil on an April morning in 1882. The crofters of Braes had long been denied the right to graze their flocks on the slopes of Ben Lee. The lease was due to expire in 1882 and although the crofters agreed to pay a higher rent than the sitting tenant, their offer was refused by Lord MacDonald's factor. Provoked by what they saw as an injustice they decided to let their sheep graze on the hill and some of them refused to pay rent until their claims were recognized. The leading agitators were marked down for eviction, but when the Sheriff's officer and his assistant in Portree went to serve notices of ejection they were forced by a mob of infuriated Braes folk to burn the documents. Sheriff Ivory of Inverness asked the Chief Constable of Glasgow to dispatch 50 policemen to Skye to quell this insubordination.

When it reached Braes this expeditionary force was met by about a hundred men, women and children, and a pitched battle of sticks and stones took place. A group of crofters were taken prisoner and subsequently convicted and fined in Inverness. The whole island was in such a state of discontent that warships were dispatched and marines were landed at Uig. It was directly as a result of the Battle of the Braes that Gladstone decided to set up a Royal Commission to inquire into the grievances of the crofters.

Brandy was commonly used in eighteenth-century Skye as a specific against the climate. Says Martin Martin:

> The Air here is commonly moist and cold, this disposes the Inhabitants to take a larger Dose of Brandy, or other strong Liquors, than in the South of Scotland, by which they fancy that they qualify the Moisture of the Air; this is the Opinion of all Strangers, as well as of the Natives, since the one as well as the other, drinks at least treble the quantity of Brandy in Skye and the adjacent Isles, that they do in the more Southern Climate.

Whisky has now replaced brandy and seems to 'qualify the moisture' quite satisfactorily.

Breakish (BRECH-kish) – a hamlet 3 miles east of Broadford. Although small it is divided into Upper B and Lower B. The place is said to have derived its name from the number of people who lived there pitted by the scars of smallpox, in Gaelic *a'bhreac*. In the seventeenth and eighteenth centuries smallpox was a great killer in Skye and *breac* described very well that pock-marked aspect of the face (still frequently seen in Asia) which marked the smallpox survivor. *Breac* is also the poetic Gaelic name for a trout.

Broadford 8 miles west of Kyleakin, Broadford is a sizeable town with hotels, retaurants, a youth hostel and a hospital. It has splendid views across to Raasay and the mainland and is a fine centre for visiting both the Cuillins and the Southern part of Skye. In 1843 it was a very small place indeed. Anderson's *Guide* noted: 'Broadford consists of only three houses and the inn, which is a comfortable one. The charges, as in most parts of Skye, are moderate. In one article only are they higher than in the mainland highlands, namely, whiskey [*sic*], of which not a drop is made in Skye, either by smuggler or regular distiller.'

Brochel Castle On the isle of Raasay, was once a 'curiosity whose attractions draw from many a tourist the expenditure of a day's excursion'. It stands on a small bay on the east coast.

On the lower ledge of the rock and rising from its very edge [ran an 1844 account] stands a small building of two low stories, and a narrow interior court; and on the summit of the rock, and occupying all its area, stands another small building, and two triangular and loop-holed recesses – the building disposed in two low stories, of each a single apartment, and in surmounting battlements, and a warder's room. The only access is up an approach which has been cut on the side next to the sea, and which is so steep that it can be climbed only on all-fours, or at least with the aid of the hands; the entrance is by a narrow, steep-roofed passage between the lower building and the base of the upper stage of the rock; and altogether, the combinations of strong natural position and artificial fortalice is so complete as to exhibit the very beau-ideal of adaptation to security and defence in the ages preceding the invention of gunpowder.

The thing that tickled Boswell about Brochel Castle was that it had a lavatory whereas Raasay House hadn't got around to such a convenience. There was one small room, Boswell observed on 10 September 1773:

in one of the towers quite entire. It was a little confined triangular place, vaulted as in the ancient manner. In a corner of it was a square freestone in which was cut an exact circular opening such as in every temple of Cloacina, and from it there appears a clear communication to the bottom, that is to say anything will be carried by the outside of the rock to the bottom. They call this room the *nursery*, and say the hole was for the children. But I take it to have been the necessary-house of the castle. It was much to find such a convenience in an old tower. I did not imagine that the invention had been introduced into Scotland till in very modern days, from our connexion with England. But it seems we have forgotten something of civilized life that our ancestors knew. It is strange how rare that convenience is amongst us. Mr Johnson laughed heartily and said, 'You take very good care of one end of a man, but not of the other'. One should think it requires very little reflection to provide such a convenience. Raasay has none. I told him that it was a shame to see it at the old castle and not at his new house. He said it would be better. But I doubt many generations may pass before it is built.

Donald MacLean, Schoolmaster of Staffin, a man of great mental ingenuity, has suggested to me that Boswell may have been wrong: 'Could it also', he writes, 'be a "convenience" for pouring molten lead or boiling oil on unwelcome visitors arriving by sea?'

Brochs Fortified round towers built in the Scottish Iron Age many of which were still in use when the Norsemen began their Hebridean raids. As none is left extant it is impossible to estimate their height accurately, but they probably reached 40 to 50 ft. They were chimney-shaped with an internal diameter of 25 to 40ft. and between the inner and outer walls were small rooms or galleries ventilated from the inner courtyard. Some of the galleries were five or six stories high. The entire construction was of dry walling. The best preserved and most easily accessible example of a *broch* in Skye is perversely call a *dun* – Dun Beag at Struanmore, a couple of hundred yards' easy stroll from the road. Here one can still see a stairway leading down to one of the chambers. Internal evidence suggested that the people who inhabited these *brochs* (or *duns*) were farmer-fishermen.

The outstanding example of a Hebridean *broch* is in Lewis, at Dun Carloway and is well worth a visit if only to give one a picture of what the Skye *brochs* were like before dilapidation set in.

The Royal Commission on the Ancient and Historical Monuments of Scotland in their ninth report published in 1928 list about 60 defensive constructions in Skye, of which they classify 24 as *brochs*. The rest are galleried *duns*, having long narrow galleries within the thickness of the wall; promontory forts (of which there's one in Skye at Ullinish); a numerous number of seashore forts, and loch forts, of which there is only one in Skye, Dun Maraig. Of the disposition of these *duns* and *brochs* Martin Martin wrote: 'All these forts stand upon eminences, and are so disposed, that there is not one of them, which is not in view of some other; and by this means when a Fire is made upon a Beacon, in any one Fort, it's in a few Moments after communicated to all the rest, and this hath been always observed upon sight of any number of foreign Vessels, or Boats approaching the Coast'.

Although mortar wasn't used in the construction of these forts, when limestone rock was available the stone was often vitrified by building huge fires against the outer wall until the fused material flowed down and welded the stones beneath into a solid mass. This elemental process can be seen in the remaining stones at Skudaborg near Uig.

One of the reasons why the Skye *duns* and *brochs* are in such a lamentable state of decay is that in the last several centuries their stones have been used for building walls, cottages, bridges and roads.

Bruach-na-frithe (BROO-u<u>ch</u> na FREE) (3,143 ft.) – the brae of the forest. One of the most northern peaks in the Cuillins offers an easy walk up to the top from which there are some splendid views.

C

Cairidh (KARRY) – the Gaelic name for the weir or horseshoe of stones built to catch herring, saithe and other fish. The remains of quite a few of these *cairidh* can still be seen in various lochs. There was a very famous *cairidh* nearly a quarter of a mile long on Loch Snizort, and it was free for all to take fish from except for a pocket in the bend which was reserved exclusively for the tacksman. Fishing began in May and went on until November or later depending on the weather. Salmon were fished from May until the end of August and there would be a lull until the herring shoals came into the lochs at the end of September. It was not uncommon to catch up to a hundred salmon on one floodtide and sometimes as many as 50 or 60 cran of herring would be caught at one time. Most of these weirs were broken down by landlords who wanted the salmon for their fishing tenants. A Skyeman writing in 1930 of the Snizort weir said: 'It was broken down and today not a trace of it is seen, inevitable through progressive encroachments on sea and land by the privileged class'.

Caisteal Uisdein (KASHT-yal OOST-yen) – Hugh's Castle. Built by Hugh MacDonald of Sleat in the time of James VI, the castle overlooks the entrance to Loch Snizort Beag and is half a mile north of the Hinnisdal river mouth. To find it leave the Portree-Uig road three-quarters of a mile after crossing the river Hinnisdal. A cart track leads down to a house now used as a farm building and from here one should cut across the moor to the shore – it's about ten minutes' walk depending on how spry you are. What is left of the castle stands within 3 ft. of the cliffs about 45 ft. above the shore. It is 52 ft. long by 32 ft. broad, and the walls are between 7 and 9 ft. thick. It is difficult to enter as

51

there are only two openings, one very small at shoulder level and the other 8 ft. above the ground. The only way into the castle would have been up a ladder which could then be drawn into the fortress in the event of an attack.

Hugh, the son of Archibald the cleric, who built the castle came to a gruesome end. He conceived a plan to get rid of his chief by inviting him to the house-warming of his new castle and then murdering him. Unfortunately the invitation went to one of his accomplices and the letter intended for the accomplice, which described in lurid detail how the Chief was to be dispatched, went to the Chief himself at Duntulm. Hugh was apprehended, brought to Duntulm and thrown into a dungeon. In the corner was a pewter jug and a platter with a piece of beef on it. Hugh, by this time relatively peckish, began tearing at the beef but found it very salty. To quench his thirst he seized the jug and raised it to his lips. It was empty. Even as he put it down he heard the hammer and chiselling of stone masons as they began walling up the door to the dungeon. They say that years later when the vault was broken open they found Hugh's skeleton and in its jaws was clamped the pewter jug from which pieces had been crunched in the terminal agonies of thirst. A Victorian minister of Kilmuir always claimed that the skull and thigh bones of Hugh were preserved in a window of the parish church and were objects of curiosity for many years until they were given Christian burial in 1827. The shell of this church still stands at Bornaskitaig.

Calpa was the iniquitous system which survived in Skye until well into the nineteenth century whereby on the death of a subordinate his superior, if he were so disposed, might help himself to part of the property of the deceased, a cow perhaps or some horses. Writing in 1841 the Rev. John MacKinnon said: 'Until recently the custom of the laird to take the best horse from a tenant's farm, on the death of the occupier, was observed.' One ground officer in Strath who took advantage of the practice came to an untimely end. After the death of a tenant he demanded the best horse on the holding from the widow. The widow put a curse on him, vowing vengeance through her year-old son. The son, seventeen years later, hearing that the same functionary had maltreated another widow, gave him such a savage beating that he died of his injuries. The boy cut off the dead man's head and laid it at the laird's door. According to legend, and the whole story sounds pretty shaky, the lad was appointed ground officer in place of the man he had eliminated. Tradition relates that this happening was responsible for the ending of *calpa*.

Camasunary (kam-a-SYOO-na-ri) – Bay of the white, fair, or beautiful shieling. It is hemmed in by mountains and lies on the northern shore of Loch Scavaig. It was of Camasunary Sheriff Nicolson wrote enthusiastically in the nineteenth century:

> Here undoubtedly is the place where, were it Switzerland, would be a *Grand Hotel de Blàveinn*, a *Grand Hotel des Cuchullins* and probably also a *Grand Hotel et Pension de Camusunary*. Why should there not be one there, it may well be asked, and echo from Blàveinn answers 'Why?' That it is much needed is as plain as the cleft in the head of Blàveinn; that it would ultimately pay, if well managed, cannot be doubted. It is not well to disturb the sacred solitude of Nature's great scenes. But we should be reasonable, and if people will go, and ought to go, to see such places as Coruisk, it were better that they should be enabled to do so with some degree of comfort. The true votaries of nature will never grudge fatigue and privation for her sake, but they should not be made martyrs of more than is inevitable. As for scaring away the crowd of tourists, that is hopeless, even were it laudable.

Camasunary is as void of hotels and pensions today as it was when Nicolson dreamed his dream.

Carbost on the shores of Loch Harport, an arm of Loch Bracadale; a small township dominated by a distillery. The distillery was established in **1830** and at the time a strong advocate of temperance described it as 'one of the greatest curses that, in the ordinary course of Providence, could befall this or any other place'. It was built by the brothers Hugh and Kenneth Macaskill who were given a 60-year lease by MacLeod of MacLeod. In 1895 the present company, Dailuaine-Talisker Distilleries Limited, was formed, and in 1900 they were granted permission to build a pier and tramway to the distillery. In 1914 a feu charter was granted to take water from the burn in Carbost and peats from the parish of Bracadale. The Distillers Comapny acquired an interest in Dailuaine-Talisker in 1916 and today own 99.9 per cent of the shares. The still-house was destroyed by fire in November 1961, but by 1962 almost the whole distillery had been rebuilt at a cost of £250,000. The distillery is operated for the company by Scottish Malt Distillers Limited, and 35 people are employed in the production of Talisker whisky. Barley comes from the mainland, the peat used for drying and flavouring the malted barley is local. The casks come and go mainly by road across the ferry at Kyle, but supplies of barley and coal still come in to the old pier by sea. Although the great bulk of Talisker goes to Scotch whisky blending houses a small proportion is bottled as Talisker Pure Malt Whisky. The largest export market for Talisker is surprisingly – Italy. Robert Louis Stevenson, who once visited Skye, singled Talisker out for mention in his poem "The Scotsman's Return From Abroad" written in 1880:

> The king o'drinks, as I conceive it,
> Talisker, Isla, or Glenlivet.

Talisker has a pleasant peaty flavour, and like all single malts is best drunk neat or modified with a little spring water.

Carn Liath (KAARN LEE-u<u>ch</u>) The grey or hoary cairn on the shore of Loch Eyre near Kensaleyre is 40 ft. high and 400 yds. in circumference. Legend says that at one time the Skeabost river was the boundary between the MacLeod and MacDonald lands. Each clan claimed the island, which was formed between two tributaries of the river. A battle was fought for the island, and such was the slaughter that it was eventually agreed that it should be made into a common burial ground. The dead were collected and the cairn built over their remains.

There is another Carn Liath which I have never seen referred to in any guide book and which is virtually unknown to tourists unless they stumble on it by accident. It lies a mile north of the Old Man of Storr and it is possibly the wildest *carn* in the Scottish Highlands. John Mackenzie of Portree tells me that it presents an awesome spectacle. It is composed mainly of gigantic blocks of basalt, some as large as two-storeyed houses, the result of a vast geological upheaval. Murdo Campbell, a **Rigg** shepherd, told Mackenzie that he found stone steps hewn out of one of these rocks which led to an underground chamber. Its floor was thick with ash – although born to the hills he has never been able to find the place since. Roddy Lamont, a local foxhunter, claims that this is a suicidal place to enter when snow is on the ground – if you once slipped between these giant rocks you would never be able to extricate yourself unaided.

Caschrom (kass-HROME) – the traditional Hebridean spade-cum-plough. Wrote an early nineteenth-century visitor:

> It is a clumsy substitute for a plough with which an active man will sometimes prepare about a fourth of an acre in a day; and it is certainly of advantage in the cultivation of their miserable crofts, which are frequently altogether scarcely equal in value to the purchase price of a plough. The *caschrom* is formed either of a stout obtusely angled knee of wood, or two pieces bound together with iron; the upper limb or handle is four or five feet long; the lower about two and a half feet, and shod at the point with a sharp flat piece of iron, which is driven into the soil by means of a lateral wooden peg projecting from an angle, on which the right foot acts.

The *caschrom* was in use in some of the Outer Islands until comparatively recently.

Castle Camus – *see* Knock Castle

Castle Maoil (KASHT-yel MURL) – Stands on a promontory a few hundred yards from the Kyleakin slip. For centuries it belonged to the MacKinnons as vassals of the MacDonalds of Sleat. Legend says that it was built by Saucy Mary, the daughter of a Norwegian king, for the purpose of levying a toll on ships passing through the Kyles. Legend also says that she stretched a chain across from Kyleakin to Kyle to make sure that no ship sailed through without paying up – thus defying not only belief but all the known laws of engineering. A portion of the castle fell during the very bad gale of February 1949.

Ceilidh (KAY-lee) – the traditional *ceilidh* was a gathering held round a peat fire at which songs would be sung, stories told and music made. William Mackenzie of Culnacnoc in Skye described a typical *ceilidh* in his book *Old Skye Tales:* the sort of *ceilidh* which would have occurred in an old thatched house in the middle of the last century:

> The inside is cosy and clean, with the fire in the middle of the floor, and around the blazing peat-fire sit young and old, listening to their elders' stories of the past. The gudeman sits in a corner twisting heather rope, and the gudewife sits in the opposite corner at her spinning wheel. Popular songs are sung, all joining in the chorus. Tales of the past are related. Beliefs of the past – fairies, ghosts, the water-horse – are listened to in mingled awe and wonder. Guessing has a place. The gudeman and gudewife, from their corners strike in now and again with a word, bringing a tear or raising laughter. The memories of the nightly *ceilidhs* round the peat fires are treasured by Highlanders all over the world, and treasured with regret at the changes now being made.

The oral tradition – the art of telling, and even more important, listening, to the folk-lore and legends of the past has died out. A *ceilidh* nowadays ('come up for a *ceilidh*') means little more than a cup of tea and a chat and the *ceilidhs* organized during the tourist season by hotels and local bodies are almost entirely devoted to music, much of which is non-Gaelic.

Chambered Cairns A large number are marked on the Ordnance Survey maps. Thomas Pennant records that when he was in Skye he was presented by Flora MacDonald with an urn found in a stone chest beneath 'an immense cairn' and he noted that the urn 'was of excellent workmanship'. In Broadford one of these cairns was opened in 1832 and its burial chamber contained human bones and a few stone implements.

Clachamish (klu<u>ch</u>-AM-ish) – About half a mile south-west of this small township on the shores of Loch Snizort Beag is what's claimed to be one of the best preserved *brochs* in Skye. It's almost a perfect circle, about 42 ft. in diameter with walls 10 to 12 ft. thick. Dun Suledale, as it's called, is less derelict than most *brochs* and quite a lot remains to be seen.

Clach Ghlas (KLU<u>CH</u> GLUSS) (2,590 ft.) – the grey stone – a prominent peak of Blaven which was first climbed in May 1880 and has been called the Matterhorn of Skye.

Clans The clan system came into existence about the middle of the thirteenth century. The clan (the children) of a Chief didn't necessarily bear his name. Anyone who placed himself under a Chief and abided by the rules became a member of the clan. When he signed a Bond of Manrent a man was bound to serve his Chief 'as his master, by land and sea'. In return the Chief was pledged to protect and maintain him as he would his own kith and kin. In the early days of the clan there was no rigid observance of hereditary rights. The son of a Chief would quickly be passed over if another more suitable relative presented himself. The clan was divided into two classes, the warriors who were the *samurai* élite, and those who were not fit to be warriors – lesser men who grew the crops and looked after the cattle.

The commonest clan names in Skye are MacDonald, MacLeod, Mackinnon, Macaskill, Nicolson, Martin, Beaton, MacQueen, MacInnes, MacCrimmon, MacArthur and MacPherson. The clan system was destroyed after Culloden, and the emergence of the Chief as a landlord and his clansmen as tenants established a new relationship which in Skye inevitably led to a wave of emigration, and towards the end of the nineteenth century to the unrest which flared into open defiance. Clan gatherings are still held in Dunvegan Castle by far-flung MacLeods looking for their roots; and the clan Donald has similar functions.

Climate Skye is a place from which one can return sunburnt in November and rainsoaked in August. For the visitor, planning a holiday is about as risky as playing Russian roulette. I am indebted to the Superintendent of the Meteorological Office in Edinburgh for the following information on the climate of Skye which I have supplemented by the observations of Donald MacLean of Staffin, Schoolmaster and local authority on Skye weather.

Rainfall In common with the Welsh hills and the English Lake District, Skye has a high rainfall. Even the driest parts of the island (lying along the narrow coastal strips) have an annual rainfall of between 50 and 60 in. This is similar to Keswick and low-lying places in Snowdonia but more than places like Glasgow and Plymouth which have about 40 in. in a year and considerably more than London and Edinburgh, which have an annual average of 23 to 27 in. There is a rapid increase in rainfall over the high ground backing the coastal strips, and the highest parts of the Cuillins have more than 125 in. a year. The following figures show the long term averages of rainfall for Duntulm during the 35 years between 1916 and 1950.

January	5.84	May	2.87	September	5.05
February	3.93	June	3.35	October	6.00
March	3.24	July	3.83	November	5.63
April	3.40	August	4.41	December	5.58

Most rainfall is associated with the prevailing moist westerly winds from the Atlantic. However, a period of light easterly winds from the North Sea, which have a long track over the high ground of the Scottish mainland before reaching Skye, occurs with surprising regularity in the spring and early summer, and the onset of easterly winds in May and June usually signals a spell of brilliantly fine dry weather. From time to time Skye does experience prolonged spells of fine dry weather during the late summer and early autumn – better weather than resorts on the south coast of England. However, the probability of a prolonged spell of dry weather occurring in Skye during the late summer and early autumn in any particular year is much less than on the south coast. As an instance of the variations for year to year of Skye rainfall, 11.41in. fell in Staffin in January 1962. In January 1963 the rainfall was 1.41 in.! The most recent wet years have been 1954 and 1967 when Broadford received an unwelcome bonus of 113 in. of rain. Those who think that Skye is wetter now than it used to be can take heart from the three years of 1861-63 in which a total of 400 in. of rain fell, and earlier than that in the first decade of the nineteenth century MacCulloch the geologist noted peevishly: 'When the reader is told that I made seven (unsuccessful) attempts, and in five successive summers, to ascend the Cuchullin hills, he will form some notion of the nature of the climate'.

Temperature The predominant maritime influence results in a remarkably mild temperature régime especially when the high latitude of Skye is taken into account – the average winter in

Skye is typified by a low frequency of frosts or days with snow
lying on the ground. Winters at places on or near the coast are
usually much less severe than in east and south-east England.
The moderating influence of the sea also results in an 'equable'
temperature régime during the summer months with a relatively
low daily range of temperature – the rather low maximum
temperatures experienced during the day are offset by high
minimum temperatures at night. Here are the averages of the
daily maximum, minimum and mean temperatures at Duntulm
during the 30 years between 1931 and 1960:

	maximum	minimum	mean
	(All temperatures shown in Celsius)		
January	6.5	2.4	4.4
February	6.6	2.2	4.4
March	8.1	3.3	5.7
April	9.6	4.3	7.0
May	12.4	6.5	9.4
June	14.3	8.7	11.5
July	15.4	10.4	12.9
August	15.7	10.7	13.2
September	14.2	9.4	11.8
October	11.5	7.2	9.4
November	9.1	5.1	7.1
December	7.6	3.6	5.6
Year	10.9	6.2	8.6

The rather low maximum temperatures during the tourist
season between May and September may not be ideal for
sunbathing but they are perfect for the more energetic kind of
outdoor activity – hiking, climbing or pony-trekking – and are far
more comfortable for relaxing in than the often enervating heat
which characterizes a summer holiday in the Mediterranean. On
average the maximum temperatures on the warmest day of
summer on or near the coast usually reaches 21°C (70°F)
compared with 24°C (76°F) in Edinburgh and 27°C (81°F) in
Birmingham. In recent years there have been some extremely
warm spells – in August 1968, for instance, there were ten days
with an average temperature of 66°F. The latest snowfall that Mr
MacLean has noted was on 9 May 1943 when 4 in. lay on the
ground at Stein 'with tulips in full bloom and the cuckoo cheer-

fully (or crazily) singing from the cliffs beyond Lochbay!'

Sunshine The long-term figures for the 30 years between 1930 and 1960 are given below for Duntulm, and they are fairly representative of the coastal regions where the horizon is not unduly obstructed by nearby high ground:

	hours		*hours*
January	34	July	125
February	61	August	131
March	109	September	103
April	136	October	69
May	200	November	41
June	171	December	24

To put Skye's sunshine in perspective this is how it appears when placed in a league table with eight other locations in Britain:

	hours
Bournemouth	1,726
Birmingham	1,404
Royal Observatory, Edinburgh	1,384
Regent's Park, London	1,353
Manchester Airport	1,263
Glasgow Airport	1,243
Keswick, Lake District	1,232
Inverness	1,228
Prabost, Skye	1,204

There are exceptions to this relatively low level of sunshine. Prabost had 1,448 hours of sunshine in the *Annus Mirabilis* of 1968, and Donald MacLean writes to say 'visual observation has frequently shown in Staffin that many days were brighter, *by hours,* than the "Brightest in Britain" as recorded, for example, in the *Daily Express.*'

Winds As a general rule the relatively dry western and northern coastal strips are also the mildest and sunniest places on the island, but on the debit side these coastal strips tend to be windswept, and in common with many other places along the western seaboard the high frequency of gales and strong winds from the Atlantic, particularly during the winter months, is perhaps the most unpleasant feature of the local climate. It is the south wind which reaches the greatest strength although the north-east and east winds do tend to be less fierce. Donald MacLean recorded an average of 68 days in the year during the five-year period 1964-68 with wind forces above 30 m.p.h.

Mist and Fog Although Skye is referred to as 'The Misty Isle' it should be emphasized that the island experiences very good visibility and its remoteness from the industrial and populous areas of Britain and their filthy air means that smoke (apart from the burning of heather in the spring), fogs and atmospheric pollution are unknown. Patches of sea fog sometimes affect the coastal regions particularly in the south of the island but much more often than not the 'mist' is low cloud obscuring the higher ground. Donald MacLean writes: 'Misty isle is a romantic myth, except for hill fog, when places up to 500ft. above sea level may have 50 miles plus of visibility in brilliant sunshine.

Seton Gordon once recalled the celebrated Emperor whose philosophy was summed up in the words 'for a thousand days that are gloomy and tedious console yourself with one that is beautiful.' The ration of good to bad days in Skye is by no means as miserable as that, but if you are reading this in Skye and the gentle rain is beating against your window-pane take courage from these words of Seton Gordon written after a prolonged spell of rough weather:

> Without warning the wind falls light, a star at midnight shines at the zenith and the moon struggles to pierce the mists. You retire to bed with hopes that a change in the weather is at last at hand. In the morning you awake, and as you look from your window, even perhaps without moving from your bed, you see revealed a fairy land of beauty. You have experienced it all before, yet it is always fresh, always wonderful, always inspiring.

Cnoc (KROCHK) – a knoll. *Cnocan* is a little knoll.

Coire (KORR-a) – a hollow surround by hills, once the site of a glacier. The word occurs in Welsh as *cwm*, in English as *coombe*. There are over 70 corries named in Skye, of which the most famous is Coruisk. 'No feature in Highland scenery,' said Archibald Geikie the geologist, 'is more characteristic than corries or cirques.'

Coire na Creiche (KORR-a na KRAYCH-ya) – Corry of the spoils – (*see Handfasting*).

Colbost On the south-west shores of Loch Dunvegan, Colbost, 4 miles along the Glendale road, is well worth visiting to see the *Tigh Dubh* or black house which the enterprising proprietors of the Three Chimneys Tea Room (snacks, afternoon and high teas) have re-created. The house, which contains old implements and bygones, has a central hearth, and the peat smoke rises through a hole in the roof. With its earth floor and thatched roof it gives a very good idea of how a crofter's family would have lived in Skye in the early nineteenth century.

Collie, Norman I remember in the long, hot summer of 1939 hearing talk of the coming war and a strange white-bearded scientist who spent his days walking the moors. He was, said gossip in Portree, the world's leading expert in poison gases and he had come to stay in Sligachan Inn while he worked out even more deadly formulae in his mad, brilliant brain. It wasn't until long after the war that I realized that the gentle man who had given rise to these fantasies was Norman Collie, a former Manchester Professor of Organic Chemistry. He first came to Sligachan in 1886 to fish. From fishing he graduated to climbing, and for a quarter of a century he haunted the Cuillins whenever he could take time off from his work. Collie, although he was spurred on to climb in the Alps and the Himalayas, never lost his first passion for the mountains of Skye. This greatest of all Skye climbers spent his last years in Sligachan, and when he died there in November 1942 his body was taken for burial to the old churchyard at Struan in Bracadale.

Coral beaches, really banks of coral sand, are found at Claggan and near Staffin. The coral is made by a plant, a seaweed called Lithothamnion. The weed lies a little way out from the shore and forms a semi-circular cushion about 4in. across. Bits break off and are thrown up by the sea on to the shore.

Cormorants (*Phalacrocorax carbo*) An old tradition relates that the Cormorant had a life span of 21 years and was 'seven years a scart, seven years a speckled loon and seven years a cormorant'. In 1703 Martin Martin reported that 'On the south side of Loch Portry there is a large *cave,* in which many Sea Cormorants do build: the natives carry a bundle of straw to the door of the cave in the night-time, and then setting it on fire, the fowls fly with all speed to the light, and so are caught in baskets laid for that purpose'. The cormorant, if caught young enough, was reckoned to make a tasty broth. Martin was probably referring to the Shag or Green Cormorant. The Shag feeds entirely on fish, and the taste of its flesh must be unusual to say the least.

Coruisk (Kor-ROOSHK) The corrie of water, the cauldron, lies at the head of Loch Scavaig. Scooped, according to a Victorian geologist, out of the solid rock by ice some 280,000 years ago, Coruisk is the most famous corrie in Britain. It has been so over-written that actually seeing it at first hand can be a disappointment. Writers from Scott onwards have romanticized it as dark, brooding, wild, weird and stern. A typical description of Coruisk was given in 1842 by James Wilson in his *Voyage Around the Coasts of Scotland and the Isles:*

> The dead, dull lake lay beneath; the ruins, as it were, of a former world were scattered on all sides; and above as far as the eye can pierce through the murky clouds, rose the vast rocky pinnacles, their extremest heights obscured at intervals, when we could behold the grim and awful giants keeping their eternal watches. There was nothing within the visible diurnal sphere that breathed the breath of life – no sound, nor the sight of any moving thing – nothing but a dead and stony, seemingly, a God-forsaken world. We almost longed, in this cloud-capped thunder-stricken region, to hear the voice of gladsome bird, or even of murmuring bee – but all, so far as regarded living nature, was silent as the grave. The whole scene from first to last exceeded in its sterile grandeur whatever had previously been seen in this, perhaps in any other, country.

Alexander Nicolson, a Skyeman himself, wrote:

> It is impossible for a person with any tincture of imagination not to feel slightly eerie in looking at these grotesque but grim, sometimes awful-looking craters, like 'Monsters of the Primal' turned into stone, yet with a stony life and conscious-

ness in their fixed look and stern sphinx-like repose. The silence of the place, and of all the corries in the Coolins, is intense, and to many minds the effect is depressing.

Coruisk can be approached either by motor-boat from Elgol (the charge is reasonable), on foot from Sligachan or round the shore. There are many people, particularly climbers, who have for long had a proprietary interest in keeping the Cuillins as inaccessible as possible, who were shocked into action in 1968 when it was discovered that the Army had been asked to construct a 2-mile jeep-track to the fishing and shooting lodge of Camasunary. This might not have excited much public attention but the Army were also asked to build a foot-bridge across the Camasunary River, improve the track to Coruisk and fling a bridge across the River Scavaig. This Rape of the Loch, as one Sunday paper called it, escalated in the public imagination from vandalism to sacrilege when it was revealed that the Army were proposing to dynamite the Bad Step, an enormous rock which makes walking to Coruisk along the shore relatively hazardous for the ordinary tourist.

Mountaineers, who regard Coruisk as an inner temple of holiness and the Bad Step as a symbolic guardian of its secret mysteries, brought pressure to bear on the authorities and the invitation to the Army to blow up the Bad Step was withdrawn. The jeep-track and the two bridges were, however, built, and you must make up your own mind whether they constitute an eyesore. The bridge over the Scavaig river is a simple construction of teak and wire and perhaps fits more into its surroundings than the hut with a corrugated iron roof which the climbers themselves erected many years ago. The main argument for the jeep-track was that it would make mountain rescue easier, but some mountaineers deny this and insist that building a road and bridges, far from aiding mountain rescue, will encourage inexperienced walkers and climbers to enter the area and perhaps run into difficulties that before would not have been open to them. There is no evidence so far that this is happening. Coruisk remains as remote and as inviolate as ever.

Creag (KRAYK) and **Creagan**: Rock – rocks or little rock. So *Creag a' Chaisteil*, the castle rock; *Creagan Dubha*, the Black Rocks; *Creag na h-Iolaire*, the Eagle Rock; *Creag an Stoirm*, the rock of the storm.

Crofting was introduced into Skye about the beginning of the eighteenth century when a MacDonald Chief divided some large parcels of land among a community of tenants. Unfortunately so much of the men's time was taken up discharging their obligations either to the tacksman on whose land they lived or the Chief, that their own land was very often worked by the women. Because a tenant could be thrown off his land without a moment's notice the land was never cultivated to the best advantage and few improvements were made – why spend a lot of time draining land, for instance, when the fruit of your labours might easily be given to someone else? When in 1879 the discontent among the Skye crofters broke out into open revolt (*see* **Braes)** a Royal Commission was talked of, but it wasn't until 1883 that Gladstone appointed one. The Commission's report resulted in the Crofters' Act which came into operation in June 1886. It conferred security of tenure on small landholders, protected them from eviction and made provision for a land court to fix fair rents.

The Napier Commission defined a crofter as 'a small tenant of the land with or without a lease, who finds in the cultivation and produce of his holding a material portion of his occupation, earnings and sustenance, and who pays rent to the proprietor'. Today a crofter is a smallholder who invariably supplements his income in other ways – by running a shop, fishing, taking in holiday guests, working as a civil servant or even, as one Skye crofter does, free-lancing for the B.B.C. Today many crofts remain unworked, others which once grew arable crops are now only used for grazing. Much of the island's milk is imported from the mainland, corn is no longer grown in such large quantities as it was in the past, and in really bad years even hay is imported. Some crofts are self-contained, but the majority of crofters share common grazing land with other crofters in the community. This land is run by a committee which keeps the fanks (the pens where the sheep are dipped and clipped) and the fencing in good order and decides general policy. A croft can be less than an acre or run into hundreds of acres, but no croft can be assigned or transferred without the permission of the Crofter's Commission which was set up in 1955 to organize, develop and regulate crofting in the seven crofting counties of Argyll, Caithness, Inverness, Orkney, Ross and Cromarty, Sutherland, and Shetland. There are many grants and subsidies to assist the crofter, who has been described as a farmer with too little land, and his croft as a small area of land surrounded by regulations.

The Secretary of State owns 674 of the 1,894 crofts in Skye, and the next biggest landowners are Lord MacDonald (422 crofts with a croft and grazing acreage of 26,241), John MacLeod of MacLeod (131 crofts, 13,626 acres), Major J. L. MacDonald, Tote (125 crofts, 9,728 acres), and Donald MacDonald, Waternish (114 crofts, 8,635 acres).

The census in June 1969 showed that 106,000 acres were owned in Skye and 183,000 rented. There were 250 acres of potatoes, turnips and swedes, and 1,000 acres of oats. Most of the land is, of course, used for grazing, and it supports 154,000 sheep, 640 dairy cattle, 9,700 beef cattle, 13,000 chickens and five pigs. Of the 2,000 holdings in Skye only 73 are operated on a full-time basis.

Tourism, which has given Skye a tremendous shot in the arm, has also weaned many part-time crofters off the land and into summer employment in the service industries. Crofting has therefore declined in importance. A man who knows what he's talking about told me: 'The Skye crofters are very reluctant to abandon the old traditional form of sheep management, which meant that you just left the sheep to fend for themselves in the late winter and spring, when there's little natural feeding. In Lewis they feed their sheep and they get better results. In Skye at tupping and lambing time the sheep are widely scattered over the common grazing land, but, of course, you'd get much better results if you had the sheep in enclosures. This way of managing sheep was all right in the old days when there was plenty of cheap labour and crofters had time to move their sheep on the hill. But nowadays the crofter has more profitable ways of spending his time – if part-time crofting is to improve, the crofter will have to be shown less time-consuming ways of doing his work'.

The last Royal Commission on Crofting, which reported in 1954, unanimously agreed that 'in the national interest the maintenance of these communities is desirable because they embody a free and independent way of life which, in a civilisation predominantly urban and industrial in character, is worth preserving for its own intrinsic quality'. For over a century now crofting has hardly been a viable way of life, and the substantial grants which a crofter receives from different agencies underline the unrealistic position he occupies in modern Britain. A recent solution to the crofters' problem, supported by the Crofters' Commission, is to make the crofter an owner-occupier. The Highlands are now split on this issue, some feeling that it would accelerate the exodus from the glens and be only a partial answer to a situation which requires profounder attention. Margaret MacPherson, wife of a Skye crofter and a writer of distinction, suggested at the 1969 Labour Party Highland conference that one solution might be 'to take acres away from the landlords and give them to young men.' Whatever happens many people feel that the Crofters' Commission in its admittedly short life has still not grappled constructively with the question.

Crotal (KROT-tul) – was a russet-coloured dye obtained from the lichen on rocks. Because crotal was thought always to be seeking its way back to the rocks it was believed that anyone venturing out to sea in crotal-dyed clothes would sink like a stone if he fell overboard and his body would never be recovered. This is probably why you don't see many Skye fisherman wearing russet-coloured jerseys.

Crow, Hoodie (*Corvus cornix*) The Hoodie feeds mainly on fish offal and any flotsam and jetsam it can pick up. Skye crofters claim that a hoodie will often peck out a sheep's eyes in its search for food. It has also been known to swoop down and bite out the tongue from a young lamb's mouth moments after it has been born – the tongueless lamb unable to suck is soon dead. It certainly likes gulls' eggs and seems to be aware that farmers regard it as vermin. There's a saying which runs: 'All the birds of the air have been taught to fly by the Hoodie; but she kept one little secret to herself – *a turn* – a trick of flying and fighting like a cat on her back.'

Cuchullin, Cuchulinn or **Cu Chulainn** This top Irish warrior-hero died at the age of 27, but not before he had reputedly built Dunscaith castle.

Cuckoo It was Wordsworth who wrote of

> . . . the Cuckoo-Bird
> Breaking the silence of the seas
> Among the farthest Hebrides . . .

The cuckoo uses the meadow-pipit as a foster parent for its outsize progeny. You will find singularly little information in this book about our feathered friends, a lacuna which will be amply compensated by delving into any of the works of that eminent nature writer Seton Gordon. However, I would like to include an observation here which demonstrates amply the breath-taking excitement of birdwatching in Skye. It was made by the Rev. H. A. Macpherson on 20 June 1890: 'Standing in the plantation at Orbost, I heard a *Cuculus canorus* sing out "cuckoo, cuckoo, cucker-cucker-cucker", and immediately after he alighted on a tree above my head. There I had an excellent opportunity of observing his movements. Perching athwart a bough near the top of the tree, he proceeded to rearrange his plumage, and first he raised his long right wing and preened the feathers with care. Next he rearranged the feathers of the left wing. The breast followed, and then bending his neck backwards he expanded the tail in fan fashion, passing each of the long rectrices carefully through his bill. What more might have followed I know not, for a passing cart disturbed him and away he hurried, much to my regret.' Who said birdwatching was dull! Birds seen by one ornithologist at Sligachan and Glen Brittle, during a single summer holiday were: song-thrush, blackbird, ring-ouzel, wheat-dear, whinchat, stonechat, redstart, robin, willow wren, dipper, wren, pied wagtail, grey wagtail, meadow pipit, tree pipit, rock pipit, spotted flycatcher, house sparrow, tree sparrow, chaffinch, linnet, twite, corn bunting, yellow-hammer, reed bunting, star-ling, carrion crow, hoodie crow, rook, raven, skylark, cuckoo, tawny owl, buzzard, golden eagle, kestrel, cormorant, shag, gannet, heron, mallard, widgeon, eider duck, red-breasted merganser, rock dove, red grouse, ptarmigan, corncrake, golden plover, ringed plover, lapwing, turnstone, oyster catcher, snipe, dunlin, sandpiper, redshank, greenshank, curlew, whimbrel, tern, gull, herring gull, lesser black-backed gull, kittiwake, razorbill, guillemot, black guillemot, puffin and a black-throated diver.

Cuillins (KOO-linz) – This, the finest range of mountains in Britain, appears in a variety of names – Cuilfhionn, Cuildhean, Cuilionn, Culinn, Quillin, Coolins, Cuilluelum, Cuchullin, Gulluin and Cullaelum. There are something like twenty four peaks in the range of which the highest are:

Sgurr Alasdair	3,251	Am Baisteir	3,070
Sgurr Dearg	3,206	Sgurr Dubh na Da Bheinn	3,069
Sgurr Thearlaich	3,201	Sgurr Fionn Choire	3,065
Sgurr a' Ghreadaidh	3,190	Sgurr Thormaid	3,040
Sgurr nan Gillean	3,167	Sgurr nan Eag	3.037
Sgurr na Banachdaich	3,167	Sgurr a' Mhadaidh	3,010
Bruach na Frithe	3,143	Sgur Mhic Coinnich	3,017
Sgurr Sgumain	3,104	Gars-bheinn	2,934
Sgurr Dubh Mor	3,084	Bidean Druim nan Ramh	2,850

The first thing to be remembered about any excursion into the Cuillins is that they constitute an area of risk. The nature of the rock and the treacherous changes of weather mean that the inexperienced climber can all too easily get into difficulty. Before attempting any climb or walk beyond your powers remember that between 1945 and 1968 there were *thirty* fatalities in casualties – an average of four accidents a year. Over and above the recorded accidents sixty-five people were lost in the Cuillins during that period, and through their foolishness the volunteer rescue teams spent long and arduous hours unnecessarily in the hills. It is not unusual for a Skyeman on these occasions, having worked hard all week, to spend Saturday and Sunday in the hills searching for a climber and then, perhaps without sleep, report for work on Monday morning.

Never climb in the Cuillins with less than three in the party, so that if there is an accident one can stay with the injured person while another goes for help. In winter, it may not be possible to complete many of the more lengthy climbs before nightfall and they should on no account be attempted. Wear warm windproof clothing, carry adequate supplies of food, take a torch, a whistle and a contour map. Let someone know exactly where you are going and when you hope to be back and do not deviate from your chosen route. The Cuillins were at one time covered with ice and they are characteristic of post-glacial scenery. Opinions vary about the etymology. Were they named after Cuchullin, the Irish hero, or were they the hiding-place (Cuil Fhinn) of Fingal, or perhaps their prickly shape led people to call them sea-holly – *cuilionn-mara?* The Cuillins, remnants only of a high tableland which rose to a height of 15,000 feet, have formed the backdrop of hundreds of paintings ranging from the impressionist and irrelevant vision of Turner down to the lower slopes of talent. Poets have been inspired and some who weren't poets. Tennyson had a go –

Leave the monstrous ledges there to slope.
And spill their thousand wreaths of dangling water-smoke
That, like a broken promise, waste in air . . .

as Walter Scott had before him; even Cecil Day Lewis, Poet
Laureate, has felt them worth mentioning:

Land's End to Lewis I know, but I love best
My Western Islands where the rain purrs on
Blue profound anchorage, where the moon climbs
Over the Coolins.

Pennant called them *savage;* Johnson, *malignant;* Ruskin,
inferior, Black, jagged, monstrous, grim, much of their fascina-
tion derives not from their bulk but from the interplay of clouds
and the peculiar quality of light and shade which is found in
Skye. Rising in many places from the seashore, the Cuillins,
although not high by climbing standards, are impressive enough
to startle most travellers into silence. Many people have
recorded their first impressions of the Cuillins; this account by
Lord Cockburn in September 1841 captures the feeling of
delight and surprise many ordinarily prosaic people experience
on first encountering this strange combination of the savage and
picturesque.

At last at the distance of about seven or eight miles,
across a sheet of calm bright water, the Cuillin Hills stood
before us – seen from their bases to their tops – some of
their pinnacles veiled in thin vapour, but most of them in
the light of a brilliant meridian sun. I gazed in admiration,
and could not for a long time withdraw myself from the
contemplation of that singular assemblage of mountainous
forms. The beauty that shone over all these objects was the
beauty of mere light and form: for there was little visible
vegetation, not one tree, no verdure, no apparent house, no
ruin, no sound. But the positions and the forms of the
objects were admirable, and a depth of interest was
impressed upon the whole circle around me, by its universal
hardness and sterility, which no softening could have
increased.

D

Deer exist but do not abound in Skye. The Red Deer (*cervus elaphus*), the largest mammal still roaming wild in Britain, is

difficult to see in the summer – when the midges and flies arrive the deer depart for higher ground and don't descend until the autumn. Although there are deer scattered all over Skye most of them are in the Coruisk district, in Sleat and on the hills to the north of the Kylerhea ferry. Deer tend to lie up for long periods during the day and are most accessible when they are feeding, either in the early morning or in the afternoon and evening. At the peak of the fashion for slaughtering deer, just before the first world war, there were about 180,000 deer in the Highlands and the annual bag was about 15,000. Today there are only about 60,000 in the Highland counties – no individual survey has been carried out in Skye.

Diatomite is a dry earth formed by microscopic unicellular algae. The tiny cell walls of the algae are almost pure silica which is deposited on the bed of a loch or wherever the algae are when the plant dies. Because it is highly absorbent (it can hold three times its own weight of water) diatomite is used in pressure filtration, and heat and sound insulation. Toothpaste, silver polish, explosives and cosmetics are some of the products which contain diatomite. There are deposits at Digg, Sartle and Kilmuir, but the most extensive are on the bed of Loch Cuithir which lies in the shadow of Creag a Lain in Trotternish. The loch can be approached by road but there is nothing to be seen there now except a ruined building and the rusting remains of an army lorry. A light railway once ran from the loch to the Staffin road at Inver Tote. There is an account by Dr. J. A. MacCulloch, Rector of St. Columba's Portree, of a visit he made to the works in Edwardian times. Leaving Portree in a boat which was going to collect diatomite they anchored off Inver Tote and were ferried ashore in blazing June sunshine:

> A drying and grinding factory has been erected at the water's edge; great sheds stand on the upper slopes at a precarious angle; while a miniature railway, the continuation of one which runs inland to the diatomite beds, connects the edge of the cliff with the landing-stage and factory far below. When we arrived the work-people were all at the loch and there was scarce a sign of life round this lonely bay. But presently a long train of men and women began to zigzag down the path on the face of the slope and transformed this solitude into humming activity. They must get the cargo embarked while the tide served. Each one carried a bag of diatomite from the grinding-house to the boat slip, till the coble was piled up with sacks. Then it made a slow journey to the steamer, where the sacks were transferred to the hold. Meanwhile a second coble was a-filling, and so all day long, for there were hundreds and hundreds of sacks to be removed, the work went steadily on.

During the first world war the industry gave employment to quite a few local people, but production stopped between the wars. A recent attempt to revive the industry (the diatomite was taken by road to Uig for processing) proved uneconomic. In 1969 a feasibility survey into the prospects for exploiting the Loch Cuithir diatomite was halted when the man who commissioned the survey became convinced that even with a government grant the industry would not pay its way. There are those, however, who still believe that with initiative and inventiveness diatomite could once again be quarried profitably.

Diet in Skye, before people began importing manufactured food-stuffs from the mainland, was simple and wholesome: barley, oatmeal, milk, butter, cheese, salt beef, fish and mutton. In the large houses of Skye in the eighteenth century travellers were entertained lavishly. Boswell records, among other dishes, enjoying venison pasty, barley bannocks, chicken pie, fricassee of fowl, liver pudding, minced collops, ham, roast turkey, goat's whey and buttermilk. He drank tea, chocolate and coffee and toasted his hosts in port, Frontignac, claret, Scotch porter, punch brandy, Holland's gin, and mountain – a variety of Malaga. Today diet in Skye is less varied than it is in the south. The long and costly journey north makes perishable fruit and vegetables relatively expensive and difficult to obtain. Whereas in England there has always been a tradition of growing vegetables in gardens and on allotments, the Skye crofter is not a great market gardener. Although there is ample evidence that with proper cultivation any fruit and vegetables that grow in other parts of Scotland will grow in Skye, most families seem content to plant a patch of potatoes and grow a few cabbages and leave it at that. Convenience foods like fish fingers, instant potato powder and other expensive time-saving substitutes for fresh food achieve a higher than average regional popularity. Local mutton and fish are superb when properly cooked, but it is often difficult to find indigenous food, and an entire meal may consist of packet, tinned, frozen or in some way preserved food. There is no great tradition of cooking in the island and those expecting gastronomic delights may leave Skye disappointed.

Digg (DEEG) – a township on the north edge of Staffin Bay – the name means a ditch or dyke. William Mackenzie in his book on Trotternish reported that 'A man at Digg got all his work done by the Flodigarry fairies. He was at a loss how to get rid of them. A neighbour told him to give them a sieve and order them to bale the sea.' The people of Digg had a nickname (eke-names, as they were called, were liberally bestowed in olden days) of *Na Boguis* – the Bugs; not unpleasant bugs, but bugs all the same.

Diseases that were prevalent when Martin Martin wrote about Skye at the beginning of the eighteenth century included: 'Feavers, Stitches, Collick, Head-ach, Megrim, Jaundise, Sciatica, Stone, Small-pox, Measles, Rickets, Scurvy, Worms,

Fluxes, Tooth-ach, Cough and Squinance'. The 1841 Gazetteer of Scotland noted: 'Agues, fevers, rheumatism, and dysenteries, as might be expected, are prevailing distempers; yet the climate is far from being aggregately unhealthy, and nurses as large a proportion of the inhabitants to a good old age as many a climate of sensible balminess and amenity.'

Duirinish (DOO-rin-ish) – One of the four districts into which the Norsemen divided Syke north of the Cuillins. The others were Minginish, Waternish and Trotternish.

Dulse Soup Before the arrival of green pea soup in packets this was a great Skye favourite and was recommended for its medicinal and health-giving properties. William Mackenzie of Trotternish recalled in the 'thirties: 'I remember people coming from Snizort to Holm for supplies of dulse, a distance of twelve miles.' Dulse contains iodine, and before iodine itself was discovered it was considered very efficacious as a sweetener of the blood and for warding off or curing scrofulous and glandular afflictions. Dulse was also eaten raw; chopped into small pieces and boiled with a little butter, flour and seasoning it wasn't at all bad.

Caragheen, an even finer type of seaweed, purple in colour and becoming yellowish-white when dried, is still boiled with milk in Skye to make a very tasty pudding. 'Curly seaweed' (*Feamainn Chirein*) used to be boiled and fed to cattle.

Dun Arkaig (DOON AR-keg) – see **Ose**

Dun Ban (DOON BAHN) – see **Aird of Sleat**

Dun Beag (DOON BEG) – see **Struanmore**

Dun Fiadhairt (DOON FEE-uch-ursht) – This *broch* on the shores of Camalig Bay, a mile or so north of Dunvegan castle, was excavated in 1914. Among the objects found were pieces of pottery, an amber necklace and a terra cotta model of a bale of goods of Roman origin. It was intended to be placed on the altar of a Roman deity as a kind of travel insurance against ill-luck on a journey – and especially one so fraught with danger as a voyage to the *Haebudes*.

Dun Gerashader (DOON GERR-a-shutter) – the fort of the little dwelling. The *dun* here, a mile north of Portree on the right-hand side of the Staffin road, was a one-time powerful fort with walls 14 ft. thick in parts – most of the *dun* went to make dry walls on nearby farms, but traces of the walls are still recognizable amid the rubble.

Dun Sleadale (DOON SLAY-dul) – see **Talisker**

Dun Suledale (DOON SOOL-y-dul) – see **Clachamish**

Dun Taimh (DOON TIVE) – see **Gesto**

Dunara Castle – was one of the longest-lived steamers that ever sailed among the islands of the west. Her maiden voyage was on 21 June 1875, and for nearly 73 uninterrupted years she served the Hebrides. She made her last voyage in January 1948 and was broken up in Port Glasgow during that summer. With twin funnels and tall masts fore and aft she left Glasgow every Thursday at 2 p.m. for Greenock, Colonsay, Iona, Bunessan, Tiree Carbost, Struan, Colbost, Dunvegan, Stein, Uig, Tarbert, Obbe, Lochmaddy Benbecula, Lochboisdale and Barra.

Dunringill – in Strathaird. On the shores of Loch Slapin (nearest point is Kirkibost on the Elgol road) lie the ruins of Castle Ringill, 900 years ago the seat of the Clan Fingon. Dean Munro in his description of the Western Isles (*circa* 1549) mentions 'the castill Dunringill perteining to the said Mackyn-noun'. Dunringill must have been in a fairly good state of preservation then; today it's just another mass of rubble.

Dunscaith (doon-SKAA) – the fort of gloom. The castle, one of the oldest fortified headlands in the Hebrides, occupies the summit of an isolated rock on the north corner of Ob Gauscavaig on the southern shore of the mouth of Loch Eishort and is only a couple of minutes' walk from the road. There is a ravine between the castle and the mainland crossed by two arched walls which once no doubt were bridged over with wood – with that long since gone, those suffering from vertigo shouldn't attempt to enter the castle. Although this is the best preserved ruin in Skye the building is only of random rubble and every year that passes sees a little more decay. As the Royal Commission on Ancient Monuments pointed out over 40 years ago: 'As the mortar disintegrates under the influence of the sea, air and wind, the stones at the foundations loosen and fall away, and the upper courses then collapse from their own weight.' As with all Skye's ruined castles one has the sad feeling that if only they were in Hampshire or Sussex they would be in a better state of preservation – people in the south seem to have more energy and time on their hands to organize preservation pressure groups and prevent the past from crumbling away by default and neglect.

MacPherson, the midwife of Ossian, relates that Cuthullin, son of Semo, and grandson of Cathbaid and at some time in the third century Chief of Skye, had his headquarters at Dunscaith. An old Skye legend, about as reliable as any other old Skye legend, claims that the castle was run up in a single night:

All night the witch sang, and the castle grew
Up from the rock, with tower and turrets crowned;
All night she sang – when fell the morning dew
'Twas finished round and round –

In a twelfth-century manuscript it is related how Cuchulainn mounted an expedition against the castle upon each of whose seven ramparts was a palisade of iron spiked by nine human heads. In the fastnesses of Dunscaith was a pit guarded by ten snakes. Having slain the snakes, Cuchulainn was then set on by a tribe of beaked beasties like malevolent toads who clung to his nose while dragon-type monsters harried him elsewhere. Our hero beat them all, put out to sea in his coracle laden with treasure but unfortunately was wrecked in a storm. The treasure sank to the bottom of the sea but Cuchulainn, undaunted, swam ashore, carrying 30 men on his head, nine on each of his mighty palms and a further four brace hanging on to his thighs. Other legends tell of Sgathach, a Queen in the days of Fingla, with whom Cuchulainn fell in love. She evidently was something of an Amazon, keeping a military school at which Cuchulainn learned his skill with arms. She also possessed a magical three-stringed harp, one string of which when plucked caused singing and merriment. A large boulder, known as Clach Luath, near the castle, is still pointed out as the rock to which Cuchulainn tied his dog Luath when he returned from the chase. All this is fiction; what we do know for certain is that Dunscaith was the ancestral home of the MacDonalds of Sleat. The earliest written mention of the castle is contained in a charter of 1505. The last documentary evidence of the occupation of Dunscaith is 16 January 1572 when Donald Grom, son of the sixth Chief, signed at 'Dounsceiche' an obligation to the Bishop of the Isles. Dunscaith remained the home of the MacDonalds until the closing years of the sixteenth century. Why they left for Duntulm in the first two decades of the seventeenth century is not known, but it may have been to consolidate their right to lands in Trotternish, where they were being leaned on rather heavily by their traditional enemies the MacLeods.

Duntulm the fort of the island of Tuilm. This ancient seat of the MacDonalds of the Isles occupies the seaward end of a ridge about a mile from the northern tip of Skye. It is approached from the road through the fields of a farm and is in a poor state of repair. The ruins look across the Minch to the hills of Harris - legend says that on this site stood the Dun of David, a Viking chief. The cliffs drop sheer to the sea on three sides and on the beach below can be seen a long indentation in the rocks which many people fondly, but perhaps erroneously, believe to have been made by the keels of Viking galleys.

The main part of Duntulm is fifteenth century and the earliest mention of it occurs in the Description of the Isles appended to Skene's *Celtic Scotland* published in the 1580s: 'Thair was an castell in Trouterness callit Duncolmend quhair of the wallis standis yet.' They standeth still but largely through luck – a nineteenth-century tenant of the farm of Duntulm had large portions of the castle blown up with gunpowder to get stones for a wall he was building. The territory of Trotternish was fought over for more than a hundred years by the MacLeods and the MacDonalds of Sleat, but in the early years of the seventeenth century the lands of Trotternish were finally settled by the Crown on the MacDonalds and it was then that Sir Donald Gorm began to build himself a dwelling amid the earlier ruins of Duntulm. Their stay in Duntulm was relatively brief – Armadale in Sleat was where they spent most of their time until it was burnt by government troops hunting for Sir Donald after the battle of Killiecrankie. With the failure of the 'Fifteen' the Chief returned to Duntulm a broken man. He died on 1 March 1718, and his estates were confiscated by the Crown. The castle was finally deserted in the early 1730s. At this time Sir Alexander MacDonald began to build a house at Monkstadt using stones from Duntulm. No doubt while the castle was in the hands of the Commissioners of Forfeited Estates it had begun to decay, and rather than repair the chilly family dwelling the young Lord decided to build himself something a bit less exposed and a lot more comfortable. Tradition, however, gives two reasons for the move. The first story is that Donald Gorm, a black sheep of the family, died in Edinburgh and began haunting the place in such a beastly way that the family were forced to leave. The second story concerns a clumsy nurse who, holding a young member of the family up at a window to see a galley arriving, dropped the child on to the rocks below. The family, shattered by this tragedy, decided that they could no longer bear to remain in a place with such unhappy associations. You must decide for yourself what authenticity attaches to these stories, but the Nurse and Baby incident is also said to be the reason why the MacLeods left their castle at Glenelg - of course it could have been the same accident-prone nurse employed in both castles, but this is unlikely as the MacDonalds gave *their* nurse notice in a most original way: the Chief arranged for her to be cast adrift in a boat drilled full of holes.

The last Chief to have lived in Duntulm was Domhnull a' Chogaidh (Donald of the Wars). He once invited all the quality to a grand ball in Duntulm and it must have been quite a ball. Even at the beginning of this century the memories lingered on: 'What happened to all the fifty young ladies on that night' wrote an exiled Skyeman, 'was not forgotten when I left Eilean a' Cheo!'

Dunvegan Skye's most famous building, said to be the oldest inhabited castle in Britain, takes its name from an Icelandic settler called Began – at least that is one theory. There is a tradition which states that Dunvegan was built in the ninth century, but the main edifice which presents itself to the eye of the tourist today is largely nineteenth century. In 1812 when the MacDonalds were contemplating the expansion of their house at Armadale into a mock-Gothic castle, the twenty-fourth Chief of MacLeod commissioned a battled mound at his front door and also built the main hall, the flanking towers, and a drawbridge which was removed by his son. It was this Chief who entertained Sir Walter Scott. His embellishments cost £4,000 and during the hungry 'forties, Norman, the twenty-fifth Chief, lavished a further £8,000 on pepper-box turrets and other flights of fancy. This pseudo-baronial conversion, breathing the spirit of Scott's *Lord of The Isles,* was quite unlike the castle in which Dr. Johnson was so lavishly entertained. Today the outer walls of the castle are covered with a porridge-coloured stucco such as is widely favoured by Inverness County Council for its public housing schemes - a drab and prosaic exterior to the ancient stones within.

The interior of the castle contains hunting trophies, all manner of weapons and curiosities and three prize showpieces – the Fairy Flag, the Dunvegan Cup and Rory Mor's Drinking Horn. The Cup was made at the end of the fifteenth century by 'Katharina, daughter of King Neil, wife of John, grandson of Macguire, prince of Firmanagh'. It is ten inches high and made of wood ornamented with silver; each side has a unique design and it stands on four legs. Sir Rory Mor's Drinking Horn rimmed with silver was used as a test of endurance in the past – every Chief on succeeding to his title was required to drain the horn in one gulp. Also on view are letters from Scott and Dr. Johnson, Stuart relics and Flora MacDonald's stays.

In the eighteenth century there were no trees at Dunvegan, but in the last decade of the century General MacLeod began tree-planting and it has been computed that at one time at least a third of the British flora was represented in the Dunvegan policies. In the great hurricane of March 1921 over 40,000 of these trees were blown down.

Duvegan itself is a small township with good hotels dominated by a pretentious motorway which sweeps up to the gates of the castle and abruptly ends.

E

Eaglais Bhreugach (ECK-lish VREE-ack-uch) – the false or lying church. This rock on the shore three-quarters of a mile south of the Lealt Waterfall in the north end of Skye is so called because of its similarity to a church. Here the Clan MacOoian (Clann 'Ic Cuithen, or MacQueens) are supposed to have performed diabolical ceremonies involving the roasting of cats and generally raised the devil. The ceremony was known as *Taghairm*. The clan (said to have been absorbed into the Clan Donald) were not highly thought of – a rhyme concerning them and their friends runs:

> Clan MacOoian, thievish experts,
> Clan MacOoan, quick to flatter
> Clan Buchanan, theft promoters
> Though as short as a dagger shaft.

Eagles The golden eagle (*aquila chrysaetos*) is a comparatively rare bird but there are quite a few still to be seen in Skye – one eyrie is within three miles of the main street of Portree. The bird can be confused with the buzzard, but its thickly feathered legs make identification fairly easy. The eagle weighs about the same as a good-sized Christmas turkey and has a formidable wing span of more than six ft. It makes its eyrie out of heather roots, and branches of mountain ash. The eagle prefers a north-facing cliff commanding a wide area of country from which it can swoop down for its food – rabbits, hares, grouse, young birds, young deer and sometimes, so farmers say, new-born lambs. Mating takes place from January until the middle of March, and the eggs are usually laid in clutches of two. On many occasions the first eaglet to hatch monopolizes the food supplied by the parents and the weaker eaglet starves to death. John Mackenzie of Portree, a keen amateur ornithologist, has in his time climbed up to various eyries and hand-fed the weaker bird to ensure that the eagle population of Skye continues to exist.

An earlier age was more concerned with protecting its investment in the land than cosseting what was regarded as a rival predator. Sheriff Nicolson in the 1880s was 'afraid the chance of a sight so appropriate to the scene (an eagle soaring aloft) is becoming small by degrees, if the Glen Brittle gamekeeper wages war on the kingly bird as successfully as he did a few years ago when he could boast of having killed sixty of the royal creatures in thirty-six months'.

With the arrival of sheep in Skye, keepers and poachers were paid as much as a guinea for a dead eagle because it had acquired a reputation for scooping young lambs from the hills and bearing them off to be devoured at leisure. Martin Martin relates the story of a native of Skye called Niall Iolair - Neil Eagle –

> who when an infant was left by his Mother in the Field, not far from the Houses on the North side *Loch Portrie*; an Eagle came in the mean time, and carried him away in its Tallons as far as the south side of the *Loch,* and there laying him on the ground, some People that were herding Sheep there perceiv'd it, and hearing the Infant cry, ran immediately to its rescue; and by good Providence found him untouch'd by the Eagle, and carried him home to his Mother.

The golden eagle is, of course, a protected bird, and John Mackenzie estimates that there are still as many as fifty breeding pairs in Skye. The sea eagle ceased to breed in Skye towards the end of last century.

Edinbane or **Edinbain** a small village six miles from Dunvegan. It derives its name (The Fair Face) from its pleasant situation. It was here that a MacLeod of Gesto who made a fortune as an indigo planter in India built the first hospital in Skye – now used for geriatric cases.

Elgol Tradition says that Vortigern sent a warrior called Aella with five ships; he fought a battle against the Picts and Scots at this place – hence Aella-gol. Elgol, on the shores of Loch

Scavaig, attracts quite a few tourists because it's from here in the season that motor boats leave for Loch Coruisk – weather permitting. Weather often doesn't permit, which can be disappointing if you've driven specially from the north end of the island. Half a mile to the south of Elgol on the promontory of Suidhe Biorach (The Sharp Seat) where childless married women sat in the forlorn hope of achieving fertility, is Prince Charlie's Cave where he was hidden before leaving Skye for good.

Emigration from Skye began in the middle of the eighteenth century. There were several reasons why people were forced to the conclusion that if they would be no better off elsewhere they certainly couldn't be worse off. The clan system in which the Chief assumed responsibility for his 'family' had begun to break down. The young Chiefs sent south to receive expensive educations at Eton and Oxford found Skye a dull and uncouth place on their return. They soon returned to the south, where they needed money to live in the manner to which they had been accustomed. 'Sucked into the vortex of the nation,' wrote a later MacLeod of his eighteenth-century forebears, 'and lured to the capitals, they degenerated from patriarchs and chieftains to landlords; and they became as anxious for the increasing of rents as the new-made lairds, the *novi homines*, the mercantile purchasers of the low-lands.' The increasing demand for black cattle in the abattoirs of the south meant a corresponding rise in the value of grazing land; rents were sometimes doubled and trebled.

Carolina in the New World was the first area of settlement to attract Skyemen. In September 1771, 370 set sail from Skye for North Carolina. The black winter of 1771-72 encouraged many more to follow in their wake. In June 1771, a minister, a Portree merchant and several tacksmen presented a petition to the Privy Council asking for 40,000 acres of land in North Carolina. Alarmed by the growing exodus of the Scots the request was refused. In October 1773 the people of Skye were so enkindled by the prospect of leaving for a better life that Boswell recorded that he took part in a dance called 'America':

It goes on till all are set a-going, setting and wheeling round each other . . . . It shows how emigration catches till all are set afloat. Mrs Mackinnon told me that last year when the ship sailed from Portree for America, the people on shore were almost distracted when they saw their relations go off; they lay down on the ground and tumbled, and tore the grass with their teeth. This year there was not a tear shed. The people on shore seem to think that they would soon follow.

There had already been a mass emigration in the spring and summer of 1772 caused by bad harvests, the cattle blight and rising rents, but the most striking departures came in 1769 and the following years. In 1769 Sir Alexander MacDonald's tenants formed an association to purchase 100,000 acres of land in South Carolina, and so many people left that Sir Alexander was forced to bring in tenants from the mainland. Between the years 1771 and 1790 eight large transports are estimated to have carried about 2,000 people from Skye to the New World.

The greatest wave of emigration began with the Clearances. Sheep graziers from the south began to offer far higher rents than the indigenous tenants and the temptation to accept a fat secure rent was seldom resisted. Whole communities were turned out to make way for the Cheviot sheep, the shepherd and the collie dogs. Several wealthy mainland farmers took possession of tacks in the island, and the western side of Skye was soon being converted into sheep runs. It has been calculated that 2,000 people were dispossessed from the MacLeod estates and altogether 3,500 were forced to move in various parts of Skye. Some found homes on inferior or exhausted land too poor to provide grazing for sheep, but a large majority left for good. In 1837 a party of 459 set sail for Australia; in 1840 and 1841 as many as 600 left for America and Australia from the parish of Portree alone.

It cannot fail [wrote the Portree minister] to afford the highest satisfaction to every well-regulated mind to see the effort now made by noble men, proprietors, and others connected with the Highlands of Scotland for transferring the poor and labouring classes of the community to the British colonies . . . the highest praise is due to Lord MacDonald for his liberality in this beneficent work and patriotic enterprise, he having expended large sums of money, both this year and last in conveying the poor people on his property to America.

To send an emigrant from Skye to Cape Breton in the 1840s cost £2. 5s.

I calculate the voyage at 35 days [a witness told the Select Committee on Emigration] the expense of food during those 35 days, at 9d. a day, is £1. 6s. 3d.; then in addition, I calculate that they require assistance in the shape of clothing and blankets to the amount of £1 per head. That would bring out an amount of £4. 11s. 3d. for a single person. But if you care to remove a great population it can be done for less.

This same witness, John Bowie, a Writer to the Signet, suggested that 9,000 of the 22,796 population of Skye should be assisted to emigrate. Emigration was not accomplished without a high toll in human lives. Speaking about one year's havoc on board ships sailing to Canada and New Brunswick an M.P. told the House of Commons: 'Out of 106,000 emigrants from Ireland and Scotland, 6,100 perished on the voyage, 4,100 on their arrival, 5,200 in the hospitals and 1,900 in the towns to which they repaired.'

In 1851 when destitution was widespread in Skye a 'Skye Emigration Society' was formed. Its aim was to 'procure help for those who wish to emigrate but have not the means of doing so, to afford information, encouragement and assistance to all for whom emigration would be a relief from want and misery'. The Society intended to help unwanted islanders to settle in Australia and Canada for something between £1 and £11: 'Let each consider well and answer the question for himself. Is it not his duty to endeavour to remove to a country where his services would be valued, and would readily procure for him not only plenty of food and clothing, but the means of rising to a comfortable and respectable independence?' The Society blossomed and Queen Victoria became its patron. The first ship to sail under the auspices of the Society was the *Georgiana* which left Greenock for Melbourne in May 1853 with 312 emigrants, most of them from Skye. They sang the 23rd Psalm as they sailed away, the great majority never to return.

It has been estimated that between 1840 and 1883 the number of families evicted in Skye was 6,940 or, taking each family at five, 34,700 people. Whole areas were ruthlessly cleared, some from end to end. In 1852, for instance, Ballingall, the inflexible factor employed by Lord MacDonald, cleared Borreraig and Suisnish, in many cases physically destroying houses so that the people would be forced away. Had these people been going to a better life than the miserable one they were leaving there might have been some charity in the concept of assisted emigration, but in many cases terrible privation awaited the settlers. An article in the *Celtic Monthly* in 1879 talked of 'Fathers, mothers, and children (who) bound themselves away as virtual slaves in some settlement for a mere subsistence. Some lived in huts with only bushes as roofs, and had to walk some eighty miles through deep snow, and through trackless forests, in order to obtain a few bushels of potatoes, or a little flour, in exchange for their labour, dragging the commodities back on their backs.'

The manifest cruelty and injustice of the Clearances came to a head in the district of Braes where the activities of Lord MacDonald's factor and the resistance of his tenants eventually led to a Royal Commission.

Emigration still continues – mainly a drift to the mainland towns. The figures for the 1960s reveal how Skye is slowly emptying; as the old people die and the young people turn towards the cities the population follows the steady downward decline that began one hundred and thirty years ago:

1961 – 7,700		1965 – 7,250	
1962 – 7,650		1966 – 7,150	
1963 – 7,600		1967 – 7,000	
1964 – 7,400		1968 – 6,700	

F

Fairies The names bestowed on fairies derive from the Gaelic word *sith* (pronounced *shee*). *Sith* means peace or silence; fairy folk go about their ways quietly, unlike humans who are a clod-hopping lot at the best of times. The most noise they ever make is no louder than a gust of wind or the swish of silk or the whistle of a sword cutting through thin air. They are keen on musical instruments and songs. There are fairy banners, fairy cows, cats and cuckoos. They come in all sizes, small enough to enter through a keyhole, large enough to be mistaken for a human. Average height is about 4 ft. They live by preference within grassy knolls and in rocks, but for some reason avoid caves. Their favourite colour is green; fairy men wear any colour but prefer red, dying their clothes with *crotal*. Fairies have foibles similar to humans – they can even get drunk. Favourite occupations are spinning, weaving and grinding meal or making fairy arrows. Some fairies are poorer than others, and reading old descriptions of fairy life gives rise to the impression that being a fairy is every bit as tedious as being human. Like rain, fairies usually come from the west and are a thieving lot, even though they only take what men deserve to lose.

Fairy Bridge where three rivers and three roads converge between Waternish and Dunvegan.

Once upon a time a Chief of the MacLeods married a fairy, but after some years had passed nostalgia overtook Mrs. MacLeod, a longing so strong that she announced she must return to the land of Faerie – sadly MacLeod walked with her from the castle and they parted by the burn now spanned by Fairy Bridge.

Many meetings were held here during the period of the Disruption and vast congregations would assemble to be instructed in the evils of the Established Church and the virtues of the Free Church. Here, too, at a later date, the crofters met to discuss Land Reform and listen to the fierce oratory of John MacPherson, 'the Glendale Martyr'.

Fairy flag Formed of yellow silk, the flag which is displayed in Dunvegan castle is said to have been taken by a MacLeod from a Saracen chief during the Crusades. When the flag was being prepared for its present frame it was examined by experts who gave this report:

> We believe that this silk was woven either in Syria or Rhodes, and that the darns it contains were made in the Near East. In our opinion these darns suggest that in its original home it was regarded as something very precious, a holy relic perhaps, such as the shirt of a Saint. We know that Harold Hardrada from whom Leod 1st Chief of Clan MacLeod was descended was in Constantinople in the eleventh century, and here may lie the explanation of how the flag came into the MacLeod hands.

The flag is thought by MacLeods to possess miraculous powers and to have been presented to them by the fairies; that it has a continuing tradition of potency was revealed by a letter which Dame Flora MacLeod of MacLeod received from a member of the clan during the second world war, who told her that his remarkable record of luck in bombing missions over Germany was due to the photograph of the flag which he carried in his pocket.

Sir Walter Scott when he visited Dunvegan was told that the flag had three properties: 'produced in battle, it multiplied the numbers of the MacLeods – spread on the nuptial bed, it ensured fertility – and lastly, it brought herring into the loch'. Other traditions say that it must be waved only when the clan was in grave danger on the battlefield, when the heir of the family was at death's door or when the MacLeods were in danger of extinction. In any of these extreme emergencies the day could be saved by unfurling the flag. But there was a minor penalty attached – an invisible being would carry off the standard and the standard-bearer never to be seen on earth again. It is small wonder that people didn't exactly tread on each other's toes in the queue to become the MacLeod standard bearer, despite the fact that a gift of free lands in Bracadale went with this dubious post.

Fertility 'It is a general Observation', wrote Skyeman Martin Martin in 1703, 'of all such as live on the Sea Cost, that they are more prolifick than any other People whatsoever.'

Fingal's Seat overlooking Portree has a golf course on its lower slopes. There is a race to the summit held during the annual Games. Fingal is supposed to have come to Skye where he organized a vast deer drive in Strath during which 6,000 deer were slain. Tradition says that he sat on top of the hill directing the chase in the valleys below and must therefore have been a giant of remarkable vision.

Fish The commonest caught in the waters round Skye are the whiting, saithe (or coalfish), lythe (or pollack), cod, herring, haddock and mackerel. Dogfish abound but are seldom eaten. Although the great majority of Skye's 182 townships lie on the coast there are only about a hundred men engaged in whitefish or shellfish fishing. The landings in Skye during 1968 totalled 422 cwt. of whitefish worth £364 and 2,067 cwt. of shellfish worth £27,211.

Recently the high prices fetched by prawns have encouraged several Skye fishermen to make prawn-fishing a full-time job. The prawns (they are really what the French would call *langoustines)* are caught in baited creels and eventually find their way into the kitchens of fashionable restaurants in Paris,

Brussels and London. They can be bought locally from the fisherman but are fairly expensive. Grilled in butter or poached lightly they make a memorable meal. Poaching is not uncommon in Skye – while the police keep an eye on the rivers, fishery protection vessels patrol the waters around Skye to enforce the prohibition on seine-netting for whitefish and on beam and otter trawling within three miles of the shore. This ban has been in force since the end of the last century and was designed to protect the local fishermen from the ravages of the trawl. Crabs and lobsters are also protected and since 1966 it has been illegal to land, sell or possess crabs less than 4½ in. in breadth or lobsters less than 9 in. long.

Fladday Chuain (FLAD-ay <u>CH</u>OO-in) - a small group of islands about three miles north-west of the most northerly point of Skye, Hunish point. Sir Donald MacDonald of the Isles is said to have hidden his title deeds here before setting off to take part in the ill-fated rising of 1715. Here also are the ruins of a chapel dedicated to St. Columba – its blue altar stone used to be bathed with water by superstitious fisherman becalmed near the island in the hope that the Saint might vouchsafe them a fair wind. In the nineteenth century the islands were frequently visited by the men of Kilmuir in search of seabirds' eggs to supplement their diet.

Flodigarry A mile north of Staffin Bay, Flodigarry was the home of Flora MacDonald for several years and five of her seven children were born here. The house, beside the present hotel, looks a little too modern to have been standing there in 1750, but that's what they say. Flodigarry was once famed for its large fat herds of cattle. A legend relates that a woman who lived here lost her husband through witchcraft. After his death she saw him sitting by the fireside – but all he could think of to say was 'Why didn't they shave me before I was buried?'

The hotel was built as a private house by a wealthy Skye-man and descendant of Flora's, Major R. L. MacDonald – the interior, Moorish in parts, bears witness to the years he spent in the Middle East. A crack in the wall of the billiard-room was once pointed out out to me as evidence that Flodigarry House was gradually sliding into the sea. It was built on clay, I was told, and it was only a matter of time before the whole battlemented edifice was under the waves. That was nearly sixty years ago and the house is still there – it's a slow slide.

Forestry There is a strong tradition that much of Skye was at one time heavily wooded. Martin MacDonald of Achacork, near Portree, was recently collecting material for a B.B.C. Gaelic programme in Raasay, and in conversation a Raasayman, pointing across the Sound to the shores of north Skye, said 'Of course all that part of Trotternish was forest once,' and he added reflectively, 'The Vikings burnt it all down.' Whether burnt by Norsemen, cut for timber or inhibited by sheep, there is little natural wood left in Skye today and yet the oral tradition of a thick treescape persists. Writing in 1934 William MacKenzie of Culnacnoc quotes a letter he received from an old friend who had emigrated to Australia: 'When my great-grandfather's great-grandfather, Angus Nicolson, Marishadder, used to visit his son in Grealine (a mile distant) he could only see sky above him at one spot for the density of the wood. When the cows were let out in the morning they were not seen again till they came in for their calves at milking time.'

Where trees have been established, round the castles of Dunvegan and Armadale and the gardens of houses like Talisker, Tayinloan, Glen Brittle and Kingsburgh, they grow without difficulty, but the oases of trees are few and far between. The tree-planters today are not well-off lairds and tacksmen but the employees of the Forestry Commission. The Commission started planting trees in Skye in 1932 in Glen Brittle, and today in Skye and Raasay they have 17,740 acres of land of which just under 8,000 consist of plantations. They are planting new trees at the rate of 900 acres a year. Their policy is to acquire only upland grazing of poor quality, but even so there is a feeling in Skye that some of this land might be better used for sheep-grazing, indeed, that some of the money expended on planting trees to produce timber for the pulp mills might be better employed in improving the land for agricultural use.

Land is prepared for planting by ploughing furrows 6 or 7 ft. apart, which not only reduce the growth of weeds but also improve drainage and the richness of the soil. Sitka spruce, a Western North American tree, is the most widely planted variety because it grows relatively fast. Lodgepole pine is less productive but flourishes better on poorly drained peat and infertile stony ground.

So far the only plantations in Skye to yield timber for industry are the oldest established ones at Glen Brittle but the profitability of the timber, which goes to the pulp mill at Fort William, is substantially reduced by haulage and ferry charges. To keep out sheep, cattle and red deer over 100 miles of 6ft.-high fencing have been erected by the Forestry Commission, and it is perhaps surprising to find that all this activity gives employment to only four foresters and a workforce of just over thirty. There is a strange theory that the activities of the Forestry Commission have a depressing effect on the landscape, but I find the young trees growing in glens like Varragill and Hinnisdal a refreshing addition to a bleak moorland landscape. The Commission is fairly sensitive about this sort of critisism. 'In fact,' they assured me, 'modest efforts are being made to improve the amenities of the forest areas by planting groups of larch throughout the main mass of the plantations and by retaining broadleaved species along the sides of streams and in irregular groups on areas in public view.'

Forestry on a voluntary scale was started by the pupils of Portree High School at the beginning of 1969. In the glen through which the Leasgeary river enters Loch Portree they are busy planting shrubs and trees which in a few years time will turn this area into a small beauty spot. It's an example which, if emulated in other parts of the island, might well restore some of Skye's lost arboreal charm.

Fosterage was a common custom in bygone times, especially when the clan ties were at their strongest. The child of a superior family was often handed over to a family lower in the social scale to be brought up until the age of 14 in the case of a girl and 17 in the case of a boy. Very often this foster-bond became stronger than a blood tie; as the Gaelic proverb says: 'Beloved by a man is his friend, but as the marrow of his bone his foster-brother.'

Foxes are still a menace to Skye farmers. In the pre-sheep days when cattle were the main grazing animal the problem was not so acute, but with the arrival of sheep in the eighteenth century and the conservation of game in the nineteenth the fox, as a voracious predator, became Enemy Number One. Professor Walker in his *Hebrides* (1808) noted:

> Before the year 1764 the stock of sheep in the Highlands was very confined, and that chiefly by the havoc occasioned by the fox. In the year 1764 the gentlemen in Skye for the first time entered into a resolution to diminish the number of foxes, and for this purpose offered a premium of three shillings for each fox that was destroyed; in consequence of this offer, no less than one hundred and twelve foxes were killed in the year 1765 in the single district of Trotterness.

Fox hunters, known in Gaelic as *Brocair,* were paid an agreed sum by every farmer and a fee for every fox exterminated.

By the time Johnson arrived in Skye the price on the head of the fox had risen to a guinea, 'a sum so great in this part of the world, that in a short time Skye may be as free from foxes as England from wolves'. But the fox is a very persistent opponent. Today there are four fox-clubs operating in Skye not for the amusement or entertainment of foxes but for their extermination. Each crofter pays an amount of money into the club proportionate to his sheep-stock. This money (matched by a grant from the Department of Agriculture) goes to pay a professional fox exterminator who works with guns, traps and terriers. The Forestry Commission also carry out fox control on their plantations and several hundred foxes are killed in Skye every year.

G

Gaelic – pronounced *Gallic*, not *gaylic* or *garlic* – was dismissed by Dr. Johnson as 'the rude speech of a barbarous people who had few thoughts to express, and were content, as they conceived grossly, to be grossly understood', the sort of remark which didn't exactly make Johnson the Highlanders' favourite Englishman. Gaelic belongs to the Goedelic branch of the Celtic languages and was introduced into Scotland from Ireland around the end of the fifth century.

In 1616 an Act was passed by James VI proscribing the language and declaring that it should be extirpated. This attitude persisted for over a hundred years and came to a climax with the persecution of the Highlanders after the risings of 1715 and 1745. From being a nation which was predominantly bilingual, much of Scotland, particularly the Lowlands, became monoglot. The use of Gaelic in schools was officially discouraged and Scotland's first Education Act passed in 1872 made no provision for the teaching of Gaelic. *An Comunn Gaidhealach* (AN KOAM-un GUY-ull-uch) was founded in 1891 as a language protection society by a small group of people in Oban. In the following year they held their first National Mod and began to make representations about the future of Gaelic. Allied with the Highland Society of London and the Gaelic Society of Inverness they were successful in having a clause inserted in the 1918 Education Act which said that Gaelic would be taught in Gaelic-speaking areas. But the idea of Gaelic as a barrier to a full education was so ingrained that it took a long time to eradicate. As a result of the activities of the B.B.C., education authorities and the various Highland societies, a new awareness of the value of Gaelic has been noticeable in recent years. *An Comunn*, under the dynamic leadership of Donald J. Mackay has put forward six aims to improve the status of Gaelic. Gaelic, the society maintains, is the longest established institution in Britain, it superseded Norse in the Hebrides and resisted the incursions of English from the fifth century to the present day. It enshrines Europe's most continuous living literature and culture – a culture older than even Icelandic. Gaelic, even so, remains the only spoken language in Britain without legal recognition or adequate State aid. *An Comunn* believes that Gaelic could have as striking a renaissance as Faroese. Fifty years ago Faroese was dying. Danish was the language of administration and commerce. The revival of the Faroese language set off new ventures and renewed morale among the people. 'We too could parallel the Faroes' success commercially, economically, socially and culturally,' Donald Mackay has claimed, and his arguments are convincing. In 1958 the Education Committee for Inverness-shire decided to introduce a bi-lingual policy, and Gaelic began to be taught in primary schools in Gaelic-speaking areas and used as a medium of instruction. But the greatest danger to Gaelic at the moment is the emigration of Gaelic-speakers and the arrival of predominantly English-speaking incomers. Although at the moment Gaelic is studied in the Universities of Aberdeen, Glasgow and Edinburgh, and is taught to teachers in training in the Colleges of Education in Aberdeen and Glasgow it will be only through the increased use of the language in significant places – in government, business, councils and the courts – that a case for the official recognition of the language can be made. Official support seems marginal. The government recently gave a grant of £25,000 over five years to start an historical Gaelic dictionary and the Secretary of State also gave a grant of £20,000 to form a Gaelic Book Council.

The percentage of Skye people having Gaelic varies from 52 per cent. in Portree to as high as 94 per cent. in the Trotternish area. Although the 1961 census revealed that about three-quarters of the people spoke Gaelic, only one in five of the primary school children in Portree knew any Gaelic in 1968. The proportion of Gaelic-speaking children would, of course, be higher in country districts than in Portree with its large population of incomers from the mainland. Even so, Gaelic is losing its ground every year. Patricia Campbell, a pupil at Portree High School contributed an article to its excellent publication *Skye*

'68 which must have made depressing reading for those trying to promote a renaissance of interest in the language:

> In our own school [she wrote] here in Portree, Gaelic is
> never heard in the playground . . . in the school hostels
> even keen Gaelic speakers are forced into English due to
> lack of fluency in their friends, or from courtesy if two
> Gaelic speakers are in a group in which English is spoken.
> I would say that very few of the younger generation in Skye
> converse among themselves in Gaelic.

Geology Just as television producers make programmes for other television producers so geologists seem to write books which only a geologist could understand. I despaired of finding a simple account of how Skye came to look the way it does until one fine day in Uig I met George Black of the Nature Conservancy. It turned out that he had written his doctoral thesis on the geology of Skye and he promised, when he got back to his headquarters in Reading, to write a child's guide to the island's geological evolution. He sent me this simple non-technical account which explains quite painlessly how it all happened:

> The Isle of Skye shows the relationship between
> geology and environment more clearly than any others area
> of comparable size in Britain. Geological factors determine
> the obvious contrasts of the island – the stark montane
> grandeur of the Cuillins, the open treeless vistas of
> Trotternish, the sharply undulating, partly wooded, craggy
> topography of Sleat and the croft lands and gentle moors
> of Strath.
> The rocks which build Skye fall into three broad groups.
> The first, and youngest, belongs to the wreck of a great
> volcano active some 60 million years ago. Beneath lie the
> sandstone, limestone and clays of the second group, laid
> down some 135–180 million years ago in warm seas, teeming
> with life. The third and oldest group is more heterogenous,
> ranging in age from 500–2,500 million years. Its members
> have all shared deep burial in the Earth's crust where they
> were squeezed and broken by earth movements which, about
> 400 million years ago, raised the Scottish Highlands into a
> mountain chain comparable with the Alps or the Himalayas.

The volcanic rocks occupy most of the island. Lavas form the Duirinish and Waternish peninsulas and half of Trotternish; they extend south as far as the isthmuses between Loch Sligachan, Harport and Brittle and reappear in Strathaird.The root of the volcano from which the lavas were erupted is marked by the main mountain group of Skye. The Cuillin Hills and Blaven have been carved from a large mass of coarse-grained rock known as gabbro which is the congealed reservoir from which the lava flows were fed. To the north and east the 'red' hills of Glamaig, Marsco, Beinn Dearg and Beinn na Caillich have been cut from granite which was formed deep within the volcano.

Some liquid rock material left the volcanic reservoir but failed to reach the surface. Instead it was intruded as molten sheets into the foundation of the volcano, where it cooled and consolidated. The most prominent of these intrusions is the great, almost horizontal, sheet or sill which extends along the eastern coast of the Trotternish peninsula, while the most numerous are the vertical sheets or dykes, usually only a few feet in width, which can be seen on most of the rocky shores of Skye.

The sandstone, limestone and clays which lie below the lavas are soft and friable, and owe their survival to the protection of the hard volcanic rocks. In consequence they tend to outcrop near the steep edges of the island between the lavas and the sea. Their most extensive occurrence runs from just south of Portree up along the eastern and northern coasts of Trotternish as far as Uig. Here they are not only protected by the lavas above but are buttressed by the very hard and resistant Trotternish sill which has been intruded among them. The same rocks build the southern half of Raasay, where they are also reinforced by resistant volcanic masses. An extensive tract extends down the western shores of Loch Slapin, and a fourth forms a broad arc from the Island of Pabay through Breakish and Broadford to the eastern shores of the same loch. Elsewhere smaller patches are found. The sandstones, shales and limestone give better soil than any of the other rocks of the island and consequently their distribution has influenced the pattern of human settlement.

Rocks of the third and oldest group built all Sleat and
Rona and the northern part of Raasay; they also occur here
and there around the ancient volcanic root. The rocks
themselves are very varied. Most of Sleat is built of hard red
sandstone similar to the rock from which the Torridon
mountains have been carved, but its eastern seaboard from
Isle Oronsay southwards is formed of gneiss, a gnarled
granite, the oldest rock in Britain. Near Ord are to be
found outcrops of a spectacular pure white quartz rock,
while south of Tarskavaig occur highly altered rocks, once
impure sandstones similar to those which build the mainland hills. Massive limestone, its outcrops marked by
unusually green and lush vegetation, forms Beinn Suardal
and underlies Torrin to the south of Broadford and occurs
in strips around Ord in Sleat. In places it has been baked by
the volcanic rocks and converted to marble, which, to the
south of Broadford, once gave rise to an industry. A
remarkable scenic contrast between the hard red sandstone
and the gneiss can be seen when looking east from the A855
halfway between Staffin and Portree. Rona and the northern
tip of Raasay show the complex hummocky topography characteristic of the gneiss, while further to the south on Raasay
the red sandstone builds the much simpler slopes of Beinn na
Chapuill.

All the rocks of Skye were heavily eroded by glaciers
during the Ice Age which ended some ten thousand years ago.
The effects of the ice are most spectacularly seen in the
Cuillin and Red Hills, where great corries have been scooped
in the hard gabbro and granite and where the dividing ridges
have been shattered into their present serrated form by intense
frost. Glaciers flowing from the corries dug the deep and
partly flooded valleys of Glen and Loch Brittle, Glen Drynoch
and its continuation, Loch Harport, Glen and Loch Sligachan
Loch Ainort, Strath Mor and, most impressive of all, Lochs
Coruisk and Scavaig. The remainder of the island also shows
the work of the ice. A great glacier, nourished from the mainland, flowed northwards along the eastern coast of Skye goug-
ing out the Sound of Raasay, while another moved south-
westwards down the Sound of Sleat grinding the hollow
which now separates Skye from the mainland. Other glaciers

cut Loch Snizort and Dunvegan in the north and Lochs
Slapin and Eishort in the south.

The glaciers produced the deep U-shaped valleys which
now add greatly to the wild scenery of Skye. In some parts
of the island, when the glaciers melted, they left almost
vertical valley walls consisting of great thicknesses of lavas
resting on weak clays – too weak to bear the weight of rock
above. The clays gave way under the strain and landslipping
on a colossal scale occurred. The Trotternish landslips, the
largest in Britain, consist of vast blocks of lava which are
still slowly and intermittently moving downhill, leaving a
high line of cliffs above. The blocks, often several hundred
yards across, give rise to a curiously jumbled terrain which
includes in places fantastic pinnacles. This type of scenery
is well seen at the Storr, where the lava hills reach their
greatest height of 2,358 ft. They are terminated by a great
eastward facing 600-ft. cliff at the foot of which lies a
jumble of slipped material, including the high pinnacle of
the Old Man of Storr, 160 ft. high. Similar pillars and
slipped blocks form the Quiraing.

A feature of the lava scenery of central and northern
Skye is its terraced appearance caused by variations in hardness in the individual flows. Each flow has a hard and
durable central portion, very often characterized by being
divided into vertical columns like those of the Giant's
Causeway or Fingal's Cave with much less resistant rock
above and below. When exposed to erosion, the hard central
position stands out as a cliff, while the soft base and top form
relatively flat, and often waterlogged, ground. The overall
result is the production of a stepped hillside, each step representing one flow. Such natural staircases are well seen on the
flanks of MacLeod's Tables, whose flat tops have been determined by a particularly hard flow.

Since the departure of the ice the sea has been cease-
lessly modifying the coastline. Where the rocks are resistant
high cliffs have been developed especially along the exposed
south-western shores where they culminate in Dunvegan
Head, 1,205 ft. and Waterstein Head, 967 ft. above the sea.
In places areas of resistant rock have been isolated from the
cliff by the waves and left as stacks (MacLeod's Maidens

being the best known example), while less resistant rocks have been eaten away to form caves and inlets. On sheltered parts of the coast beaches have been built up. In some of the western beaches the main constituent is fragments of broken shell and 'coral', but the most unusual beach sand on the island is found in the bay to the south of Duntulm Castle. Here the sand has a marked greenish hue and consists largely of the mineral olivine, obtained by the sea breaking down nearby cliffs of the Trotternish sill. This beach sand, like so much of Skye geology, is unique in Britain.

Gesto - On the shores of Loch Harport lie the ruins of one of the oldest houses in Skye, famed for a family of MacLeods to whom the *Gesto Collection* of Highland music was dedicated by Dr. Keith Norman MacDonald of Ord. Half a mile from Gesto Bay on Beinn Dubh stands the ruined fort of Dun Taimh. It is defended by a curved wall; inside is a somewhat anachronistic cairn assembled in 1887 to commemorate the jubilee of Queen Victoria.

Glaistig (GLASHT-yig) – a name partly derived from the Gaelic *glas,* grey or wan. It's applied to a guardian of supernatural powers. The glaistig was, perhaps is, a meagre, grey little person with long yellow hair falling to her feet, dressed in green. Once upon a time she was a human, but she became enchanted and from then on manifested a special interest in cows and the dairy. She was known to haunt houses and castles and was something of a social climber in her choice of abodes, preferring affluence to poverty. The glaistig of the old Castle of Sleat was often seen as dusk fell, standing near the *Gruagach* stone where kindly disposed persons used to leave her evening milk.

Glamaig (GLAA-meck) (2,537 ft.) – a beautifully shaped conical mountain descending to the shores of Loch Sligachan. In 1899 a Major Bruce, who was later to become well known for his exploits in the Himalayas, brought a Gurkha to Sligachan, and this Gurkha, Harkabir Tharpa or Herkia as he was also called, carved his own niche in Skye's history by being the first, and undoubtedly last man to ascend Glamaig in 37 minutes. Percy Caldecott, who timed this astonishing feat, wrote a letter to

Alasdair Alpin MacGregor in 1936, recalling the scene:

> As you will know even better than I do, the land between
> the bridge and Glamaig is very rough going – the heather,
> water-courses, pools etc. To this day I can see in my mind
> the spray thrown up by Herkia as he ran along, regardless of
> pools or any other obstruction. The speed with which he
> climbed Glamaig was incredible, more like a spider than
> anything else. On reaching the top he waved his arms to us,
> and then immediately started the descent, which he made at
> the run. As you probably know, on that side of Glamaig there
> is much fine loose scree. He came down this in what one
> might call a series of jumps, and each time his foot landed,
> he slid for some distance as the scree moved with him. The
> most wonderful thing about it was that he arrived at the
> bridge barely out of breath.

The actual time that Herkia took was just under 55 minutes
from door to door of Sligachan Inn. The average time today for
the ascent alone is about an hour and a half.

Glasgow Fair – traditionally the most notable week of the Skye
year, for it was then that sons and daughters, nieces and
nephews and grandchildren white with pallor came home from
the offices, factories and tenements of Glasgow to visit the old
folks. Those who had jobs in Glasgow could get away only for a
week, but the children would often be sent to summer in Skye
on the family croft and to help bring in the hay – this practice
still persists although with the new mobility many exiled Skye
families are taking packaged tours south to the sun. Before the
first world war when there were no such opportunities, Skye
used to be full at the time of the Fair. An Edwardian report
described the scene:

> There are thousands of Skyemen in St. Mungo holding
> responsible positions in every branch of industrial activity and
> all of them trustworthy reliable men. On Fair Friday and
> Saturday literally hundreds of Islemen reach Portree with the
> Mail and other steamers. The Mail coaches for Dunvegan,
> Uig and Sligachan are packed with passengers and Mr.
> MacDonald the energetic mail contractor relieves the pressure
> by bringing into requisition motor cars which make the trip to

Dunvegan in a little over a couple of hours instead of five by ordinary coach.

Glebe the lands belonging to a parish church. A manse, or minister's house, is known as a *glebe-house*.

Glencoe If you mention *Glencoe* to a Skyeman over the age of sixty he will think not of the 1692 slaughter of the Macdonalds by the Campbells but of a MacBrayne paddle steamer which for a quarter of a century sailed on the Portree-Mallaig run. When I first sailed from Kyle to Portree on the *Glencoe* in 1925 she was 79 years old. With her single funnel, for'ard mast, great splashing paddles and open bridge she was by then a part of history. She was built for Sir James Matheson of Stornoway, the man who amassed a vast fortune in the East and founded the firm of Jardine, Matheson. He named her *Mary Jane* after his wife and she made her first voyage on 18 June 1846 from Glasgow to Portree. She passed into the ownership of the Glasgow and Lochfyne Steam Packet Company in the year of the Great Exhibition. In 1857 she was lengthened, fitted with a saloon and emerged as *Glencoe*. *Glencoe* had a superb model of a golden eagle over the entrance to her dining saloon where one ate kippers and bacon and egg and drank strong tea. But the greatest treat of a trip on the *Glencoe* was to be taken to the engine room to watch the pounding of the two great pistons which drove the paddle wheels. Part of this engine is preserved in the Kelvingrove Museum in Glasgow.

Glencoe left Portree for the last time in May 1931 and was broken up in the summer. She was then, with the *Premier* of Weymouth, one of the two oldest ships in the world. B. H. Humble, in his book *Tramping in Skye*, recalls a notice in the third-class cabin of the *Glencoe* which epitomizes the dual nature of the island steamer: 'This cabin has accommodation for 90 third-class passengers, when not occupied by sheep, cattle, cargo or other encumbrances.'

A splendid story, probably apocryphal, is told of the *Glencoe's* most colourful master, a Captain Baxter. On hearing the cry one day 'Minister Overboard!' Baxter inquired: 'What denomination?' The answer was 'Wee Free.' Without a moment's hesitation Baxter ordered: 'Full speed ahead!'

Glendale a valley, not a town, lying in Duirinish and dominated by the 1,500-ft. heights of Healaval Mhor. The glen's life once centred round Loch Pooltiel, which had a regular steamer service, and the people of the glen were in many ways insulated from the rest of the island. But it was in this isolated glen in the 1880s that John MacPherson, 'the Glendale Martyr', and a group of like-minded men made a firm stand against the gradual erosion of their rights. The factor, a man of dictatorial leanings, even forbade the crofters to remove driftwood from the shore or keep dogs. On 7 February 1882 the crofters met at Glendale Church to present a united opposition against further clearances and to press for the reinstatement of those who had been turned off their land. A gunboat, H.M.S. *Jackal*, was dispatched to Glendale to intimidate the people and accept the surrender of the four ringleaders. Subsequently some of the crofters were imprisoned in Edinburgh, an act which fanned the flames of resistance even higher. The Royal Commission brought the whole story into the open. In 1904 the Congested Areas Board bought most of Glendale and the crofters became the only ones in Skye to own the title deeds of their land.

Gold has been found in Skye. A century ago a special type of collie dog was bred which had a very smooth coat. At the age of three it would be killed and its skin hardened with alum in the sun. The prospector would then take it down to a likely burn and after tying a wire to the tail it was left in the water for a few days in the hope that any gold dust flowing in the stream might be trapped. I am indebted to the Skye *Clarion* for this curious piece of information and the story that a Staffin man's father had once handled a wedding ring made by a travelling tinsmith from gold retrieved in the Staffin river. It was this article which provoked the following letter from a *Clarion* reader:

> When Mr. Coulle Lotts, Portree was a gamekeeper he heard shooting gentry discussing details of their various gold rings and jewellery. Among them was Lord Dunmore. One titled gentleman among them said it would be difficult for them to guess where his gold ring came from. He then revealed that it was originally extracted from rock-ore discovered in the Allt Dearg in the vicinity of the Cuillin hills.

John MacPherson, 'the Glendale Martyr', addressing a crofters' meeting in 1884.

In 1956 two German geologists spent some months in the Cuillins prospecting for diamonds and uranium, but nothing seems to have come of their labours.

Grange Of Ann Chiesley who had the misfortune to marry James Erskine, Lord Grange, Boswell wrote: 'The true story of this lady is as frightfully romantic as if it had been the fiction of gloomy fancy.' Ann was a hot-tempered hard-drinking Hanoverian: her husband, Lord Grange, was an ardent Jacobite and brother of the Earl of Mar who raised the rebellion of 1715. Today Ann would certainly have been under psychiatric care and sedation, but in the 1730s she was just thought to be abnormally quick-tempered. Lord Grange was at the centre of Jacobite intrigue in Edinburgh and his home was the rendezvous of those who were plotting to restore the Stuarts to power. Ann got hold of some documents which incriminated not only her husband but also Fraser of Lovat, Sir Alexander MacDonald of Sleat and Norman MacLeod of Dunvegan. Stupidly she hid under a sofa and eavesdropped on her husband and his fellow-conspirators. Discovered by a sneeze she was blindfolded, trussed up and spirited away from Edinburgh. Next morning it was given out that she had suddenly died. A mock funeral was held and amid great lamentation an empty coffin was solemnly lowered into a grave in Greyfriars' Churchyard, Edinburgh. Meanwhile . . . as they say in all the best soap-operas . . . Ann had been taken to Idrigill in Skye. While here she managed to get a note, concealed in a skein of wool, to her relatives. Another version of the story says that this note was smuggled out of St. Kilda. From Idrigill Ann was removed to the island of Heisker on the west coast of North Uist. After two years she was transferred to St. Kilda. She languished here for seven years and then when her captors once again feared that she was about to be rescued they moved her first to Assynt and then finally to a cave near the Point of Idrigill where her trials had first begun. She began to lose her mind and towards the end of her life was accorded a degree of freedom. She died in a miserable cottar's hut in Waternish and a second false funeral took place. A coffin weighted with turf was buried in Duirinish, but the wretched Ann's body was taken to Trumpan and buried secretly in the churchyard there. A grey rectangular slab marks her grave.

The Great Moss *A'Mhointeach mhor,* lies about one mile from Portree on the Dunvegan road, and in the days before coal and electricity it used to supply Portree with all its peat. At the Portree end of the moss a dam was built so that when in winter the water behind the dam froze it could be cut up and carted into Portree to be stored for summer use in the salmon house.

Gruagach (GROO-ag-uch) – or literally 'long-haired one' (*gruag*, a wig) is a Gaelic name for a young woman. In parts of Skye the *Gruagach* is a tall youth with flowing flaxen hair who carries a stick in his hand. He may wear a long coat and knee breeches and frilled white shirt. He was attentive to cattle and kept them from doing themselves an injury among the rocks. Milk had to be put out for the *gruagach* at night in a hollow of a stone (the *gruagach* stone – *Clach na Gruagaich*). If you forgot to do this you wouldn't get any milk from the cows the next morning. The *gruagach* was a sort of *Till Eulenspiegel* and one of his merry pranks was to let cattle loose at night and enjoy the confusion. Apart from tittering at the result of this jape he was relatively harmless. At Tottrome, a mile north-east of the Old Man of Storr, outside Portree, a *gruagach* once annoyed a woman who was trying to drive some calves into a byre. The woman, losing her temper, cursed him and he gave her a slap on the face which surprisingly killed her. All that night he is said to have kept the fire alive for the women who came to watch over the corpse.

As late as 1794 the poor *gruagach* was credited with the fathering of a child born at Shulista, near Duntulm – a libel no doubt assiduously fostered by the real father.

Handfasting or contracting what was known as a 'left-handed marriage' was once very common in Skye. As Martin Martin recorded: 'It was an ancient custom in the Isles that a man take a maid to his wife, and keep her for the space of a year without marrying her; and if she pleased him all the while, he married her at the end of the year, and legitimized her children; but if he did not love her, he returned her to her parents.' This custom, convenient for a man but hardly satisfactory for a woman, led to one of the most savage feuds ever fought between the MacLeods and MacDonalds. Donald Gorm Mor handfasted with Margaret MacLeod, carried her off to Duntulm castle, gave her a trial, found her sadly wanting and packed her off back to her brother Rory Mor at Dunvegan. This incident occurred at the beginning of the seventeenth century and precipitated what came to be known as the 'War of the One-Eyed Woman'. Margaret had injured her eye and this seems to have been the main reason why Donald decided to opt out. Unfortunately he did it in a pointed way – the poor deflowered girl was returned to Dunvegan, very much a picture of damaged goods, mounted on a one-eyed nag, escorted by a one-eyed groom and followed by a one-eyed moth-eaten dog. The resultant war lasted for two years, with raid and counter-raid, foray and counter-foray. The burning, slaying, desolation and wholesale massacre ended in the battle of Coire na Creiche where the MacDonalds routed the MacLeods. The year was 1601 and it was to be the last clan fight ever fought in Skye.

Harta Corrie Drained by Sligachan river and a mile to the north of Coruisk, a much painted scene which some have suggested is sublimer in its beauty than Coruisk itself. It was here that yet one more bloody battle was fought between the MacLeods and

MacDonalds. It lasted all day and ended, legend reports, only when the last MacLeod had been massacred. The bodies were piled round the base of a huge rock called the Bloody Stone, and it is reported that here the fairies fashioned their bows and arrows from the ribs of the dead.

Hebrides an invented mistaken name. It arose when some unsung scribe mistranscribed the name *Haebudes* or *Hebudes* which Pliny applied to the islands in the first century. *U* became *ri* and so was born what for islanders is still the most evocative name in the world . . . 'and we in dreams behold the Hebrides', thanks to the bad eyesight of a medieval scholar.

Herring The herring fisheries in Skye were at one time so productive that in Strath alone 60 or 70 boats were employed. Fish merchants in Glasgow and Greenock used to send their sloops to receive and cure herrings on the spot. The herring would visit the west coast in June for about six weeks and an early nineteenth-century report described how they appeared in prodigious shoals in Kilmuir:

> not only around the coast of the parish, but in all the lochs, creeks and bays of the island; it then formed an extensive and lucrative source of traffic, and the benefits derived from it by the country in general were very great. It was caught at comparatively little expense, as the natives could for the most part make their own nets. In every creek and bay large fleets of schooners, brigs, sloops, wherries and boats of all sizes and descriptions were to be seen eagerly engaged in the securing of stores for private families, and of cargoes for the southern market; now the irregular appearance of the migratory fish, together with the small quantities of it which frequent at the present day its wonted haunts, have deprived the natives of one of their most lucrative sources of support and have been in no small degree the means of reducing the redundant population to poverty and of unfitting them to meet such seasons of destitution as those of 1836 and 1837.

The failure of the herring, Their irrational decision to forsake western waters for the east coast, brought a great deal of distress to Skye. There are still herring to be had and it is generally reckoned that the best herring of all are those caught in West Hebridean waters. Martin Martin claimed that eighteenth-century Skyemen believed that 'if a quarrel happen on the Coast where Herring is caught, and that Blood be drawn violently, then the Herring go away from the Coast without returning, during that Season'. If the herring was thought to dislike physical violence he was also believed to like bright lights and it was once a custom to light bonfires on headlands at the beginning of winter to try and attract shoals of herring.

Highland Missionary Society was only one of many organizations which laboured in Skye and other islands to bring the Christian message home to the natives.

> They subsist on hard fare [the Society noted in
> a nineteenth-century report] lodge in uncomfortable huts
> and are exposed to the rude blasts of an unpropitious
> climate. Let us endeavour to alleviate their temporal suffer
> ings by conveying to them the knowledge and counsel of the
> Gospel and direct their minds beyond the snowy mountains
> and gloomy lakes to that better land where there is no storm,
> no tempest, but quiet and peace and assurance forever.

Hugh's Castle – See **Caisteal Uisdein**

Hunglader the farmstead of Hung, a Norse princeling; or perhaps derived from *Unga,* an ounce of silver, or the area of land which could be rented for an ounce. This small hamlet half a mile north-east of Kilmuir church was once occupied by the MacArthurs, hereditary pipers to the Lords of the Isles and the MacDonalds of Sleat.

Hunish (HOO-nish) – in Kilmuir, the most northerly point of Skye. Here at Hunish House lived Donald MacLeod of Bernera, three of whose sons became generals in the British army.

Hunter River which rises in the Liverpool range of New South Wales has some relevance to this book for in the nineteenth century so many Skye families settled in one particular place of its three-hundred-mile course that it became known as Skye district.

Hydro-electric power In 1938 a group of experts approached by the Scottish Economic Committee proposed 84 schemes for utilizing water power in the Highlands and Islands. They considered that four catchment areas were capable of development in Skye: Glen Uig, the Kilmartin River in Staffin, the River Snizort at Carbost and the Storr Lochs north of Portree. The cost of these four power stations would, in those pre-inflationary days have been £334,100 and between them they would have produced an annual output of 17 million units of electricity. The war came and the plans were shelved, but in 1947 the North of Scotland Hydro-Electric Board (referred to locally as 'The Hydro') published a scheme to build a 170 ft. gravity dam, 36ft. high, from which the water would be piped 2,800 ft. to a power station on the beach below the Storr Lochs. The station was built and officially opened in June 1952. Its estimated average output today is 7 million units a year. Other supplies come into the island by submarine cable from Kyle of Lochalsh to Kyleakin. Today about 99 per cent of all potential consumers have been supplied with mains electricity.

Before the station was built the outflow from Loch Leathan provided one of the finest waterfalls in Skye. 'A streamlet,' wrote a nineteenth-century observer, 'falls sheer over an extraordinary high precipice, and forms a cascade which, though but a toy in bulk of water, appears as seen from the sea below to be singularly beautiful and grand.' It is worth descending the flight of 674 concrete steps to the beach, no longer, alas, to view the waterfall, but to examine the beach composed of beautifully shaped stones of all sizes, rounded and smoothed by the action of the sea and a rich source of ammonites of all sizes.

$$I$$

Ichthyosauria or fish-lizards – were in a way forerunners of the whale and porpoise still to be seen round the waters of Skye. They were smooth skinned, fed chiefly on fish and were last seen alive and well about 70 million years ago. A few years ago the finest specimen of a fossilized ichthyosaurus ever found in Scotland was discovered by the engineer in charge of the Storr Lochs hydro-electric station. Fishing one day, he reached down to pick up a knife and saw outlined in the rock what he first took to be the backbone of a sheep. As Mr. Gillies looked closer and saw that there were 21 vertebrae and that the length of the fossil was nearly 10 ft, he realized that this was no sheep. He contacted the

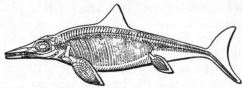

royal Scottish Museum in Edinburgh, and a team of excited geologists shortly afterwards arrived in Skye, cut the headless fossil out of the rock and took it back to Edinburgh.

Ilica Passio or Twisting of the Guts had a drastic seventeenth-century treatment in Skye: 'it has been several times Cured by drinking a draught of cold water, with a little Oatmeal in it, and then hanging the Patient by the heels for some time. The last Instance in *Skie* was by *John Morison*, in the Village of *Talisker*, who by this Remedy alone Cur'd a Boy of fourteen years of age.' – Martin Martin.

Innsegall the name applied by the Celtic people of the main-

land of Scotland to the Western Isles: 'The isles of the Strangers
or Foreigners.'

Isay (EE-sha) the ice-isle, lies at the entrance to Loch Bay,
about a mile and a half offshore from the village of Stein. In the
early part of the sixteenth century Roderick MacLeod of Lewis,
whose daughter had married twice, decided to eliminate two
entire families so that his own grandson should inherit the island
of Raasay and the lands of Gairloch. He invited the members of
the two families to a banquet on Isay at which, he led them to
believe, they would hear something to their advantage. Avid as
most people are for personal gain, they all turned up expectantly.
At an appropriate point in the meal Roderick announced that he
would like to hear the views of everyone present on a matter of
considerable importance. He left the room and each guest was
summoned from the table in turn. On entering the apartment
where Roderick had placed himself each was stabbed to death.
The island belonged in the eighteenth century to MacLeod of
MacLeod and on 23 September 1773 he proposed to Dr.
Johnson that he should accept the island as his own –

> on condition [Boswell reported] of his residing on it three
> months in the year, nay, one month. Mr. Johnson was
> highly pleased with the fancy, He talked a great deal of this
> island – how he would build a house, how he would fortify
> it, how he would have cannon, how he would plant, how he
> would sally out and *take* the Isle of Muck; and then he
> laughed with a glee that was astonishing, and could hardly
> leave off. MacLeod humoured Mr. Johnson finely as to his
> island; told him that as it was the practice in this country to
> name every man by his lands, he begged leave to drink him
> in that mode: 'Island Isa, your health!' – Ulinish, Talisker,
> Mr M'Queen and I all joined in our different manners,
> while Mr. Johnson bowed to each, with much good humour.

At one time Isay was thickly populated. There is a letter
extant from a Mr. Melvill who lived on Isay and who wrote on
10 December 1813: 'Sir, I received your favour and observe the
contents, and herein enclose two pounds. The article I got from
Holmes was Debenture Rum cleared out at Liverpool for
Archangel. This is the fact, and you will please state the matter

as you think best. At all events spin out the time as long as
possible. . . .' Why the time was to be spun out we'll never know
but as one looks at the deserted island today it's difficult to
imagine it as a big fishing station with a general store and a relatively large population. There was a final clearance of the population (twelve crofter families) in 1860 and since then the island
has been unproductive. It was bought a few years ago by
Donovan, the folk singer.

Isle Oronsay ebb tide island, the Norse name for an island
which at low tide is joined to the mainland. There are about
twenty *Ornsay* or *Oronsay* islands on the west coast of Scotland.
Skye's Isle Ornsay in Sleat has a lighthouse, a white tower, built
in 1857. It is unmanned, can be seen from 12 miles away and
stands on a rock formed of hornblende schist full of crystals
about the length of a matchbox – garnets are reputed to lie
about for the taking. The last time I was there they all appeared
to have been taken. The village of Isle Ornsay has a pier, an inn
and a road leading to the attractive beach of Camus Croise.

J

James IV (1475–1513) who raised Scotland to the highest position it had ever attained in Europe and who died with the flower of the Scottish nobility on the field of Flodden, should not go unrecorded in this book. It seems highly likely that he was the last British king to have a knowledge of Gaelic. 'He speaks,' wrote a contemporary historian, 'the language of the savages who live in some parts of Scotland and on the islands.'

Jesters were maintained both by the MacDonalds at Duntulm and by the MacLeods at Dunvegan. The honour of being the last Scottish Chief to employ a full retinue of bard, harper, piper and jester goes to Ian Breac, the sixteenth Chief of MacLeod who succeeded to the title in 1664. Another member of Ian Breac's household was certainly no man's fool – the celebrated Martin Martin.

Johnson, Samuel (1709–84) arrived in Skye shortly before one o'clock on Thursday, 2 September 1773; it was the nineteenth day of his Highland Jaunt with James Boswell. Johnson, overweight, touched by hypochondria and a whole misery of distressing maladies, suffered great privations on his journey and his reception at Armadale by Sir Alexander MacDonald was not what he had become accustomed to expect. Sir Alexander was living in relatively humble circumstances in the house of one of his tenants which to Johnson 'seemed very poor for a chief'. From Armadale the travellers rode to Corriechatachan near Broadford where 'Mr. Johnson was much pleased' by the hospitality of the MacKinnons. Raasay was next on the itinerary and here again they received a gratifying reception. On Sunday, 12 September, they landed at Portree and in the afternoon, after a meal at the inn where the present Royal Hotel stands, they rode to Kingsburgh where Johnson had his celebrated encounter with Flora MacDonald. They left Kingsburgh for Dunvegan, where they stayed for a comfortable week before leaving for the farmhouse of Ullinish. They stayed here and also at Talisker before returning to Corriechatachan. Their last few days were spent at Ostaig and Armadale and on 3 October, after four weeks in Skye, they sailed away to Mull. The full account of the visit is contained in Boswell's *Journal of a Tour to the Hebrides* and Johnson's own *A Journey to the Hebrides*. Would Johnson's rather sombre view of Skye have been different if he'd had better weather? And why did he delay his visit until so late in the year? The first question can't be answered but as Boswell was an advocate and the Court of Session in Edinburgh didn't rise until 11 August the jaunt could not have been made earlier. Johnson was an extraordinarily dogmatic and didactic man and his pronouncements are distinguished by a refreshing lack of self doubt. Some of his dicta throw as much light on the eighteenth century as they do on Skye:

On gardens 'of their gardens I can judge only from their tables. I did not observe that the common greens were wanting, and suppose, that by choosing an advantageous exposition, they can raise all the more hardy esculent plants. Of vegetable fragrance or beauty they are not yet studious. Few vows are made to Flora in the Hebrides.'

On brogues 'In Skye I first observed the use of brogues, a kind of artless shoes stitched with thongs, so loosely that though they defend the foot from stones, they do not exclude water.'

On conversation 'Such is the laxity of Highland conversation, that the inquirer is kept in continual suspense, and by a kind of intellectual retrogradation, knows less as he hears more.'

On taboos 'The vulgar inhabitants of Skye, I know not whether of the other islands, have not only eels, but pork and bacon in abhorrence and accordingly I never saw a hog in the Hebrides, except one at Dunvegan.'

On cuddies 'The cuddy is a fish of which I know not the philosophical name. It is not much bigger than a gudgeon, but is of great use in these islands, as it affords the lower people both food and oil for their lamps. Cuddies are so abundant, at some times of the year, that they are caught like white bait in the Thames, only by dipping a basket and drawing it back.'

THE
J O U R N A L
OF A TOUR TO THE
H E B R I D E S,
WITH
SAMUEL JOHNSON, LL.D.
BY *JAMES BOSWELL*, Esq.

CONTAINING

Some Poetical Pieces by Dr. JOHNSON, relative to the TOUR, and never before published;

A Series of his Conversation, Literary Anecdotes, and Opinions of Men and Books:

WITH AN AUTHENTICK ACCOUNT OF

The Distresses and Escape of the GRANDSON of KING JAMES II. in the Year 1746.

THE SECOND EDITION, REVISED AND CORRECTED.

O! while along the stream of time, thy name
Expanded flies, and gathers all its fame,
Say, shall my little bark attendant sail,
Pursue the triumph, and partake the gale? POPE.

L O N D O N:
PRINTED BY HENRY BALDWIN,
FOR CHARLES DILLY, IN THE POULTRY.
MDCCLXXXV.

On cattle 'They go from the islands very lean, and are not offered to the butcher till they have been long fatted in English pastures. Of their black cattle some are without horns, called by the Scots humble cow, as we call a bee a humble bee that wants a sting.'

On milk 'In the penury of these malignant regions, nothing is left that can be converted to food. The goats and the sheep are milked like the cows. A single meal of a goat is a quart, and of a sheep a pint.'

On the chiefs 'Their chiefs being now deprived of their jurisdiction have already lost much of their influence, and as they gradually degenerate from patriarchal rulers to rapacious landlords, they will divest themselves of the little that remains.'

On visits 'Visits last several days and are commonly paid by water; yet I never saw a boat furnished with benches, or made commodious by any addition to the first fabric. Conveniences are not missed where they never were enjoyed.'

Jones, John Paul (1747–92) a native of Kirkcudbright, became a midshipman in the Royal Navy, a captain in the American Navy and an admiral in the navy of Catherine of Russia. He was a slaver and a murderer. He finds himself in this book because during the War of Independence he spent some time in British waters taking prizes and generally harrying the shipping lanes. On the last day of August 1779, Jones appeared off the coast of Skye in the *Bon Homme Richard* (named by Jones in honour of Benjamin Franklin and his *Poor Richard's Almanack*), an old 42-gun French East Indiaman. When the enemy ship was seen to enter Loch Dunvegan there was consternation in the castle. General MacLeod was away on military service in America, but his factor started evacuating all the moveable plate and valuables. As the *Bon Homme Richard* neared the castle there hove into view on the skyline a large party of mourners bearing the body of Donald MacLeod, the tacksman of Swordale, to his interment in Kilmuir graveyard. Jones mistook the funeral party for the MacLeod army in full battle array and, his valour overcome by discretion, turned sail and fled. Which must be the only account on record of a dead Scotsman defeating a live one.

Kelp Early in the eighteenth century it was discovered that seaweed, growing on rocks or cast up by the sea – seaware as it was called – was rich in iodine, alkali, soda and potash. Its main use was to replace barilla, which the Napoleonic wars had made scarce. The supplies of barilla, which provided the alkali used in the manufacture of soap and glass and the bulk of which came from Spain, petered out and the demand for Hebridean kelp soared. At the height of the kelp boom it was estimated that the value of the output from western Scotland was £400,000 and 40,000–50,000 men and women were employed in its production. The kelp industry was so profitable to the lairds that they began to encourage early marriages so that there would be more hands to collect the seaweed. Shortly after the end of the Napoleonic wars the duty on barilla was reduced, and the demand for kelp consequently slackened. The innovation of

Leblanc alkali, which began to be manufactured in Glasgow in 1825, depressed the kelp industry even more grievously. What kelp meant in terms of wealth to a man like Lord MacDonald was described in 1841 by his agent. At the height of the boom Lord MacDonald was deriving £14,000 a year from kelp – costing as little as 30s. a ton to produce it sold in London for as much as £22 a ton. As the making of kelp became increasingly profitable the rent of farms on the sea-shore had been raised, but as wages rose too the tide of emigration began temporarily to ebb. The failure of the kelp industry meant that Skye was over-populated with mouths it could no longer feed. Emigration began afresh.

In their guide book the Anderson brothers described the manufacture of kelp, which even in 1834 was still profitable enough to produce:

> Kelp is formed by burning seaware previously dried in the sun, in small circular and oblong pits attended by men to rake the crackling ingredients. The smoke of these pits spreads during the summer months in dense volumes round the shores, and diffuses a disagreeable pungent odour. The alkaline substance, as is well known, is chiefly used in the manufacture of glass. The best kind is made from the seaweed cut from the rock, which is generally done every third year; that made from the driftware is naturally more impure.

Kensaleyre (KEN-za-LYRE) – head of the sea, or the upper reaches of a long tidal bay. On the left of the road from Portree to Skeabost just by the old Kensaleyre manse are two standing stones placed in a line running north-north-west and south-south-east. Local tradition says there were three such stones and on them Cuchullin's venison cauldron used to be placed.

Kilchrist (KILL-krisst) – Christ's church. Here on the road between Broadford and Torrin are the ruins of an early church; the only other pre-Reformation church whose walls still stand is in Dunvegan. The rising ground between the church and the loch is still called the Hill of the Mass. The last service was held in the church in about 1843 when the congregation removed to the new church at Broadford. The ivy-clad ruins are surrounded by numerous burial stones and vaults and contain the family graves of the Mackinnons of Corriechatachan. Nearby is a loch which is reputed to have been haunted by a monster exorcised by Saint Maolrubha.

Kilmore (*A' Chill Mhor* – the big church) Four miles north of Ardvasar in Sleat is the small township of Kilmore. It is highly likely that the church stands on a site long given over to Christian, and before that, pagan rites. The first church on this ground was built by a priest called Crotach Mac Gille Gorm – a canon from Beauly, who visited Skye early in the thirteenth century. The church he founded stood until the early seventeenth century. The present church was built in 1876. The first church was set on fire by the MacLeods, destroying in the process a whole congregation of militant MacIntyres who had taken refuge there after losing a battle.

Kilmuir four and a half miles north of Uig the district and hamlet of Kilmuir called in Gaelic *Am fearann stapagach* – the land of cream, but also from its comparative fertility, long dubbed the Granary of Skye. Kilmuir churchyard contains the granite memorial to Flora MacDonald and Johnson's tribute: 'A name that will be mentioned in history and, if courage and fidelity be virtues, mentioned with honour.' Also in Kilmuir is the burial place of the MacArthurs, the hereditary pipers of the MacDonalds. But the most interesting tombstone is a long, thin slab on which lies a mailed figure not dissimilar to the tombs of the crusaders found in many English country churches. It lies at the east end of the cemetery and if you go in high summer you may have to brush aside waist-high grass to find it. It marks the burial place of the celebrated Martin family. This particular stone was brought back from Iona by a wild member of the family called Angus of the Wind. He is reputed to have carried it up on his own back from the shore. Angus of the Wind (wind used here in the sense of *storm* and not a reference to any digestive troubles) was alive in the early years of Queen Elizabeth's reign, and his second wife was a sister of the Chief of the MacDonalds. His brother-in-law had married a MacLean whom Angus loathed heartily. She, aware of Angus's skill as an amateur versifier, kept nagging him to compose an ode in her honour. Angus eventually got so fed up that he wrote a quatrain which made him markedly *persona non grata* for a long time to come:

You promised not to get enraged
You red-eyed, pockmarked ruddy-faced old bag.
We paid dearly for your dowry
Woe to him who's got you for life!

A Kilmuir man who used to live near the churchyard always said that he heard dogs howling before a funeral: 'It was because they saw the wraiths of the living,' he would say. The estate of Kilmuir was purchased by the Congested Districts Board in 1904 when £80,000 was paid for the land and another £27,628 for the stock – the object of the purchase was to divide the farm lands among the crofters. Kilmuir, like Kilmore, derived its name from the presence of a church dedicated to the Virgin Mary.

Kilt Rock Stop at Loch Mealt on the Portree–Staffin road and walk to the edge of the cliff. Look north and you'll see the vertical black, columnar basalt folds which give this cliff its name. Its resemblance to a kilt is heightened by the varied colours of the horizontal strata which provide the 'sett' for the kilt pattern. Do not walk too near the edge of the cliff. In the early 1960s a young Indian couple came to Skye on their honeymoon. It was a wild day when they got out of their car to admire the view and one particularly violent gust of wind seized the young bride in her billowing sari and hurled her to a violent death on the seawashed rocks four hundred feet below.

Like much of Skye's more spectacular scenery the cliff is best seen from the sea. In stormy weather when the east and northeast winds are blowing, the fall formed by the water flowing from Loch Mealt is blown back over the edge of the cliff across the road and into the loch from which it came. An inspiring sight but dangerous in winter if the spray freezes on the road.

Kingsburgh The *cisborg* or tax-town was built at the entrance to Loch Snizort for the purpose of levying taxes on passing ships. The present house of Kingsburgh, pleasantly situated amid woods, was built near the site of the old house in which Prince Charles was sheltered for a night and in which Boswell and Johnson were entertained. They were received by Kingsburgh and had their celebrated meeting with Flora MacDonald herself (*see* Anthology).

Kirkibost Four miles from Elgol, in the district of Strath, Kirkibost derives its name (church-steading) from the church built by Norse invaders after they were converted to Christianity around the year 1,000. From here one can walk three-quarters of a mile to the shore and the ruins of Dunringill Castle.

Knock Castle also known as Castle Camus or Camys, can be approached easily from the road and lies on the northern point of Knock Bay in Sleat. It commands a splendid view over the Sound of Sleat to the hills of Knoydart. The site on which the ruin stands once held Dun Boravaig or the *Dun* of the Bay of Thor. Today the 4ft. -thick walls stand fairly high and are picturesquely overgrown with ivy. The castle is thought to be fourteenth century. Tradition says that at the end of the fifteenth century it was besieged by the MacLeods and that a MacDonald heroine, who subsequently was christened Mary of the Castle, inspired the defenders to victory. James MacDonald, fourth son of the fourth Chief of Sleat, lived at Knock during the first half of the sixteenth century and may have built the tower. The last piece of documentary evidence is on 31 August 1632 when a McConillreich signed a bond in the castle declaring that Sir Donald MacDonald was his undoubted Chief. Much of the stone from the castle was cannibalized for the building of Knock House.

Kyle of Lochalsh the main road and rail terminus and jumping-off point for Skye. In June 1893 the Highland Railway received powers to complete its line to Kyle by extending the railway a further 10^1/$_2$ miles from Strome Ferry. The extension, winding along the shores of Loch Carron, cutting through sheer rock for much of the way, cost the astonishing sum, for those days, of £250,000. Although the government chipped in with a subsidy of £45,000 the shareholders must have wondered whether they'd ever see their money back. The fast new motor road has made the railway almost redundant; despite local opposition it seems only a matter of time before the lines will be removed and the stations closed, leaving Mallaig as the only remaining rail route to Skye.

It was in the straits here that on a September evening in 1263 the Norwegian king and his unconquered fleet of a hundred brown-sailed galleys anchored on their way to defeat at the battle of Largs – a defeat which ended Norse domination in Scotland.

Kyleakin (KILE-ack-in) – Acunn or Haco's Strait. This small township, the nearest to the mainland, is the Skye terminal of the most widely used ferry. The current here is so swift flowing that in 1690 a certain Captain Pottinger styled it 'the horrible sound of Kellachie'. At the beginning of the nineteenth century Lord MacDonald conceived a grand plan to create a model town at Kyleakin which he proposed to call New Liverpool. A contemporary engraving shows the ambitious project which would have been about the same size as present-day Portree. The plans were grandiose and too far-fetched to be realized. The houses themselves, two-storeyed (compared with the traditional one-storey cottage) would have remained empty even if they had been built – the economy of the island could not have supported such an extravagant folly (*see* **Castle Maoil**).

Kylerhea (KILE-RAY) – The oldest ferry from Skye to the mainland operates from here to Glenelg, but only in the summer-time. The road to Kylerhea is narrow, steep and fairly hair-raising, and the ascent of Mam Ratagan on the mainland side should not be attempted by L-drivers or the faint of heart. Johnson noted that descending Ratagan to Glenelg 'was the only moment of my journey in which I thought myself endangered'.

The fast flowing straits here are supposed to have been named after a Fingalian called Readh who attempted to leap across to the mainland but didn't quite make it. Hugh Miller described how in the 1840s he navigated through the straits – a difficult feat under sail:

> Never, except perhaps in a Highland river big in flood, have I seen such a tide. It danced and wheeled, and came boiling in huge masses from the bottom; and now our bows heaved abruptly round in one direction, and now they jerked as suddenly round in another; and though there blew a moderate breeze at the time, the helm failed to keep the sails steadily full. But whether our sheets bellied out, or flapped right in the wind's eye, on we swept in the tideway, like a cork caught during a thunder shower in one of the rapids of the High Street.

It was through these waters at slacktide that the island cattle were swum on their way to the slaughter-houses of the south (*see* **Roads**).

Law in Skye is administered through the Sheriff Court in Portree. The Sheriff is a legally qualified professional judge who visits the island at regular intervals and has jurisdiction in both civil and criminal cases. He has other administrative functions, such as hearing appeals against decisions made by local authorities and acting as a Returning Officer at Parliamentary Elections. The investigation and prosecution of crime is undertaken by a resident Procurator Fiscal, who is a qualified advocate or solicitor appointed by the Crown. The police are the Procurator Fiscal's agents and in criminal investigations act under his instructions.

When information about a crime comes to the notice of the police it is the Procurator Fiscal who decides whether to prosecute, and it is he who will, if necessary, eventually conduct the prosecution in the Sheriff's Court. He is also responsible for the investigation of sudden and suspicious deaths, but such investigations are carried out privately and not, as in England, in the presence of a jury. England, which doesn't have the Scottish system of public prosecution, except in a limited number of serious crimes, has no equivalent to a Procurator Fiscal; the closest parallel would be the American District Attorney.

The present tourist office in Portree, which is seen to advantage in William Daniell's engraving, (see Plate 8) at one time housed both jail and court for the whole of Skye. It continued to be used as a court-house until the present one was built in 1867 in Somerled Square. This is a handsome, dour building, which is more than can be said for the new police headquarters next door – completely out of keeping with the rest of the Square.

Lazybeds or Feannagan are more peculiar to the Outer

Hebrides than Skye. They were platforms of soil and seaweed sometimes no larger than a double bed in which oats and potatoes could be grown. The outlines of former lazy beds can be seen in Skye, but there was never as much need for them in comparatively fertile Skye as there was in the barren rocky ground of a place like Harris. The hardship involved in growing minute quantities of corn or vegetables in such a way makes the name for this type of cultivation a fine example of irony.

Loch a lake. A **lochan** is a small loch. Including sea lochs, of which the largest are Snizort, Bracadale, Dunvegan, Scavaig and Eishort, there are nearly 200 lochs in Skye.

Loch Chaluim Chille (<u>CHA</u>Lum <u>CHEEL</u>-ya) – St. Columba's loch in Kilmuir. The loch was 2 miles in length and two attempts were made to drain it in 1715 and 1760 without permanent success. It was finally drained in 1824 after 6 years' hard work. The architect of the scheme was the celebrated Doctor Alexander MacLeod (*An Doctair Ban*),who also planted trees on the Meall in Portree. On two slightly elevated plateaus in the middle of what was once the loch are the remains of beehive dwellings described by one authority as the best example of a monastic establishment in Britain. An advocate of land reform described how the labour of the workers was later taken from them:

> For some time after the loch had been drained the land thus reclaimed was allotted to the crofters, who, by dint of hard work converted it into splendid arable land. But mark the sequel. No sooner had the bed of the loch been made available for agricultural purposes, than the proprietor took it away from the crofters, through whose exertions the result had been achieved, and added it to the already large sheep-farm of Monkstadt. It was simply the old story – the proprietor appropriating the labour of the reclaiming crofter.

Loch Scavaig (SKAVV-aig) – the loch which guards the entrance to Loch Coruisk. In his *Nautical Descriptions of the West Coast* published in 1776, Murdoch Mackenzie said of Scavaig: 'There is no safe anchorage in this loch, or rather bay, being liable to violent squalls of wind from the *Culin Mountains*, and the bottom rocky in many parts.' A song concerning Scavaig used to be sung by women 'waulking' cloth; it celebrated the risks attending upon those who sailed in the loch because of its sudden storms. A tale, too, is told of a woman who saw a funeral procession passing along a hillside near the loch where there was no road. After the woman died a boat was lost in the loch and the bodies of the three drowned men were buried near a shepherd's house at the loch side. Their bodies were afterwards disinterred and carried along the very path the woman had described in her vision. Boatmen taking tourists from Elgol

across the Loch exercise great care and never set off if there is any likelihood of a storm arising before they can complete the trip. 'We might almost imagine,' said the geologist MacCulloch, 'that Dante had visited Scavaig. Numerous projecting points and rocky islets vary the scenery; and the extremity is a deep basin, enclosed seawards by promontories and islands, all equally rugged and bare, rising in a solid wall to the height of some hundred feet on the land side.'

Locks could be opened in olden times by anyone possessing the right rhyme or incantation. The last man to know the charm in Skye was Archibald the Lightheaded, but unfortunately when he repeated it he spoke so fast that no one was able to learn it. Dogs were terrified of Archibald, and no wonder – as a contemporary report said: On their offering the slightest sign of hostility, Archibald would knock out their brains without as much as looking at their masters.'

In the old days no one ever locked the door of his cottage –
a locked door was always associated with inhospitality and
meanness, from which stems the Gaelic expression *mosach ris
a'ghlais* – 'as mean as the lock'. If anyone desired privacy they
would place a wand across the open door. Even to this day in
Skye no one has any need to lock a door against his neighbour
and many a Skye housewife would be hard put to it to find the
key to her front door. An old Gaelic saying, which defines the
very lowest form of theft runs: 'From the theft of salt or seed,
never can a soul be freed'.

Lon an Eireannaich (LONE un AIR-nee<u>ch</u>) – Lon has many
meanings but in Skye it usually means a burn, so this is
Irishman's Burn. An Irish pedlar took a night's lodging at
Garslapin neat Portree. He overheard the son of the house say to
his father 'Isn't it about time for us to be killing the wedder-goat?'
The Irishman took this to be a metaphorical allusion to himself
and fleeing from the house fell into the nearby burn and was
drowned. Other experts suggest that *Eireannaich* really stands for
eirchinneach which means 'lay stewards of the church who seized
and held church lands in absence of monks who had died or been
dispossessed, and constituted themselves hereditary possessors'.
So from a semantic confusion a legend is born. I record this entry
not for the intrinsic importance of Lon an Eireannaich (which
flows from the foot of Ben Skriaig into Loch Snizort Beag) but as
a classic example of the extraordinary interplay of imagination,
muddle, myth, misinformation and poetic invention that lies at
the root of much of the naming of places in Skye.

Lorgill the glen of the deer's cry. A track, 5 miles south of
Glendale as the crow flies, leads from Ramasaig to this deserted
glen. Here in the summer of 1830 life in Lorgill came to an end.
One day a small party consisting of the factor, the sheriff officer, four policemen, and the minister made its way to this crofting community of ten families and everyone was summoned
together. The sheriff officer pulled a document from his pocket
and read it slowly and clearly:

> To all the crofters in Lorgill. Take notice that you are
> hereby duly warned that you all be ready to leave Lorgill at

twelve o'clock on the 4th August next with all your baggage but no stock and proceed to Loch Snizort, where you will board the ship *Midlothian* (Captain Morrison) that will take you to Nova-Scotia, where you are to receive a free grant of land from Her Majesty's Government. Take further notice that any crofter disobeying this order will be immediately arrested and taken to prison. All persons over seventy years of age and who have no relatives to look after them will be taken care of in the County Poorhouse. This order is final and no appeal to the Government will be considered. God Save the Queen.

On 3 August, after singing the 100th Psalm, the children gathered flowers and laid them on the family graves in the Lorgill burial ground. Then they went home to lie down for the last time in Skye. On the following morning they began the long march over the moors to the emigrant ship and as soon as they were on board the ship set sail. There is a tradition that among the evicted crofters was a MacCrimmon who, during the two-month voyage to the New World, composed 'The Lorgill Crofters' Farewell to Skye'.

Ludag (LOO-dack) – a malignant Skye goblin which, according to Hugh Miller writing in the 1840s, 'used to be seen at dusk hopping with immense hops on its one leg – for unlike every other denizen of the supernatural world, it is not furnished with two – and that, enveloped in rags, and with fierce misery in its hollow eye, has dealt heavy blows, it is said, on the cheeks of benighted travellers'.

Lyndale (LINE-dayl) – the dale of flax. There are three Lyndales in Skye: in Snizort, Duirinish and Bracadale. Flax is no longer grown in Skye but in the last century you would probably have slept as a visitor to Skye between sheets woven from island flax. Kilmuir museum has a fine example of locally woven linen. There is a Lynton in Staffin which derives its name from flax-growing, and Linicro in Kilnuir had a large acreage also under flax.

M

MacArthurs The hereditary pipers to the MacDonalds in Trotternish. Charles MacArthur was described by the eighteenth-century traveller Pennant as 'a master of his instrument'. The family occupied Hunglader in Kilmuir rent free until the end of the eighteenth century; Angus the last of the MacArthurs died in 1800. In the Kilmuir churchyard, the same one where Flora MacDonald lies buried, is a stone slab, half hidden by grass, which is curiously unfinished:

HERE LYES
THE REMAINS OF
CHARLES MAC
KARTER WHOSE
FAME AS AN HON
EST MAN AND
REMARKABLE PIP
ER WILL SURVIVE
THIS GENERATION
FOR HIS MANNERS
WERE EASY & RE
GULAR AS HIS
MUSIC AND THUS THO
THE MELODY OF
HIS FINGERS WILL

Two stories circulate concerning the abrupt ending of the inscription. One is that the mason went on strike because he felt he wasn't being paid enough and the other is that Charles MacArthur's son was lost at sea while the stone was being chiselled and the mason on hearing the news, abandoned his task, thinking that as he wasn't going to be paid there was little point in continuing.

MacAskills One of the oldest families in Skye. It is thought that they are of Irish origin. Their forebears were forced to leave Ireland, and after they had sought protection from MacLeod of Harris he gave them lands in Skye. The ruins of the MacAskill stronghold can still be seen at Rudhaan Dunain.

MacBrayne's For over a century now the most important name in the Highlands and Islands has been MacBrayne's. An old Hebridean lament explains something of the love-hate relationship which the name inspires:

> The earth belongs unto the Lord
> And all that it contains
> Except the Western Highlands
> And they are all MacBrayne's!

Today MacBrayne's is completely government controlled, but in the early days the company was privately owned and held the islands in a mixed debt of gratitude and resentment. Steamships first arrived in the Hebrides in the early nineteenth century when such companies as the City of Glasgow Steam Packet Company, the Clyde Steam Navigation Company, the Castle Steam Packet Company and David Hutcheson and Company began to open up routes round the islands. From 1879 the activities of David Hutcheson were carried on by David MacBrayne, a founder partner of Hutcheson. The first ship built for the fleet under MacBrayne's name was the *Claymore* and she was typical of the steamers which served Skye and the other islands. She was launched in July 1881 and worked summer and winter until she was taken away to be broken up in 1931. When one considers the short hours of winter daylight, the lack of navigation facilities and the storm-tossed waters of the Hebrides one can have nothing but admiration for the officers and men of the MacBrayne's fleet. But as the people of Skye and the other islands were totally dependent on MacBrayne's for the transport of virtually everything that arrived and left, it was easy for them to become a steam-valve of discontent and the scapegoat of all the island's grievances.

The arrival of the MacBrayne's steamer in a small Skye port was an event of some significance. It brought not only supplies and mail but news and gossip from other parts of the island, it brought friends and relations and took them away – it was television, radio, newspaper rolled into one black-hulled, scarlet-funnelled event that for many Skye men and women was their only link with the outside world. Today MacBrayne's fleet of ships has shrunk to a dozen passenger steamers, four cargo ships, three car ferries and twelve small motor ferry boats. In the winter their passenger ships are far from full, at the height of the tourist season they are often so crowded that cars have to be turned away. But the bulk of the business is carried today by road – MacBrayne's familiar red lorries and coaches have become for today's islander the equivalent of last century's steamer.

At the height of its maritime enterprise MacBrayne's served seven principal ports in Skye with passenger and cargo sailings: Portree, Kyleakin, Broadford, Dunvegan, Isleornsay, Glendale and Armadale. With the slow erosion in post-war years of uneconomic services MacBrayne's has been the main target of the sort of resentment that in mainland areas has been directed at British Rail. Just as a small market town will measure its importance by a rail link, even though most people prefer to go by road, so an island community will measure out its pride in the size of the steamer which serves it and the frequency of its sailings. Although in Portree nobody in his right mind would think of going to Kyle of Lochalsh any other way than by MacBrayne's bus or his own car, there is still a great sadness that the *Lochnevis,* a large, handsome motor vessel, should have been withdrawn, to be replaced by the small *Loch Arkaig.* This in turn was there only until such time as a regular ferry service between Raasay and Skye would make it finally a romantic anachronism.

MacCoitir's Cave (ma<u>ch</u>-KO<u>CHT</u>-ya) – on the north side of Portree Bay. This Cave of the Cottar's Son is said to have been where a young man hid to save himself from the press gang. Another legend relates that MacCoitir was a brigand who used the cave, high above the bay, as a base from which to raid ships lying at anchor (*see* also **Bornaskitaig**).

MacDonalds of the Isles and Sleat are descended from Somerled of the ancient Clann Cholla, which can be traced back to Constantine Centimachus, who lived in the second century A.D. Somerled married Ragnhildis, daughter of Olav the Black, King of Man and the Isles. Olav's son Godred, a tyrant, was defeated in battle on the night of Epiphany 1156. From then on Somerled was known as King of the Isles. The first Chief of the MacDonalds of Sleat, Hugh, son of the Earl of Ross, died in 1498.

MacDonald, Alexander son of the first Lord MacDonald, succeeded to the title in 1795. Like his father before him he preferred England to Skye, but when he did come home he was full of grandiose schemes (*see* **Kyleakin**), and it was he who was responsible for the Gothic alterations at Armadale which turned a modest house into a castle. 'He lived', wrote a contemporary apologist, 'on terms of cordial intimacy with his clansmen and tenantry whose interest it was his chief pleasure to promote; while the greater proportion of his income was expended on the improvement and decoration of his estate'.

MacDonald, Flora was the daughter of Ranald MacDonald of Milton, in South Uist. Born in 1722, her father died when she was young and her mother remarried a member of the house of Sleat, Hugh MacDonald. Flora was brought up in Skye and went to school in Sleat. From there Sir Alexander and Lady Margaret MacDonald sent her to school in Edinburgh and she was a frequent visitor at their house in Monkstadt. When Prince Charles was in flight after Culloden Flora happened to be visiting Milton. Here she encountered a member of the Prince's retinue and it was arranged that Charles should accompany her back to Skye disguised as Betty Burke, an Irish servant girl. The visas for the journey were issued by Flora's stepfather, who was at that time in charge of the militia in Uist. The party landed on 29 June 1745, half a mile to the south-west of Monkstadt House, and Flora sped to Monkstadt House to inform her kinswoman Lady Margaret that the royal fugitive was in hiding on the shore. It was arranged that he should spend the night in Kingsburgh house and from there the party went to Portree, where Flora bade farewell to her Prince. After Charles had made his escape Flora was captured and taken to London where she was put in protective custody until the passing of the Indemnity Act in 1747. She became something of a celebrity in the capital and a subscription was raised on her behalf. With some of the money she hired a post-chaise to take her to Edinburgh and was soon back in Skye. Three years later she married Allan MacDonald, the eldest son of MacDonald of Kingsburgh and for the next 22 years she and her growing family lived at Flodigarry. In 1774 the MacDonalds emigrated to North Carolina where they bought land.

When the American War of Independence broke out, Flora's husband joined the Royal Emigrant Regiment and in the fighting was taken prisoner. Eventually the MacDonalds returned to live in Skye, this time at Kingsburgh. Flora had five sons and two daughters and died in 1790. She was buried in the churchyard of Kilmuir and it is said that 3,000 mourners came from far and wide to attend her funeral. It was Dr. Johnson who phrased Flora's most fitting epitaph – the one which is now inscribed on her memorial cross in the kirkyard of Kilmuir – *Quantum cedat virtutibus aurum* – With virtue weighed, what worthless trash is gold!

MacDonald, Godfrey The fourth Lord's dilemma is a classic example of a situation which seemed to render not only the tenants of a former chief incapable of governing their own destinies but reduced the Chief himself to the role of a pawn in economic games played by businessmen with no concern for anything other than profit. Extravagance forced Godfrey to sell part of his birthright in 1847, including the whole of North Uist and Kilmuir in Skye. Of him, Alexander MacKenzie wrote in his *History of the Highland Clearances*:

It is well known that in other respects no more humane

man ever lived than he who was nominally responsible for the cruelties in Skye and at Sollas. He allowed himself to be imposed upon by others and completely abdicated his high functions as landlord and chief of his people. We have the most conclusive testimony and assurance from one who knew his lordship intimately that, to his dying day, he never ceased to regret what had been done in his name, and at the time with his tacit approval, in Skye and North Uist.

MacDonald, Sir James The eighth baronet of the family must have been a remarkable man. He was born in 1741 and his mother was the Lady Margaret MacDonald who had assisted Prince Charles in his escape from the government troops. He was educated at Eton and Oxford and showed a great aptitude for languages. When he was in Rome during his final illness the Pope sent a cardinal to the young nobleman who had excited such univeral admiration. 'I addressed him in seven different languages', the cardinal is said to have told the Pope,' and he answered me in all with fluency and obvious familiarity; and when I was about to leave the room, he gave an order to his servant in a language that I am sure nobody in the world understands but themselves.'

He made the Grand Tour in the company of several distinguished contemporaries, including Adam Smith who was then Professor of Moral Philosophy at Glasgow. On his return to Skye he set about improving his lands and the welfare of his tenants. He wanted to enlarge Portree and turn it into a centre of local industry and trade, but the only one of his plans which fully matured was the establishment of a large school. In the last two centuries, this has produced many men and women who have made their mark in the world. A shooting accident in Uist weakened a far from strong physique, and in the hope of convalescence in the sun he set off for the warmth of the Mediterranean. The journey didn't have the desired effect. He grew gradually weaker and died in Rome in July 1766 at the age of 25. In the Augustan tradition of the times a fulsome monument was carved in Rome and placed in 1768 in Kilmore church. The epitaph was composed by an Oxford friend, Lord Lyttelton: 'His eloquence was sweet, correct, flowing; His memory vast and exact; His judgement strong and acute; All which endowments, united With the most amiable temper And every private virtue, Procured him, not only in his own country, But also from foreign nations, The highest marks of esteem.' 'The panegyric recorded that on his death at Rome 'such extraordinary honours were paid to his memory as had never graced that of any other British subject since the death of Sir Philip Sidney'. Sir James' outstanding abilities suggested to several scholars a Roman parallel with the adopted son of Octavius Caesar and he was given the posthumous title of 'The Scottish Marcellus'. It was tragic that a man of such culture and vision should have died so young. Skye, had he lived, would have been a very different place and, one can't help feeling, a more enlightened place, during his chieftainship. He was succeeded by Alexander MacDonald, who fell far short of his elder brother's promise.

Machair (MA<u>CH</u>-ur) A fertile coastal strip formed by the binding of sand and marram grass occurs extensively on the sandy western seaboard of the Outer Isles but is not widespread in Skye. It can be seen, however, in one or two bays like Camasunary on the shores of Loch Scavaig.

MacLeods (ma-KLOWDZ) – an ancient family whose representatives still inhabit Dunvegan castle. Whence the MacLeods originally sprang is uncertain – the traditional tale is that their remotest ancestor was Leot or Leod, son of Olav the Black, King of Man. This Leod, born about the beginning of the thirteenth century, became foster son to Paul Balkeson, the king of the Northern Isles and Sheriff of Skye. When Balkeson died Leod came into possession of Uist and Harris. He inherited Lewis from his grandfather, and on marrying the daughter of a Norse chief he secured Duirinish, Bracadale, Minginish, Lyndale and a large slice of Trotternish. Leod died about 1280 and was buried in Iona. His son Norman, the first chief of the MacLeods of Skye, assumed power about 1280 – he is the Torquil of Scott's *Lord of the Isles.* Then follow years of conflict with the MacDonalds, and the disputes and often childish feuds have given rise to a whole series of myths and legends centred on the slaughter and carnage that was a part of everyday life in the islands before the English subdued their troublesome northern neighbours. The MacLeods included Ian (1330-92) a

134

notable despot and bloodthirsty tyrant who was killed in a battle at Rodel in Harris, and William, a remarkably virile Chief who fathered a great progeny of bastards. Apart from his philoprogenitive skill William is remembered chiefly for a bloody battle with the MacDonalds at Loch Sligachan from which few of the MacDonalds escaped alive. Then there was Ian the Fierce (more battles), Black William killed in a battle in Mull . . . and so on into the comparatively peaceful days when Dame Flora MacLeod of MacLeod, the 28th Chief, embraced Moral Rearmament.

MacLeod's Maidens Off Idrigill Point at the entrance to Loch Bracadale lie three stacks, the largest of which is about 200 ft. high. They derive their name from the tradition that after a four-teenth-century Chief of MacLeod had been mortally wounded in a clan battle in Harris his wife and daughters were shipwrecked and drowned on this spot while returning to Dunvegan. The larger rock is the Mother; the smaller two, the Maidens.

MacLeod's Tables formed by the twin flat basalt promontries of Healaval Mhor (1,538 ft.) and Healaval Bheag (1,601 ft.). It has been suggested that the name is derived from *helgi fjall*, holy fell, because the two flat tops suggested great natural altars. There is a story told of Alasdair Crotach (The Hump-backed), seventh Chief of the clan MacLeod, who lived in some splendour in Dunvegan Castle and who on a visit to Edinburgh behaved with such urbanity and grace that a group of lowland nobles were discountenanced by his aristocratic bearing. They began to needle him, suggesting that the elegance of Edinburgh couldn't be found in such an uncouth place as Skye. Alasdair refused to rise until finally one noble said: 'Have you ever seen in Skye, halls so spacious as these, a roof so lofty, a table so ample and richly laden and candelabra so ornate as those around us here tonight?' The MacLeod replied that although these

surroundings were quite grand he possessed in Skye a roof far more impressive, a larger table and infinitely superior illumination. The nobleman said he'd believe it when he saw it and was promptly invited to Dunvegan. When he arrived he was escorted to the summit of Healaval Mhor where the flat top was covered with food and wine, the stars shone down, and scores of MacLeods stood around holding aloft flaming torches. After the banquet Alasdair is said to have remarked quietly: 'Truly, sir, this is a roof grander than was ever made by human hands; this table, you must confess, is more commodious than any that can be shown even in the royal court; while those faithful vassals of mine are more precious by far than any metallic contrivance, however costly and ornate it may be'. The guest was duly shamed and nobody ever tried to take a rise out of Alasdair Crotach again. Scott used this story in his *Legend of Montrose*.

Mackenzie, John (1856-1933) The first and most famous Cuillin guide was born at Sconser and climbed Sgurr nan Gillean at the age of ten. Of him Sheriff Valentine wrote:

> His independence he always retained. He had his croft and could live without the tourists. In later life he went only occasionally to the mountains, but gave most of the summer to his old and constant ally, Collie. His was a green and sturdy eld. His stride was long and his eye keen. When his companions, wearied by a hard day, had sat themselves down with relief, they would see him set forth in the dusk for the three-mile trudge to his cottage, as fresh as a youth in his prime

and that when he was already far on in the sixties. The stalker's cap, the loose jacket and knickerbockers which he wore suited the man; they seemed to grow out of him. He had the characteristic of the Highlander; the courtesy joined to self-respect that are the heritage of the clans. His accent to the end smacked something of the Gaelic speaker and the turns of his phrases showed in what language his thoughts had been moulded. His features were strong and embrowned by weather. He wore in the old style a short beard, whiskers and moustache. Always alert, always cheerful, he was a perfect companion, but it was when the mist came down on the wet rocks that his worth was known. Scottish cragsmen may be content and proud to have him as a leader and a memory.

Norman Collie always said that John Mackenzie was the only real climbing guide that Britain had ever produced:

His great love of the mountains, his keen pleasure in all the beauties of the Cuillin never fails; whether it is a distant view of the mountains, or a sunset fading away behind the Outer Hebrides or the great slabs of gabbro bending over into space, or a still pool of clear water reflecting the rowan bushes and the peaks beyond, or the autumn colour on the rolling moors backed by the hills and the sea – all these do not pass him by unnoticed. He understands not only the joy of a hard climb but can also appreciate the marvels a beautiful mountain land is perpetually offering to one.

John Mackenzie died in 1933 at the age of 76 and is buried beside Collie in the churchyard at Struan.

Macpherson, James (1736-96) – the Celtic Homer, was born in Ruthven in Inverness-shire. He studied for the ministry but subsequently became a teacher. He had written poetry from an early age and made a collection of Gaelic poetry in Skye and the adjoining isles. This was not difficult to do. John MacDonald of Breakish declared on oath at the age of 78 that he could repeat when a boy from one to two hundred Gaelic poems and that 'he had learned them from an old man of about eighty years of age, who sung them for years to his father, when he went to bed at night, and in the spring and winter before he rose in the morning'. A Highland minister of the period recalled how an old Skyeman 'repeated to him for three successive days, and during several hours each day, without hesitation, and with the utmost rapidity, many thousands of lines of ancient poetry, and would have continued his repetitions much longer, if the Doctor had required him to do so'. Macpherson therefore had no dearth of material; at that time most people in Skye seemed to be blessed with a total recall almost verging on tedium. On his return to Edinburgh from his poetical tour Macpherson began translating his material into English. In 1761 he published an epic poem called *Fingal* and a year later *Temora*. He stated these to be translations from the Gaelic of Ossian, a third-century poet. Macpherson was loaded with praise for his work, but his output seems to have been largely invented, and although the poems had a quite considerable influence in their day (Napoleon admired them intensely), their lack of genuine character soon diminished their appeal. Perhaps the best verdict is this: 'No other imposture in literary history approcaches them in the splendour of their course'. A Committee of the Highland Society looked into the whole affair and they found that Macpherson was such a great improver of what he had collected that he had undoubtedly undertaken a work of creation. But as most of the people Macpherson had taken his poems from were dead nobody would ever know how much was the Bard of Ruthven and how much traditional Gaelic poetry. Johnson's verdict on Ossiana was characteristically blunt:

> I believe there cannot be recovered in the whole Erse language five hundred lines of which there is any evidence to prove them a hundred years old. Yet I hear that the father of Ossian boasts of two chests more of ancient poetry, which he suppresses, because they are too good for the English. . . . I suppose my opinion of the poems of Ossian is already discovered. I believe they never existed in any other form than that which we have seen. The editor, or author, never could show the original; nor can it be shown by any other; to revenge reasonable incredulity, by refusing evidence, is a degree of insolence, with which the world is not yet acquainted; and the stubborn audacity is

the last refuge of guilt. It would be easy to show it if he had it; but whence could it be had?

Whatever the provenance of the poems their romantic evocation of a period which up to then the Western world had known nothing about was like a hand grenade thrown at the retreating ogre of Classicism. Ossianism had a profound influence on the new partisans of the European romantic movement and stirred their imagination to an astonishing degree. The picture of Macpherson trudging round Skye from cottage to cottage collecting the incendiary material that was to set Europe on fire makes an appeal to the imagination that disarms criticism. John Stuart Blackie always claimed that Macpherson acted with the most perfect good faith: 'He found the long-neglected Celtic Muse of the Highlands in a very forlorn, defaced, ragged and unsavoury condition; and he thought it was only his duty, before presenting her to a critical modern public to wash her well and scrub her stoutly and dress her trimly in fresh habiliments, of which himself was proud to be the milliner'.

Marble When Johnson was in Skye he mused that 'perhaps by dilligent search in this world of stone, some valuable species of marble might be discovered'. Diligent research did reveal marble in the Strath district at Torrin where it is still quarried and exported as chippings to the mainland to be used in making composition slabs. Many of the fine Gothic fireplaces in Gillespie's Armadale Castle were carved from Strath marble; the Duke of Hamilton paved the lobby of his palace with Strath marble, and the altar in Iona cathedral is also supposed to have come from Skye. The marble is more compact than Carrara and harder to work, which accounts for its comparative commercial neglect. Marble quarries were also opened in the Red Hills near Broadford, and the first miniature railway in the island ran from the pier at Broadford to the foot of Beinn-na-Caillich where the stone was quarried. The company which promoted this enterprise built cottages at the base of the mountain and imported workmen from France, Belgium and the Scottish mainland.

Martin Martin (Gent) – was the first Skyeman to write about his place of birth. His book, published in 1703, was read by both Johnson and Boswell. Johnson felt he might have done a better job and was clearly disappointed by Martin's lack of legwork:

> He lived in the last century, when the chiefs of the clans had lost little of their original influence. The mountains were yet unpenetrated, no inlet was opened to foreign novelties, and the feudal institutions operated upon life with their full force. He might therefore have displayed a series of subordination and a form of government, which in more luminous and improved regions, have been long forgotten, and have delighted his readers with many uncouth customs that are now disused, and wild opinions that prevail no longer. But he probably had not knowledge of the world sufficient to qualify him for judging what would deserve or gain the attention of mankind. The mode of life which was familiar to himself, he did not suppose unknown to others, nor imagined that he could give pleasure by telling that of which it was, in his little country, impossible to be ignorant.

Meall (MYOWL) – a heap or a lump of a hill. The Highland Games in Skye are held on the Lump or *Meall* overlooking the harbour in Portree. Names like *Meall Beathaig* (Beathag's Hill), *Meall na Cuilce* (Hillock of the Reeds) and *Meall Grioba* (Precipice Hill) are found in different parts of the island.

Mental Illness was treated in a brisk and workmanlike way in Skye in pre-Jungian days. If a man was suffering from a fit of depression well-meaning friends might row him slowly out to sea and then when his attention was distracted, sieze him and bundle him over the side. The theory was that a sudden shock like this might work wonders. Another dramatic cure was devised by a blacksmith of Kilmartin, the thirteenth in a long line of muscle-men. The patient was brought to him and laid on his back on the anvil. The smith raised his hammer on high and brought it crashing down to within an inch of the victim's skull. There is no clinical record of success using this technique but no doubt the sufferer was so glad to come back alive from Kilmartin that it may have assisted in taking his mind off more trivial matters. Dr. Martin Whittet, Physician-Superintendent of the Craig Dunain mental hospital in Inverness, has pointed out (*Scottish Medical Journal*, August 1963) that there is today a relatively high incidence of involutional melancholia in the Hebrides, but he was careful not to attribute this either to the influence of climate or religion, although his paper explores both possibilities. He quoted the crofter patient who, on being asked what was wrong said: 'It's the nerve, doctor. You'll be the doctor for the nerve. It's a difficult thing the nerve. Some professors write books about it. It's myself that's sorry for them. It's not easy for them. They'll be doing their best no doubt'. Having divulged as many of his symptoms as he thought fit he added, 'Thank you very much, doctor, and I know if it's God's will I'll get better'. As Dr. Whittet commented: 'Such an independent assessment by a natural psychiatrist not only reflects the background of Highland psychiatry but also the timelessness of the Hebrides, which bridges with ease and grace the generations and the advances in the man-made treatments of Medicine.'

For anyone who wishes to explore the Highland temperament more deeply, Dr. Whittet's article in the *British Medical Journal* (1967, 40, 1) 'Highland and Island psychiatric reflexions,' is well worth studying.

Mermaids abound in Skye. 'A man in Skye caught a mermaid and kept her for a year. She gave him much information. When parting he asked her what virtue or evil there was in water in which eggs had been boiled. She said: "If I tell you that, you will have a tale to tell," and disappeared.' This story which I found in John Gregorson Campbell's *Superstitions of the Highlands and Islands of Scotland* and is here quoted verbatim, must be the most gnomic and pointless mermaid legend extant.

A slight clue to this story is afforded by the superstition that egg-water shouldn't be used for washing the hands or face. If somebody had bad luck through their own stupidity they would say: 'I believe egg-water was put over me.'

Midges a summer curse and bane to man and beast. Only known escape is to leave. Ointments and insect repellents alleviate but don't really control the curse. Midges are found in their greatest density in and around the rotting seaweed left by the high spring tides in March and not washed away again until October. Of them MacCulloch wrote in 1824:

It is the toss up of a die whether the world shall be possessed by midges and gnats, or by man. That their teeth are sharp, is too well known, and I can answer for the goodness of their noses. We had anchored about a mile and a half from the shore; yet they scented us; and in about a quarter of an hour, the vessel was covered with this 'light militia' of the lower sky. There are not many things more ingenious than the snout of a midge.

In the Sligachan Visitors' Book 70 or 80 decades ago some winsome body miserable with a surfeit of midges wrote in Harry Lauder Scots:

> Did aebody ken
> Sic an awfu' glen,
> Wi' its mosses and mires and ridges;
> But ainst within
> The Sligachan Inn
> We forget em a' – a' but the midges.

Monkstadt (MUNK-stat) – Monk's town – stands on rising ground half-way between the sea and the road 5 miles south of the ruined castle of Duntulm. It gets its name from the monastery which once stood on the island in Loch Chaluim Chille, long since drained. It was there that Sir Alexander MacDonald on his return from St. Andrews University decided to build a new mansion. Building began in 1732 and Monkstadt was probably the first house in Skye to have a slated roof – Duntulm where the family had lived previously had a roof of thatch. Sir Alexander farmed extensively in this fertile area and employed in addition to his household staff, gardeners, a grieve, a blacksmith, a cooper, a tailor, grooms, salmon fishers, herdsmen and all the skilled men necessary to sustain an eighteenth-century rural community. Here the brilliant James MacDonald, known as the Scottish Marcellus, was born on Boxing Day 1741. On Sunday, 29 June 1746, Prince Charles and Flora MacDonald landed on the shores of Monkstadt after their voyage from Uist. Monkstadt was finally deserted by the MacDonalds in the year of the French Revolution – it was then that Alexander Wentworth, second Lord MacDonald, decided to re-establish the family seat at Armadale. Monkstadt was lived in by various tacksmen but has now fallen into ruin. The coast here has many creeks and caves which were once the haunt of smugglers. Luggers would arrive from Gairloch laden with kegs of spirit to be bartered for barley, oats and potatoes. The Gairloch moonshiners also bartered their liquor for barley with the farmers of Staffin.

Monro, Donald Archdeacon of the Isles before the Reformation, wrote the first extant description of the Western Isles from personal observation. In 1549 he noted that Skye had many woods, forests and deer and plenty of salmon for the taking. 'This Ile,' he wrote, 'is callit Ellan Skianach in Irish, that is to say in Inglish the wyngit Ile, be reason it hes many wyngis and pointis lyand furth fra it, throw the deviding of their foirsaid Lochis.'

Mountains have many different names in Gaelic and as four fairly well-known lines of doggerel have it:

A mountain's a mountain in England, but when
The climber's in Scotland it may be a *Beinn,*
A *Creag* or a *Meall,* a *Spidean,* a *Sgor,*
A *Carn* or a *Monadh,* a *Stuc* or a *Torr.*

Munro, Donald There has always been a conflict between music and the more rigid forms of evangelical religion. Donald Munro, who lost his sight at the age of 14, was born at Achtaleathan, near Portree, about 1773. He was one of the finest fiddlers in Trotternish, but he came under the influence of an itinerant preacher in the year 1805; so remarkable was his transformation that he is known as the Father of Evangelical Religion in Skye. All the skill that he had formerly expressed in music was channelled now into spreading the Word. So powerful was his oratory, so complete his conversion from the works of the Devil, that he was able to convince his flock that the only way to Eternal Reward was to renounce the wiles of music. He named a day when they were to bring their fiddles and bagpipes to the head of Loch Snizort for a big public conflagration. The response was gratifying for Munro, and he was able to warm his body and soul at a monumental bonfire. It was not only music that men like Munro objected to. They were almost entirely successful in stifling the oral tradition of story-telling and other manifestations of native culture.

To understand fully the faith and power of men like Donald you should read Roderick MacCowan's account of the rise of Evangelicalism called *The Men of Skye*. Typical of the 'Men' who were 'Saved' was John MacKenzie who lived at Galtrigil and was employed as a fish-curer. Although he had a huge sack of salt beside him which his employer provided for the curing of the fish John was scrupulous in insisting that his wife should bring down with her a few grains of salt from his own house to go with his midday egg because 'he would not take so much as a grain of salt that was not his own'. Another equally remarkable man was John MacLeod of Fasach in Glendale. MacCowan describes him as 'constant and fervent in prayer, and when lying sick on his death-bed, they had to lay bags of fodder on the floor, so that he would slip out of bed on to them to bend his knees and pray to the Lord'. The lengths to which the Men went to ensure their redemption seem perhaps fanatical in our own less religious days, but the tradition of neglecting the full pursuit of happiness in this life in order to qualify for the chance of external life in the world to come still exercises a powerful appeal to a small and diminishing minority (*see* **Religion**).

Museums If you find yourself in Inverness on your way to Skye, visit the small museum on the first floor of the new Library, and in Fort William the Highland Museum is well worth a detour. Until 1965 there was no museum in Skye but in that year an enterprising crofter, Jonathan MacDonald converted a disused cottage close to Kilmuir churchyard into a folk museum. Among the relics is an alabaster egg cup used by Flora MacDonald while living in Flodigarry in the 1750's, old crofting implements, a pewter communion cup from Trumpan church, an old baptismal font last used in a Skye church in the eighteenth century and all manners of bygones. The small relics here are overshadowed by the historic collection in Dunvegan castle but Kilmuir is worth seeing as is the thatched house next door to the tea rooms at Colbost.

Necker In an overgrown part of the old Portree Churchyard (you'll find it facing the Skye Gathering Hall) is a moss-covered stone on which are inscribed the words: 'sacred to the memory of Louis Albert Necker of Geneva who died at Portree on the 20th day of November 1861'. Charles Richard Weld met this exile's nephew in 1859:

As I was about entering my inn for the night, my attention was drawn to a strange-looking character attired in a fantastic sporting costume, standing in the doorway. He was evidently not an Englishman, but before I had time to speculate as to his country, he addressed me in French, asking whether I spoke that language. His joy when I answered in the affirmative was great, for his acquaintance with English was very slight, and you may be sure that French is an unknown tongue in Skye. Yet not entirely, for a gentleman lives near Portree whose native language is French, and it was to see him that my questioner had journeyed from Paris to the Hebrides.

This foreigner is M. Necker, grandson of the celebrated statesman of that name, and nephew of Madame de Staël. Upwards of forty years ago, distressed and disgusted by home politics, he left his country, and in the course of his wanderings visited Skye. The scenery and solitude of this island pleased him; he purchased a small house near Portree and, declining all offers of hospitality, has lived a hermit's life for many years, retaining, however, a love for science, to which he had been attached from a very early age. The gentleman who addressed me was his nephew; he had been paying his uncle a visit, and was now on his way home.

Neist Point (NEESHT) – the most westerly point of Skye, which can be reached by taking the road which branches off from Upper Milavaig in Glendale. There is a three-quarter-mile walk fairly up hill and down dale to reach the lighthouse, which commands the waters of the Little Minch, was built in 1909 and is manned by three keepers. The tower is 62 ft. high and the light, which can be seen 24 miles away is 140 ft. above sea level. It has an intensity of 480,000 candelas. The foghorn, which in poor visibility emits two three-second blasts every $1^1/_2$ minutes, is a powerful one. In August 1969 while fishing a mile or so north of Portree we clearly heard the Neist fog signal. It was a strange freak effect which carried the sound 28 miles from the west coast to the east coast of Skye.

Nicolsons are said by some historians to have come to Skye from Denmark in the thirteenth century, but another tradition states that the Nicolsons were in possession of the Isle of Lewis before the MacLeods. One authority claims that a Captain John Muldovie Nicolson fought in the Battle of Largs in 1263 and was rewarded by King Alexander III with the lands of Scorribreac, north of Portree. It was he who built the first Scorribreac House in which James V stayed a night in 1540. In the early years of the nineteenth century Norman, the last Chief of the Nicolsons, sold his land to Lord MacDonald and emigrated to Tasmania. The remnants of the clan were evicted and Scorribreac was given over to sheep. In November 1952 the *Clarion of Skye* announced that the Chief of the clan, Norman Alexander Nicolson of Scorrabreak Estate in Tasmania, proposed in his seventieth year to hold a reunion of the clan on the site of the old Scorribreac House in Portree. His last visit to the island had been in 1916 as a Captain in the Australian army. To forestall correspondence, I hasten to add that this gentleman's claim to the chieftainship did not go undisputed.

Nicolson, Alexander born at Husabost in 1827 and known affectionately as Alick Husabost. He was a brilliant Gaelic scholar and thought at first he might become a minister, but he settled for journalism. He worked for the *Edinburgh Guardian* and when that folded he edited the *Daily Express*, strangely, an extremely Liberal paper. He later took up law; at the age of 33 he was called to the

Scottish Bar and in 1872 was made Sheriff Substitute of Kircudbright. He was never happier than when in the Cuillins and in 1873 became the first man to climb the peak which is named after him, Sgurr Alasdair. It was Nicolson's articles about Skye in the magazine *Good Words* which encouraged a great influx of tourists to the island in the 'seventies and 'eighties.

It was Nicolson too who wrote the quatrain more often quoted than any other four lines of verse on Skye:

> Jerusalem, Athens and Rome,
> I would see them before I die,
> But I'd rather not see any one of the three,
> Than be exiled for ever from Skye!

Nicolson, 'Allie Willie' of Struan in Bracadale will be remembered with admiration and respect by all those who met him or subscribed to his remarkable magazine *Clarion of Skye*. *Clarion* began life in February 1951 as a single stencilled sheet – its price 2¹/₂d. In the early days its subsidiary role as an Inter-Island Advertiser concealed its real purpose. Allie Willie was a visionary who wanted to re-people the glens of Skye, and in the six years that he edited this monthly magazine he had only one aim: to awaken the people of Skye to all the wasted opportunities that lay around them. Allie Willie's dream was of indigenous industries mushrooming in every township, the young people staying in the island and a renaissance flowering in the West. The *Clarion* grew to sixteen pages and its circulation rose to a thousand copies a month, but illness overtook the editor and the last edition appeared in March 1957. The 74 issues remain not only as a memorial to a good and passionate Skyeman but as a rich mine of information for the social historian.

Norse pirates began to raid the Hebrides around the eighth century. They were independent chieftains who had thrown off the authority of the Norwegian kings. Their first recorded descent was in A.D. 794 when they laid Skye and many other islands waste. They settled in Skye and used it as a base from which to harry the Norwegian coast. They didn't wipe out the indigenous Celts but used them for menial tasks, and there was a great deal of intermarriage which produced a mixed race of

Gallgaels. Towards the end of the tenth century they were brought to heel and the King of Norway once more asserted his authority over them. For something like four hundred years Skye was dominated by the Norse and it wasn't until 1156 that Somerled defeated them. When Somerled died his sons were not strong enough to hold off the Norse, and their domination continued until they were finally defeated at the battle of Largs by Alexander III. In escaping, Haco, the Norse leader was over-taken by a gale which wrecked most of his galleys on the coasts of Lorne, Mull and Skye. He took refuge in Loch Bracadale and, sailing for home, died in Kirkwall in the Orkneys.

Norse blood flows in the veins of many Skyemen, and Norse place-names are found all over the island.

O

Ob The bay or tidal inlet.

Ord Overlooks Loch Eishort, which in 1644 was the scene of a fight between three ships of the Scottish parliament and Alasdair MacColl who escaped with the loss of his ships or galleys.

It was in Ord House that Alexander Smith stayed with his father-in-law and gained the experiences which he wove into *A Summer in Skye*.

The River Ord contains horse mussels, in one of which a pearl of great price (£20) was once found.

Osdale (OZZ-dul) – east fell. Half a mile up the Ose river about a quarter of a mile north-north-west of Osdale croft is a monolith which was probably once a standing stone. It is 7 ft. long and 12 ft. broad. Legend says that a ploughman killed a water-horse with a red hot plough coulter and buried the beast under this stone.

Ose river mouth. On the shores of Loch Caroy in Bracadale. If you walked up the Ose river about 2½ miles from its mouth you'd see a *broch* shown on the map as Dun Arkaig. It stands about 150 ft. above the southern bank of the river dominating the second largest green glen in Skye. The remnants of a gallery can still be seen but dilapidation is far advanced.

Ostaig (OSS-tig) – East Bay in Sleat – where in simple comfort, his castle at Armadale long since abandoned as a costly anachronism, lived Alexander Godfrey MacDonald of MacDonald, M.B.E., T.D., seventh baronet and Lord Lieutenant and County Convener of Inverness-shire. His son and heir Godfrey came of age in 1969.

P

Pabay (PAB-ay) – Monk or Priest Island. Forms a breakwater to Broadford bay; a low-lying island famed for its fossils and petrifactions. It contains an ancient ruined chapel and burying ground. The island was described by Dean Monro in 1549 as: 'full of woods, good for fishing, and a main shelter for thieves and cut-throats'. A century and a half later Martin Martin wrote: 'It excells in Pasturage, the Cows in it afford near double the Milk that they yield in Skie. In the Dog-Days there's a big Fly in this isle, which infests the cows, makes them run up and down, and discomposes them exceedingly'.

Peasantry In the days when the word *peasant* was not a term of abuse but a very accurate description of the unfortunate rural majority, it was a common practice for landowners and those connected with the management of estates to talk and write about the Peasantry as if they were a commodity, like sheep, deer or grouse. In a way the parallel was appropriate. Like some kind of unwanted species, the peasantry often squatted on one's land, abused one's hospitality and generally created a nuisance – especially if one wanted the land for a more profitable purpose, like letting the shooting rights to fat men from the Potteries. The Final Solution with the peasantry was usually to send them a long way away where they could fend for themselves and be a nuisance to no one (*see* **Emigration**). If the surplus peasantry couldn't be persuaded to push off somewhere else one had to set about the rather tedious task of 'improving their lot'. The mid-nineteenth-century attitude to the lower orders is crystallized in a series of articles written for the *Inverness Courier* by George Mackay, the Inverness Land Agent. His article on 'The Peasantry' went like this:

The conditions of the peasantry must interest and affect all who are concerned in the management of land. The daily increasing interest in the welfare of the humbler classes, on the part of their superiors, is a happy proof of our social advancement, and we earnestly wish it God speed. But in what direction soever we move in connection with this most difficult of problems – the elevation of the peasantry – we are met with obstacles of every possible kind, so that the utmost forbearance and untiring application must be exercised by any one who would, with success, adopt practical measures on their behalf. It seems a prevalent idea that the chief characteristic of the Highlander is laziness – inveterate laziness. Without any desire to screen our countrymen from merited aspersion, we must say that this fault is much exaggerated; and in so far as they deserve this character, we pity more than we blame them. And why? Because it is the consequence of being uncared for on the part of those whose duty it is to look after them. They are ignorant, because they have not been educated; they are indolent, because they have little encouragement to exert themselves, being furnished with no field for their ambition; they are often filthy in their habits from their extreme poverty; and they are reckless and improvident from that stupidity and want of thought natural to creatures that have been despised and neglected. In commencing a proper system of management on a neglected property, the circumstances of the people should be considered; and in so far as the peasantry are concerned in any changes, they should be approached in a kindly, conciliatory manner; their prejudices should be humoured, and their wishes consulted to some extent. This, with firmness and determination, will invariably secure the desired results much more effectually, speedily and pleasantly than by the harsh, dictatorial style too often adopted.

One can only assume that the number of ignorant, indolent, filthy, reckless, improvident and stupid peasants subscribing to the *Inverness Courier* in the 1850s was pretty low.

Peat still for many people takes the place of more expensive coal, and the piles of peat by the roadside, waiting to be taken to nearby

houses are a common sight. The peat lying in the moor can be as
much as 93.5 per cent water. It is cut in slabs and piled to dry
until it contains only about 40 per cent of water; when it's finally
ready for the fire a good peat will be bone dry. The calorific value
is only a third of good quality coal. The peats are cut in the spring
with a special instrument called a *toirbhsgir,* and a household rely-
ing entirely on peat for its fuel would burn between 15,000 and
18,000 peats a year. As one man can cut only a thousand peats in
a day this represents a considerable amount of hard labour. The
West Highland Survey edited by F. Fraser Darling estimated that
in 1955, 75 per cent of townships in Skye were using both peat
and coal, 20 per cent coal only, and the remainder relied entirely
on peat. Peat varies in quality, and there is good and bad peat just
as there is good and bad coal. Peat is, of course, decayed vegetation and the peat reek you smell as you approach a Skye township
may be coming from reeds, rushes, sedges, mosses and trees
perhaps laid down nine or ten thousand years ago.

Peinduin (pen-DOON) – the pennyland of the fort. The Norse
measured land by rentals and a penny-weight's worth of silver in
land is a description of both value and size. Unmarked on the
Ordnance Survey map Peinduin lies just less than a mile south
of Caisteal Uisdein and a ruined house can still be seen on the
shore, much overgrown by bracken and, if memory serves me,
a tree or two. It was here that Flora MacDonald died while on
a visit from nearby Kingsburgh House. Her body was carried
across the swollen waters of the River Hinnisdal during a night
of raging storm and back to Kingsburgh where it lay in state for
a week before burial. They say that 300 gallons of whisky were
consumed at Flora's funeral.

Picts' Houses long narrow tunnels flanked and roofed with
stone cut into the side of hills and sometimes as long as 90 ft.
have been found in Skye. The end of the tunnel widens into a
small circular chamber in which even a dwarf couldn't stand at
ease. Martin Martin said of them: 'They served to hide a few
people and their goods in time of war'. He also seemed to think
they were used as storehouses for corn and as winter places of
hibernation. The most elaborate of these tunnels, or Erd houses,
is at Vatten but you will have difficulty in finding it. On his way

from Dunvegan to Ullinish, Dr. Johnson was shown one of these caves, but he wasn't very enthusiastic about their antiquity:

> These caves were represented to us as the cabins of the first rude inhabitants, of which, however, I am by no means persuaded. This was so low that no man could stand upright in it. They are not the work of an age much ruder than the present; for they are formed with as much art as the construction of a common hut requires. I imagine them to have been places only of occasional use, in which the islander, upon a sudden alarm, hid his utensils or his clothes, and perhaps sometimes his wife and children.

Pigs are not looked upon with favour in Skye – the number kept could be counted on the fingers of one hand. Whether this is a religious revulsion I haven't been able to discover, but the traveller Charles Weld writing in the 1860s thought it might be:

> Why is that useful animal the pig which after doing pillow duty for Pat, pays his rent and often gives him a bit of wholesome bacon never seen in Skye, and indeed but seldom throughout the Highlands? With respect to Skye, the answer is easy. The population holds pork in Israelitish abhorrence, and not the most succulent sucking pig, nor the plumpest porker, possess charms for them.

Pooltiel (pull-TEEL) – This loch on the northern tip of Duirinish was named after a Danish prince called Diel whose body was washed ashore here. Loch Pooltiel used to be a regular port of call for steamers serving the Glendale district, but the pier now lies deserted and unused. Ian Anderson in his travel book *To Introduce the Hebrides* recalled an arrival at Loch Poolteil at the beginning of the century. The time shortly before midnight:

> The *Hebrides* soon glided alongside Pooltiel Pier and really I almost felt as if I had suddenly entered into the centre of a village 'social'. At the corner of the pier stood the Pier Master swinging his oil lantern for the ship's guidance to assist it in berthing. The open-fronted shed on the pier was filled with people of both sexes and all ages, from all parts of the surrounding district, and all actively engaged in conversation

under the feeble yellow rays of the oil lamp illuminating the shed. It was an animated scene, and the quick sound of the Gaelic and shrill laughter of the children and the soft cadence of the Highlanders' English, lent a warmth of friendliness to the gathering. The arrival of the *Hebrides* broke up this company and the business of assisting with the unloading, and the claiming of respective articles of merchandise was set to. This was seemingly an event and it appeared that all came to the pier whether for goods or not. The pier was the meeting-place for this outlying community. No sooner was the cargo unloaded than the people began to drift away in twos and threes, and as our last ropes were drawn on board, even the man with the lamp of guidance had disappeared.

About 1840 the 25th MacLeod of MacLeod tried to start a fishing station in Loch Pooltiel but, like earlier attempts to interest the islanders in fishing, his efforts, for one reason or another, met with little success.

Population density varies in Skye from as low as 6 per square mile in Bracadale to as high as 21 in Kilmuir. The average density is about 12 persons per square mile, which compares with a United Kingdom average of 567. The whole story of depopulation can be seen in the figures recorded from 1755 onwards. Because of the profits from the kelp industry and the consequent need for large numbers of willing hands to collect seaware from the rocks, the population showed an increase until the fourth decade of the nineteenth century – from then on it has been a story of decline.

1755	11,252	1881	17,680
1801	15,788	1891	16,478
1811	17,029	1901	14,561
1821	20,827	1911	13,283
1831	22,796	1921	11,584
1841	23,074	1931	10,345
1851	22,536	1951	8,537
1861	19,591	1961	7,700
1871	18,114		

Porpoise (*Phocaena phocaena*) can be seen cavorting and corkscrewing very frequently in Skye waters, especially when supplies of small fish are plentiful. They seem to be extremely fascinated by boats and will follow one, diving under it, crossing its bows and generally exhibiting great curiosity. Many people on first seeing a porpoise imagine that they've seen a small shark; apart from the triangular dorsal fin they have little else in common. They are known in Gaelic as *Mucan biorach,* or dog-fish pigs.

Portnalong the port or harbour of ships. Here on the shores of Loch Harport after the first world war the Department of Agriculture settled a number of families from overpopulated Lewis, Harris and the nearby island of Scalpay. Two waves of immigrants came, and each family was given between fifteen and twenty acres, three cows and a share in a common sheep pasture of 4,000 acres. The idea was that as crofter-fisher-weaverman they would have a better chance of making a living in Skye, where the land was relatively more fertile. Although they came without their looms they later sent for them and began weaving. Every year until 1939 a *Feill* or Gathering was held in Portnalong when the year's weaving was offered for sale. After the war an enterprising firm revived the weaving of tweed, and yarn was sent to be woven to specific instructions. Skye homespuns were exported to the United States, and a store in Memphis, Tennessee (selling Skye tweed sports coats at $75 each), had the bright idea of mailing promotional matter from Portree. The sell was enough to bring a misty tear to all but the hardest eye and was a triumph of the copywriter's art – a tasteful blend of *schmaltz* and innacuracy:

> Off the North-West Coast of Scotland where Atlantic gales exhaust their fury against the 1,000-ft. cliffs of Talisker and the sun sets soft and beautiful over Uig Bay, lies the misty Isle of Skye. . . . Skye homespun is woven in the crofters' own homes, and the clatter of the shuttle spells tangible wealth to the islander eking out a meagre existence from his few acres of croft. The sturdy Scottish sheep provide the wool from which fine yarn is spun – yarn which embodies the natural brilliance of the Skye scene . . . the birch, the bracken, the machair, the seawrack, the gabbro and the

heather all find their counterpart in the finished cloth. Mountain and moorland, sky and sea in all the moods of nature, are reflected in the unique colourings of the cloth. Tough and resilient, honest and kind, Skye homespun is a cloth to buy and to cherish as a friend.

One or two crofters are still selling lengths of homespun cloth in Portnalong and if you can't get it there you might be able to get it from an honest and kind shopkeeper in Memphis eking out a meagre existence with the help of a sturdy homespun advertising agency.

Portree (por-TREE) – In 1540 James V set sail from Leith in a fleet of 12 ships to pacify the Isles. After visiting Duntulm he sailed round the north of Skye and anchored in what was then known as Loch Chaluim Chille where the dissident chiefs had assembled to pay him court. People came from all over the island to enjoy the fun and the event made such an impression on them that they changed the name of the place from Kiltaraglen (the *kil* or cell of Talorgan, a culdee who dwelt in solitude just beyond the Black Rock) to *Port an Rìgh* – the King's Harbour. It was according to Martin Martin 'the Convenience of the Harbour which is in the middle of the Isle, made 'em chuse this for the fittest Place'. Portree is often compared to Tobermory for beauty but the metropolis of Skye, nestling in the comfort of the bay, is to my mind a much more attractive town. Like Broadford, Portree was virtually non-existent at the beginning of the nineteenth century. The oldest building was on the site of the present Royal Hotel. Here, in MacNab's Inn as it was then known, Prince Charles made his farewells to Flora MacDonald before embarking for Raasay. Here 27 years later Boswell and Johnson had 'a very good dinner, porter, port and punch' with the innkeeper, a certain James MacDonald who like many Skyemen at that time was about to emigrate to North America.

It was Boswell's friend, Sir James MacDonald, doomed to die in Rome at the age of 25, who founded the town and his work has been continued by successive MacDonald chiefs who still own the land on which it stands. Their associations with Portree are commemorated in Somerled Square (Somerled is reputed to have been the twelfth-century founder of the clan), Wentworth Street (Godfrey Wentworth, son of the 17th

MacDonald chief, eloped with an illegitimate niece of George III) and Bosville Terrace (a family name of the MacDonalds of Sleat).

Today Portree boasts five churches, three banks, a score of shops including a supermarket, a large new hospital, a library, a famous High School to which secondary pupils come from all over Skye and the outlying islands, two gaelic choirs, a pipe band, golf and tennis courts, six hotels, several guest houses and a large number of hospitable householders offering bed and breakfast. Portree is the administrative capital of Skye and an ideal head-quarters for touring.

There are boats for hire, a variety of bus tours, and a sandy beach at Camus Ban. In Loch Portree at high tide an island is isolated from the shores of Peinafeiler which is supposed to contain the remains of a church named after St. Columba. It was 26 ft. long by 16 ft. wide.

Portree is dominated by the 1,367 ft. high peak of Suidh Finn – Fingal's Seat. In the town itself and forming a hillock above the harbour is the *Meall* or Lump which was laid out with trees and shrubs by the celebrated Dr. Ban, a visionary who hoped to make Portree a second Oban. It was he who built the round lookout tower which is said at one time to have been used by an apothe-cary. On the Lump on 18 June 1742 the last hanging in Skye took place 'with the greatest Decency and without the least Disturbance'. The victim was Angus Buchanan who with an accomplice had murdered a travelling chapman.

At the entrance to the Lump is the Skye Tourist Headquarters housed in the oldest extant building in Portree (*c.* 1810) which was the first jail and Sheriff's court. It is seen to advantage in Daniell's engraving (see Plate 8) and the exterior today is almost exactly the same as it was a century and a half ago.

The population of Portree is about 1,500 and growing every year.

Prices in Skye for those used to the big city supermarkets and cut-price stores must seem high. When in April 1968 *The Scotsman* undertook a shopping survey in various parts of the country they noted that Portree shops, because they are a long way from the wholesale sources of supply, are seldom offered the competitive bulk-buying terms open to a big retailer in Glasgow or Edinburgh. On top of this, shipping and delivery charges are so heavy that on a low-priced bulk commodity (potatoes, for instance) transport costs can be as expensive as the basic price of the article itself. In 1968 a pound each of flour, biscuits, butter, margarine, cheese, bacon and lamb chops bought in Glasgow would have cost 18s. 4^{1}/2d.; the same basketload cost 28s. 6d. in Portree. It must be borne in mind that some things, fish for instance, are much cheaper and fresher in Skye than they are in the cities, but when it comes to consumer durables the Skye shopper is again faced with high transport charges, lack of choice, and no competitive price-slashing, special offers or High Street cut-price bargains. Many families find it pays to make an occasional shopping expedition to Inverness – the return journey can be done quite easily in a day and even with the cost of the fare they can make substantial savings. Anyone planning to retire to Skye on a fixed pension or any fugitive from urban life who sees the island as a cheap land of peace and plenty must face the fact that the cost of living in Skye can be anything up to 50 per cent more expensive than in a city.

Prince Charlie's Cave 4 miles north of Portree. Legend which is probably wrong says the Young Pretender was hidden here. Forty-five years before that time Martin Martin noted that 'there is a Well within it, which together with its situation and narrow Entry, renders it an inaccessible Fort, one Man only can enter it at a time, by the side of a Rock, so that with a Staff in his hand, he is able by the least touch to cast over the Rock as many as shall attempt to come into the Cave'. Another writer has described it as 'a piece of natural rock-work moulded outwardly like a cathedral window, and large and lofty in the interior'. A nineteenth-century guide book didn't care much for it at all: 'The interior is wet and damp, and not at all a spot one would choose for a residence during the winter'.

There are three other caves in which Charlie is supposed to have lain hidden: one south of Elgol, another near Loch Coruisk, a third at Dunvegan.

Procrastination is a characteristic of which the Skyeman perhaps more than the Skyewoman is often accused. A former Rector of Portree put it down to the weakening effects of tea-drinking, although he was obviously not an advocate of the hard stuff: 'If he is prone to certain diseases, like consumption, or insanity, out of all proportion to the population, that is because he subsists now so largely on boiled tea, and also because years and years of inbreeding have enfeebled the vital powers. Habits of procrastination denote a feeble vitality, and the customary submission to fate suggests that the fires of energy are burning low'. Some time ago a man called Cameron who lived in Glen Brittle composed a rhyme to illustrate what he saw as endemic apathy:

Oh that ta peats would cut themselves,
And ta fesh shump on the shore,
And that we in our peds might lie
For aye and efermore, och, och!

It is common for incomers to be exasperated beyond all reasonable measure by the leisurely approach to affairs they find in Skye. The cut and thrust of competitive city life is noticeably and pleasantly absent in Skye. But it would be unwise to equate lack of frenzy with laziness or an unhurried rhythm of life with apathy. Bustle, rush and the inability to relax are perhaps more the symptoms of an ailing civilization than the calmer, even pace of life which is still to be found in Skye.

Ptolemy The astronomer and geographer who lived at Alexandria during the first half of the second century A.D. provided the first written evidence that such a place as Skye existed. He included the island in his map of the world but stuck it halfway between Norway and Caithness under the name of Sketis.

Q

Querns or handmills, used to be employed throughout Skye for grinding corn. They consisted of two flat stones about 20 in. in diameter, selected for their toughness and grittiness. Boswell was very much intrigued with the quern and persuaded the laird of Coll to send him one from Mull 'as he has set up a mill on his estate there, and is abolishing the quern which is a very poor and tedious implement'. Called in Gaelic *Muillean-brath*, the quern was still in use in parts of Skye in the 1830s:

> Across the central hole in the upper stone is a piece of wood with a small tapering hollow, which fits a wooden pivot on the lower stone. Placing the finger, or a stick, in a hole sunk for that purpose, close to the exterior edge of the upper stone, it is with the greatest facility made to revolve with the desired velocity; and the whole machine being placed on a sheet, or sheepskin, the grain gradually poured in at the hole in the upper stone, is speedily ground into meal, which falls out at the circumference between the two stones.

Earlier, in 1772, Thomas Pennant had watched women at the quern and observed:

> The *quern* or *bra* is made in some of the neighbouring counties in the mainland and costs about fourteen shillings. This method of grinding is very tedious: for it employs two pair of hands four hours to grind only a single bushel of corn. Instead of a hair sieve to sift the meal the inhabitants here have an ingenious substitute, a sheep's skin stretched round a hoop, and perforated with small holes made with a hot iron. They knead their bannock with water only, and bake, or rather toast it, by laying it upright against a stone placed near the fire.

In 1833 Alexander Mackenzie in his account of the evictions and clearances in Skye recorded that

one of the results brought out by the evidence submitted to the Royal Commission in Skye is that nearly all the meal mills that used, in great numbers, to be constantly employed twenty to fifty years ago, have fallen into decay or are lying completely idle in consequence of the evictions and of the best portions of the Island having been laid waste to make room for large sheep farms. These silent and dilapidated buildings now proclaim the sad truth respecting the once prosperous inhabitants of the famous and soldier-producing island more eloquently than pen can record.

Quiraing (Kwirr-ANG) – the round fold or pen. It is said that this strange geological formation in Trotternish could shelter 4,000 head of cattle in time of trouble. The Quiraing is best approached by walking up a gentle slope from the Uig-Staffin road. A sheer precipice falls away to reveal a chasm on whose seaward side giant pillars rise. From the summit both the west and eastern shores of Skye can be seen. In the middle lies the Table, a grassy plateau on which in the old days an annual midsummer shinty match used to be played. The Needle is a slender rocky phallus 120 ft. in height. Although far more people visit Skye than ever before the number who don't bother to scale the Quiraing is strangely high. In Victorian times at the height of the season between 50 and 60 visitors a day would drive out from Portree to climb among these awesome rocks.

Raasay (RAA-zay) – Roe-isle. This 14-mile-long island lies along the eastern coast of Skye, its southern tip opposite the entrance to Loch Sligachan and its most northern point on a level with the Storr rock. Today Raasay is a dying island, the population has dwindled year by year and gradually, one by one, services have been withdrawn in the outlying parts: a school closed here, a telephone kiosk disconnected there. But things were not always so: the 27 square miles of Raasay flourished in the eighteenth century and Boswell and Johnson were entertained with great elegance in Raasay House.

> It was [wrote Boswell] a most pleasing approach to Raasay. We saw before us a beautiful bay, well defended, with a rocky coast; a good gentleman's house, a fine verdure about it, a considerable number of trees, and beyond it hills and mountains in gradation of wildness. Our boatmen sung with great spirit.

On the table at Raasay house they found coffee and tea,

> diet loaf, marmalade of oranges, currant jelly; some elegantly bound books on a large table, in short, all the marks of improved life. We had a dram of excellent brandy, according to the Highland custom, filled round. On a sideboard was served up directly, for us who had come off the sea, mutton-chops and tarts with porter, claret, mountain, and punch.

Raasay house was built in the 1740s and of his reception there Johnson declaimed: 'This is truly the patriarchal life. This is what we came to find'. Boswell climbed to the top of Duncaan, danced a reel in sheer exuberance and ate 'cold mutton and bread and cheese and drank brandy and punch'.

Neither Boswell nor Johnson mentioned that after the '45 virtually every house on the island, including the Chief's house, was burnt by the government troops. All the sheep and cattle, even the boats, were removed or destroyed.

The last descendant of the MacLeods of Raasay was forced by debts to emigrate to Australia in 1846. He sold the island to an Edinburgh man who shipped over 120 families to Australia in order to free their land for sheep. The island changed hands over the heads of the people several times before being bought by a man called Wood who enlarged Raasay house. In 1907 it was put up for auction at an upset figure of £45,000 and it was described in attractive terms:

The total extent of the Islands is 18,000 acres or thereby. The Mansion House which lies close to the sea occupies a charming and sheltered situation near the south end of the Island of Raasay overlooking Raasay Bay and the Cuchullin Hills and contains drawing-room, dining-room, boudoir, library, billiard-room, smoking-room, gun-room, business-room, school-room, twenty-seven excellent bedrooms with five dressing-rooms, very large kitchen and scullery complete with domestic offices. On Rona there is also a small Shooting Lodge of nine apartments. The Pleasure Grounds around the Mansion-House are beautifully laid out and ornamented, and the Flower and Kitchen gardens are well stocked and in excellent order. There are also vineries, Peach House, Hothouses and Greenhouses. The Game is plentiful and varied, consisting of Deer, Grouse, Black Game, Pheasant, Woodcock, Snipe, Hares, and Rabbits; Wild Fowl, Blue-Rock Pigeons, seals and otters are also to be had. There are several Lochs of considerable size on the Island and an Artificial Lake near the House all well-stocked with Trout . . . there is a substantial stone pier with Berth for a Yacht.

Obviously a very substantial property suitable for an Edwardian man of substance. The island passed into the hands of Baird and Company who proceeded to develop its iron ore deposits. The iron ore had been discovered in 1893 by a Fellow of the Geographical Society. The vein was between 6 ft. and 17 ft. thick and Baird and Company built a pier directly in front of the seam and began mining operations. The outbreak of the war in 1914 made the lode more economically important than it otherwise might have been and it was worked mainly by German prisoners of war. They lived in the row of ugly single-storied cottages that can still be seen on the hillside facing Skye. Many of them died in the influenza epidemic of 1918 and were buried on the island.

After the war the enterprise ground to a halt but the machinery was not removed until a second war raised the price of scrap. A survey in 1940 estimated that there were probably reserves of ore amounting to 10 million tons. Ore of a much higher grade (72 per cent iron compared with 25 per cent in Raasay) lies between Broadford and Torrin, but the likelihood of either deposits ever being disturbed is remote.

Raasay was traditionally served by the steamer plying between Mallaig and Portree, which called at Raasay pier every night and morning except upon the Sabbath. The service has been reduced in recent years and with the advent of the Raasay-Sconser car ferry will cease altogether. The island, owned now by the Department of Agriculture, supports a population of some two hundred. It remains to be seen whether the new accessibility opened up by the ferry will bring to Raasay some of the benefits of the bed-and-breakfast trade enjoyed by Skye.

Railways Until 9 August 1870 the quickest way to reach Skye was by steamer from the Clyde, but on that day the 53 miles of line linking Dingwall with Strome Ferry was opened to passengers. The Dingwall and Skye Railway, as it was known, was originally intended to run to Kyle of Lochalsh, but the prohibitive cost of blasting the extra 10 miles to Kyle deterred the promoters. There was a daily service between Strome Ferry and Portree and a weekly service to Stornoway, but in 1880 the sailings were relinquished to MacBrayne's.

In 1889 the West Highland Railway was authorised to lay a line to Fort William and there was every sign that they might seek powers to extend it, as they eventually did, to Mallaig – this would have attracted a large volume of trade away from the Inverness-Strome ferry line. It was becoming increasingly clear that because of the strong currents in Loch Carron the terminus at Strome Ferry was not an ideal one. Faced with the prospect of competition from a new terminal at Mallaig, the Dingwall and Skye directors sought and were granted permission to continue the line to Kyle and establish a pier head there. The site for the station had to be blasted out of solid rock and the undertaking was expensive. Opened on 2 November 1897 the line retained a monopoly of Hebridean traffic until 1901 when the extension to Mallaig was completed. It is only a matter of time now before the line from Inverness to Kyle is closed – its role superseded by a fast road. This was one of the two most picturesque lines in Britain – the other being the west coast route to Mallaig. No one who has travelled on either of these lines on a first visit to Skye will forget the experience.

At the time when floating a railway was regarded as a licence to print money there was a scheme to build railways on both Lewis and Skye. The terminus of the proposed Skye railway was to be at Kyleakin, running from there 14½ miles through Broadford to Torrin on the shores of Loch Slapin. After much discussion with the Skye landowners the scheme was dropped. In the following year, 1898, a London-based syndicate known as the Hebridean Light Railway Company was formed and a terminus was proposed opposite Mallaig at Isleornsay. Surveys were actually made for the railway which would run from Isleornsay through Broadford and Sligachan to Portree and then west across the island to Uig. There was to be a branch line from Portree to Bernisdale and Dunvegan. Some people in Skye saw the proposed railway as a solution to all their economic difficulties, others were equally convinced that it would never pay its way and that if a railway did come it would adversely affect the steamer services. In the end the capital (£500,000 for the railways in both islands) was not forthcoming and MacBrayne's was able to retain its Hebridean monopoly.

Ramasaig (RUM-uz-ayg) – the name may mean Raven's Bay – lies on the west coast of Skye some 8 miles south-west of Dunvegan. Take the Glendale road and turn left just after the school. It's said that Ramasaig produced Black Bess, the fastest mare ever bred in Skye. In November 1892 Magnus Murcheson of Ramasaig mounted on Black Bess left Portree Post Office at 8 in the morning and arrived in Glendale, 30 miles away, at 12.45. Black Bess served with the Lovat Scouts and died in

Ramasaig at the advanced age of 32.

Recreation in Skye three centuries ago, you may think, was limited, but the art of music was widely cultivated (Evangelicalism had not yet decreed it godless) and what with piping, harping, fiddling, singing, telling tales, enunciating proverbs, propounding riddles, putting the stone, wrestling, leaping, hunting, playing backgammon and dice there was hardly a dull moment. Now there's television.

Recruitment for the army was never difficult in Skye. Skyemen fought under Montrose at Inverlochy, hundreds of them fell at Worcester in 1651, and many hundreds more took part in the the Jacobite risings of 1689 and 1715. Alexander Smith once said:

> they have had representatives in every Peninsular and Indian battlefield. Of the miniatures kept in every family more than one-half are soldiers, and several have attained to no mean rank. The tartans waved through the smoke of every British battle, and there were no such desperate bayonet charges as those which rushed to the yell of the bagpipes. At the close of the last and the beginning of the present century half the farms in Skye were rented by half-pay officers. The British Army List was to the Island what the Post Office Directory is to London.

Dr. Norman MacLeod, writing in 1867, two years after Smith, claimed that since the beginning of the wars of the French Revolution Skye had sent forth 21 lieutenant-generals and major-generals; 48 lieutenant-colonels; 600 commissioned officers; 10,000 soldiers; 4 governors of colonies; one governor-general; one adjutant-general; one chief baron of England; and one judge of the Supreme Court of Scotland. The last two wars took a heavy toll of Skye; it was not only emigration that emptied the glens.

Religion in Skye is an historical procession from Paganism to Popery, Popery to Episcopacy and Episcopacy to Presbyterianism. From worshipping the sun the islanders were converted by Columba to Christianity. The Hebrideans remained devout Catholics until 1561 when the Reformers expelled the monks from Iona – from then on in Scotland there was a pitched battle for the care of souls between the Episcopalians and the Presbyterians. Evangelical piety came to Skye in 1805, a burning brand brought by an illiterate but powerful preacher. The new and fervid faith spread through the glens like moor-fire, all forms of secular relaxation were abjured; tobacco was out, shinty was banned and music and dancing crushed. With the Disruption of the Church of Scotland in 1843, when 193 ministers signed the Act of Separation, most of the island with the exception of Sleat and Strath went solidly Free Church. For many years their services had to be held in the open air because most of the landowners were prejudiced against the new Church, some even evicted tenants who had left the Established Church. At one time there were at least seven separate Presbyterian Churches in Scotland and the endless secessions and unitings make curious reading for an agnostic. In 1900 the Free Church and the United Presbyterian Church joined to form the United Free Church of Scotland and in 1929 the Established and the United Free Churches combined. The Free Church and the Free Presbyterian Church (the Seceders) are still opposed to the Church of Scotland and tend to regard Moscow and Rome as twin axes of anti-Christ. Seton Gordon has described how during the last war an old Skye woman talking about Hitler paused for breath and then said: 'He's a baad one; he's as – as baad as – as baad as – he's *near* as baad as the Pope!'

In Skye today, apart from a small Catholic community mainly composed of incomers, there is the Church of Scotland, the Free Church of Scotland, the Free Presbyterian Church and the Scottish Episcopal Church. In Portree on a Sunday between them these five Christian churches offer nine or ten services in both English and Gaelic. On a Sunday evening in Portree about 400 people attend the two Free Churches. The respect for Sunday is deeply entrenched and is strong enough for a group of churchgoers to have issued a communiqué in 1968 which read:

> We residents of Skye are happy to extend a cordial welcome
> to tourists to visit our island and enjoy its beauty and peace.
> We shall be still happier if you join us in seeking the more
> enduring peace which many of us enjoy in these days of stress
> and uncertainty. It will give us great pleasure to have you
> worshipping in the House of God, for we are persuaded that

we have a message which alone gives a real aim and purpose in life, and is the only answer to man's many problems. In Skye we cherish the Christian way of life which formerly made our nation great. An integral part of our Christian heritage is a deep respect and love for the Lord's Day. We therefore appeal to all not to desecrate God's Holy Day by travelling to and from the island on the Sabbath.

Roads Until the nineteenth century the only roads in Skye were vague tracks marked out usually by the passage of herds of cattle. John Knox writing in 1786 said: 'It is hardly agreed upon by travellers which is the line of road, everyone making one for himself. Even sheep follow better routes, understanding levels better and selecting better gradients.' As early as the beginning of the sixteenth century surplus cattle were being exported from Skye to the Lowlands. By the middle of the eighteenth century cattle dealers from England were frequent visitors to the island and the cattle they bought were driven along drove roads to the ferry at Kylerhea. Cattle from North and South Uist, from Harris and Barra were sent to Skye on the first stage of their journey to the English markets. The cattle from the Outer Isles were landed either on the shores of Loch Dunvegan, in Uig Bay or occasionally in Loch Pooltiel. From these three points drove roads led to Portree, where a cattle market was held. From there the cattle would be driven either along the route of the present road through Glenvarragill to Sligachan or, more usually, along the coast through Braes. At Sligachan the cattle from Portree would be joined by more cattle from neighbouring areas like Bracadale. At Broadford there would be another market for cattle from parts of Sleat, Loch Eishort and Loch Slapin.

The drove road led from Broadford through Glen Arroch and down the steep hillside to Kylerhea, the narrowest crossing between Skye and the mainland. An Agricultural Survey of Inverness-shire in 1813 described how the cattle were ferried to the mainland:

Their numbers are very considerable, by some supposed to be 5,000 but by others 8,000 annually, and the method of ferrying them is not in boats as is done from the Long Island where the passage is broad, but they are forced to swim over Caol Rhea. For this purpose the drovers purchase ropes which are cut at the length of 3 ft. having a noose at one end. This noose is put round the under jaw of every cow, taking care to have the tongue free. The reason given for leaving the tongue loose is that the animal may be able to keep the salt water from going down its throat in such a quantity as to fill all the cavities in the body which would prevent the action of the lungs; for every beast is found dead and said to be drowned at the landing place to which this mark of attention has not been paid. Whenever the noose is put under the jaw, all the beasts destined to be ferried together are led by the ferryman into the water until they are afloat, which puts an end to their resistance. Then every cow is tied to the tail of the cow before until a string of 6 or 8 be joined. A man in the stern of the boat holds the rope of the foremost cow. The rowers then ply their oars immediately. During the time of high water or soon before of after full tide is the most favourable passage because the current is then least violent. The ferrymen are so dexterous that very few beasts are lost.

An entertaining and scholarly account of these early roads can be found in A. R. B. Haldane's *The Drove Roads of Scotland*.

The Highland Society, founded in 1784, campaigned for new and better roads and when in 1801 Thomas Telford was commissioned to report on the problem he sought their advice. The Parliamentary Committee concerned decided that the cost of roads should be borne equally by the government and by local interests, and it was the Act of 1803 which really began the era of road-building which still continues today.

In 1804 Lord MacDonald and eleven other landowners in Skye proposed a small system of roads running from the new fishing village of Stein to Ardvasar with an extension to Kylerhea and Portree. In the following year they made further proposals for a road from Dunvegan to Portree, 'the line by which the cattle from the Long Island are driven to the market of Portree'. The work was initially entrusted to an Oban mason called John Faichney. He got off to a bad start in 1806 when he made a mistake in his arithmetic tendering for a road between Broadford and Portree. The Commission allowed him to raise the price by £1,000, but before long James Hope, the secretary and consulting engineer to the Commission, was suffering from diminished faith in his contractor's reliability: 'Faichney,' he reported, 'is engaging in other speculations . . . of late he has married in the Island a clergyman's daughter and I have heard that he has begun to traffic in meat.' Finally the contract was abandoned – poor Faichney became the first of a long line of contractors for whom road-making in Skye was to prove far from profitable.

The road from Sligachan to Dunvegan, Macleod's Road, as it was called, wasn't finished until 1826. In the period 1803-26 over 100 miles of road were built in Skye at an average cost of £400-£450 per mile. Today there are 230 miles of publicly maintained roads in the island, many of them still so narrow that passing places are essential, but road improvement schemes in recent years have provided Skye with a great deal of employment, and the motorist with an opportunity to drive so fast that his passengers will see even less of Skye than they might have done before the war.

The only major road that remains to be built is the Road to the Isles itself. All traffic must still arrive by boat and there is a growing agitation (always inflamed at the height of the tourist season when delays at the Kyle ferry cause many potential visitors to turn back in frustration) for a bridge to link Skye with the mainland. At the end of 1968 the Scottish Council commissioned a firm of consulting engineers to undertake a feasibility study and in August 1969 they published their report. The bridge suggested would be of the suspension type with a central span of 1,200 ft. and side spans of 400 ft. It would take three years to build and cost £2.9 million, including all the approach roads and viaducts. The report estimated that if the bridge were built by 1974 it would initially carry about 200,000 vehicles a year. A bridge would undoubtedly kill the ferry at Kylerhea and cast doubt on the necessity for a vehicle ferry from Mallaig to Armadale. The Scottish Council feel that a bridge is not only essential but would stimulate both the tourist industry and future economic development in Skye and reduce the cost of living (*see* **Prices**). Unfortunately in February 1969 the Highlands and Islands Development Board decided that a bridge was not necessary, only an efficient ferry. The discussion continues, but it is highly unlikely that any government will consider building a bridge

1/2 Shortly before Samuel Johnson and James Boswell set off on their Highland jaunt Thomas Pennant undertook a tour of Scotland accompanied by the Welsh artist and naturalist Moses Griffiths. *above*: Griffiths' impression of Duntulm Castle with Tulm island in the foreground and the hills of Harris on the horizon.
below: a view of the Cuillins from Beinn na Caillich.

Two engravings from Dr. John MacCulloch's *Description of the Western Islands of Scotland* published in 1819 (see pages 245-8).

3 MacLeod's Maidens at the entrance to Loch Bracadale.

4 Highly romanticised View At The Storr. Note the shepherd and his buxom Trotternish nymph in the foreground.

Two engravings by Moses Griffiths.

5 Dunvegan Castle as it looked in 1770 before the twenty-first and twenty-second Chiefs began their ambitious castellations.

6 'Women at the Quern and the Luaghad with a view of Talyskir.' Thomas Pennant's description of this scene appears on page ?.

7 William Daniell undertook a Voyage Round Great Britain in 1813 and his engravings of Skye appeared in 1819. He was there in the month of June and while drawing the view above of 'Kylehaken' experienced 'a considerable fall of hail and snow'.

8 Portree. The isolated house was then in use as a jail and courthouse. It is now the headquarters of the Skye Tourist Association.

9 Liveras near Broadford. Daniell noted 'The wood observable in the view was planted by Mr. M'Kinnon . . . his garden displayed the full and unchoked bloom of summer and the strawberries were already ripe'.

10 Armidel Castle. When Daniell arrived in Skye only the first storey had been built. His impression is based on Gillespies's drawings but the building was never carried to this ambitious stage.

11/12 *left*: Sir James MacDonald (1741-1766) 'The Scottish Marcellus' posed for the ancestral seat of Duntalum. *right*: Dr. Samuel Johnson dressed for the Hebrides: 'He wore a full suit of plain brown clothes . . . a large bushy greyish wig . . . and he carried in his hand a large English oak stick'.

13/14 *left*: Flora MacDonald (1722-1790) who became a national heroine as a result of the part she played in helping The Young Pretender to escape to France.
right: Prince Charles disguised as an Irish servant girl.

15 The entrance to Loch Scavaig in 1842 from an etching on steel based on the sketch books of Sir Thomas Dick Lauder – the Cuillins peaks have been heightened for dramatic effect.

16 An engraving from another sketch by Lauder of the Quiraing. In the centre the Table, 'a verdant platform about 1500 feet in height, 100 paces long by 60 broad'.

17 The traditional custom of swimming cattle from Skye to the mainland across the narrows at Kylerhea ceased in the nineteenth century. In this Victorian engraving cattle are being ferried more humanely by sailing boat from Kyleakin to Kyle of Lochalsh.

18 Poverty bordering on destitution characterised the lot of the common people in Skye at this time. This engraving of the inside of a typical crofter's house appeared in the *Illustrated London News* during the agitation for land reform and must have shocked many a genteel Southern reader.

unless a high-pressure campaign is launched. One has only to remember the years of agitation that were necessary before the Forth Bridge was even considered, to see what a long haul it's going to be. When the bridge is built it will take away some of the romance of going over the sea to Skye and for many Skye, in some indefinable way, will be diminished.

Roag (RAW-ug' – famed for its winkles and splendid views of Loch Bracadale – its road leads to Orbost and the elegant early nineteenth-century house in which Skye's authoress Otta Swire resided and from whose windows, she claimed, one could admire the most beautiful view in the island.

Rona (ROE-na) – rocky isle or isle of seals. Deserted now, South Rona can be seen to best advantage from Tote on the Staffin road.

Its surface (said the 1844 Gazetteer) is prevailingly tame and cheerless; and is separated by deep irregular valleys into a series of rocky hills. It is appropriated chiefly to the rearing of black cattle; and in proportion to its area, is among the most barren of the western uplands. To an ordinary observer, its aspect is quite repulsive; presenting no picturesque features, and but little verdure to chequer its grey and sterile surface, and hiding most of even its patches of brown mountain-pasture amid a profusion of dull and naked rocks. Nearly all its arable ground lies round a scattered village which is situated at the head of a bay and contains most of the population. Of four small harbours which occur on the west side one called Archasighirm has a double entrance, and offers a convenient refuge for coasting vessels.

Martin Martin described it as 'the most unequal rocky piece of ground to be seen anywhere', but at the time of Johnson's visit the Laird of Raasay kept a cowman and 160 head of cattle there. There are two stories concerning the origin of the light-house, manned today by keepers whose families live in Portree. The first says that at one time the only occupants of the island were a fisherman, his wife and three sons. Returning from fishing one night the men were wrecked on sunken rocks to the north of the island. From then on the widow kept a light burning in her window and when the lighthouse was built she was made keeper. The second story is that in times of drought the people of Rona had to fetch their water from Skye. A party of men and women were coming back from Skye when they were wrecked on the rocks. The widow, a Mrs. MacCrae, from then on kept a light in her house and was rewarded with a pension of £40 a year for her devotion. She eventually went to live in Braes.

Ross, William, poet, was born at Broadford in 1762; his father, like the hero of Wordsworth's 'Excursion' was a pedlar. The Gaelic scholar, Mackenzie, said of him: 'In purity of diction, felicity of conception and mellowness of expression he stands unrivalled.' Ross, like Keats, died young at the age of 28, weakened by asthma, consumption and unrequited love. Like most Skyemen forced to live away from the island of their birth Ross had frequent longings for Skye:

> How could I know else than pain
> When my heart is rent in twain?
> While in exile I remain
> Little life is left me.
> For my heart is in those hills
> Where my soul with rapture thrills
> Far from this dull pain that kills
> And of joy has reft me.

Rudha (ROO-a) – a point or promontory.

Rudha an Dunain (ROO-un-DOO-nun) – the point of the small hill. In Soay sound, south-west of Strath. Take the road to Glen Brittle and then enjoy a 4-mile walk to where on the shore about half a mile east of the point is one of the best preserved examples of a galleried *dun* in Skye – only a portion of the wall on the landward side remains. This was the stronghold of the MacAskills until a century ago. According to legend the founder of the MacAskills, Black Donald, was hereditary keeper of Dunscaith before it passed into the hands of the MacDonalds.

S

Sage was thought to be efficacious for a variety of ailments. As Martin Martin reports:

> A quantity of wild Sage chewed between one's Teeth, and put into the Ears of Cows or Sheep that become Blind, they are thereby Cured, and their Sight perfectly restored; of which there are many fresh Instances both in *Skie* and *Harries,* by Persons of great Integrity. A quantity of wild Sage chop'd small and eaten by Horses mixed with their Corn kills Worms, the Horse must not drink for 10 hours after eating it.

Saint Columba arrived in Iona with his monks in A.D. 565 and legend says that he not only spent some time in Skye but slew a boar there as well. Donald Macqueen, the eighteenth-century minister of Kilmuir, said that 'the missionaries from Icolmkill (Iona) to the Western Isles and neighbouring continent were numerous. There are remains of about thirty places of worship in this and the two neighbouring parishes (Snizort and Portree) besides monasteries.' Other Christian saints whose names are commemorated in the place names of Skye are: Maol Luag, Bishop of Lismore (Kilmaluag); Talorgan (Kiltaraglen); Martin (Kilmartin); Donan (Kildonan) and Maolrubha (Kilmolray). *'Kil'* means church or burying ground.

Saint Maolrubha was the patron saint of the central and southern portions of Skye – Columba appears to have staked out the north for himself. Maolrubha is supposed to have founded a church at Applecross in A.D. 673 and then proselytized among the highlands and islands. There are sites of chapels dedicated to him at Ashaig, Kilmaree and Eynort. The 25th day of August was observed for many years at Broadford as Maolrubha's feast-day.

Salmon (*Salmo salar*) Adult salmon return to their freshwater river in almost any month but usually grilse, salmon which have spent a year at sea, run up from July onwards. Very little is known about the deep-water habits of the salmon, but it is thought that they feed in the waters somewhere between Iceland and Greenland. In recent years salmon have been very plentiful in the summer in Skye and they have been selling for as little as 5s. or 6s. a pound. Salmon are quietly poached in the rivers and at the mouths of rivers by enterprising Skyemen, some of whom now and again get caught by equally enterprising Skye policemen.

Scalpay (SKAL-pay) – an island 12 square miles in area, 4 miles north-west of Broadford. There is a ruin, once a castle dedicated to Saint Fillans, on the island and a large white house. Mullach Carn rises to a height of 1,289 ft. It was on this island that Dr. Johnson proposed in jest that he and Boswell should build a school and an Episcopal church 'and a printing press where we should print all the Erse that could be found'. The island found a more practical if less distinguished owner in the nineteenth century who lavished large sums of money on its development. A contemporary contributor to *The Scotsman* described it as viewed from the deck of a passing MacBrayne's steamer:

> We could see the white walls of the mansion house which Sir Donald Currie has built on its shore shining from amidst a mass of foliage; on the rocks we could see the seals sunning themselves and playing; along the shore we saw the roads which he had constructed all round the island; and we could see the first fruits of the million trees wherewith he planted the dells; and with the eye of faith we saw the wooded slopes

waving all their branches in the breeze; and a few score yards from shore riding gracefully at anchor was the steam yacht *Iolair* all in white, waiting to go whither her owner willed.

Scarlet Fever appeared in Skye according to Martin Martin in 1706. It was ordinarily cured 'by drinking now and then a glass of Brandy. If an infant happens to be taken with it, the Nurse drinks some Brandy, which qualifies the Milk, and proves a successful Remedy.'

Sconser (SKON-ser) lies on the south side of the entrance to Loch Sligachan. Its present claim to attention is that it boasts a hotel and Skye's premier golf course. When it becomes the Skye terminal for the ferry to Raasay it will acquire even more significance. Its chief claim to fame in the past is that a fateful meeting was held in the old inn at Sconser in September 1745. Gathered there were Sir Alexander MacDonald, MacDonald of Kingsburgh, Captain MacLeod and the Laird of Raasay. A Glenelg man brought them the news of Prince Charles' victory at Prestonpans and this inspired Sir Alexander to promise his support for the Prince's cause. He told the company that he would raise 900 men, and on the strength of this new resolve there followed a convivial evening. But the following day he received letters from Inverness that persuaded him against this course of action and he withdrew his offer. If you subscribe to the tenuous theory that had Sir Alexander come out for the Prince he would have overthrown the Hanoverians then you might claim with some certainty that this meeting at Sconser could have changed the whole pattern of history in both Europe and America.

Sea Serpents have been seen on several occasions in the waters around Skye. In 1808 a minister called Donald Maclean saw something very peculiar while rowing along the coast of Coll. At first he thought it was a rock, but as whatever it was elevated itself above the water he distinctly saw an eye:

> Its head was rather broad, of a form somewhat oval. Its neck somewhat smaller. Its shoulders, if I can so term them, considerably broader, and thence it tapered towards the tail,

which last it kept pretty low in the water, so that a view of it could not be taken so distinctly as I wished. It had no fin that I could perceive, and seemed to me to move progressively by undulation up and down. Its length I believed to be from 70 to 80 ft.

In August 1872 the Rev. John Macrae, minister of Glenelg and a friend, the Rev. David Twopeny, vicar of Stockbury in Kent, set off in a small cutter for an excursion down the Sound of Sleat. The day was calm, the sun was shining and there was not a breath of air when suddenly they saw a dark mass: 'While we were looking at it with our glasses another similar black lump rose to the left of the first, leaving an interval between; then another and another followed, all in regular order. We did not doubt its being one living creature . . . it gave the impression of a creature crooking up its back to sun itself.' The following day the party saw the serpent again and the ferrymen on each side at Kylerhea saw it pass rapidly through the straits on the evening of 21 August: 'They were surprised and thought it might be a shoal of porpoises, but could not comprehend their going so quickly.' The serpent was also seen by a lady at Duisdale in Skye and by people living in Eigg.

In September 1893 Dr. Farquhar Matheson of London was sailing near Kyle of Lochalsh when he saw a long straight neck-like thing as tall as the mast of his boat rise out of the sea: "Then it began to draw its neck down, and I saw clearly that it was a large sea-monster – of the saurian type, I should think. It was brown in colour, shining and with a sort of ruffle at the junction of the head and the neck. I can think of nothing to which to compare it so well as the head and neck of the giraffe.'

The latest sighting of some kind of monster occurred in August 1969 when two Mallaig fishermen out in Loch Morar were attacked by a graceful sort of creature, dark brown or greyish in colour and much longer than their 18-ft. motor boat. It would be credible that a visitor to these waters might confuse a large shark or a whale or a school of porpoises with a 'monster', but most sightings have been corroborated by local people and they remain, like the Loch Ness monster, an unresolved tribute to human credulity.

Seals The common seal (*Phoca vitulina*) is found in many sea lochs in Skye; they vary in colour through blue and brown to fawn and greeny-cream. The grey seal is less common and were it not for the arrival of rubber wellingtons (which made sealskin boots no longer fashionable) and paraffin lamps (far more efficient and cleaner than seal oil) it might by now have become extinct. The grey seal, unlike the common seal is protected by law, and its numbers appear once again to be increasing. I have the common seal to thank for a memorable series of salmon meals one November a few years ago. A friend of mine was walking one sunny Sabbath afternoon round to the Black Rock along the shores of Portree Bay. Suddenly there was a great thrashing in the water and a 24-lb salmon hurled itself out of the water at her feet to escape from the attentions of a seal. The salmon was concealed in the gorse by the boathouse and retrieved first thing on Monday morning. My half, which I got two days later, was in the pink of condition and tasted all the better for having been neither poached nor bought.

Second Sight was of great interest in the Age of Reason. John Aubrey and Samuel Pepys both engrossed themselves in the phenomenon and Dr. Johnson discoursed on it at some length. The ability to presage death or calamity was fairly widespread and found fertile ground in the habitually melancholic Celtic mind. Johnson described Second Sight as –

> an impression made either by the mind upon the eye, or by the eye upon the mind, by which things distant or future are perceived, and seen as if they were present. A man on a journey far from home falls from his horse; another, who is perhaps at work about the house, sees him bleeding on the ground, commonly with a landscape of the place where the accident befalls him. Another Seer driving home his cattle or wandering in idleness, or musing in the sunshine, is suddenly surprised by the appearance of a bridal ceremony, or funeral procession, and counts the mourners or attendants, of whom, if he knows them, he relates the names, if he knows them not, he can describe the dresses. Things distant are seen at the instant when they happen. Of things future I know not that there is any rule for determining the time between the sight and the event.

There is a great tradition with those who have the gift or curse of Second Sight of seeing lights. A typical story would be of the woman who on looking from her window one night claims to see the cow byre on fire. When neighbours go to investigate they find nothing. Next day a girl is killed on the spot where the light was seen. Even horses are thought to have the faculty of second sight. A horse will rear or bolt for no reason at all and then perhaps in a week's time a funeral party will rest a coffin on the very spot where the horse had his psychic manifestation.

John MacKenzie of Portree told me the most macabre instance of Second Sight that I have yet heard. His grandmother used to make shrouds for the undertaker and sometimes she could be heard busy at her sewing machine the night before a sudden and, to all but herself, unexpected death.

Sgeir (SKAIR) – an isolated sea rock which rarely disappears under water.

Sgitheanach (SKEE-a-nuch) – a native of Skye, a Skyeman. A native of Lewis is a *Leodhasach* (LYO-a-such), a native of Harris a *Hearach* (HERR-uch) and a native of The Uists a *Uibhisteach* (oo-YUST-chuch).

Sgurr (skoor) – a large steep rock or precipice.

Sgurr Alasdair (SKOOR AL-uss-ter) (3,251 ft.) – Alasdair or Alexander's Peak – the highest of the Cuillin hills. First ascended in 1873 by Sheriff Alexander Nicolson and named after him. Before its defeat by Nicolson it was known as Sgurr Lagain, the peak of the hollow.

Sgurr Dearg (SKOOR DYERR-eck) (3,026 ft.) – the Red Peak for long considered inaccessible. The pinnacle is thought to have been first climbed by the famous Cuillin guide, John Mackenzie.

Sgurr Dubh (SKOOR DOO) (3,084 ft.) – The Black Peak.

Sgurr a' Ghreadaidh (SKOOR a GRETT-i) (3,190 ft.) – the peak of torment or anxiety. It's been called 'the great central dome' of the Cuillins and from the Coruisk side it presents the longest rock climb in Britain. Norman Collie described it in these words

> The climber will see the bare grey rocks rising out of the heath not 500 ft. above the level of the loch; and the walls, ridges and towers of weather-worn gabbro stretch with hardly a break to the summit of the mountain. He must climb up gullies that the mountain torrents have worn out of the precipices and over slabs of rock sloping down into space at an angle that makes handholds necessary; he must creep out round edges on the face of the perpendicular cliffs, only to find that, after all, the perpendicular cliff itself must be scaled before he can win back to the ridge that is to lead him to the topmost peak.

Sgurr nan Gillean (SKOOR nun GIL-yun) (3,167 ft.) – the Peak of the Young men, was first climbed on 7 July 1836 by that pioneer of Swiss mountaineering, Professor J.D. Forbes – the route he took is now regarded as comparatively easy, the 'tourist route' they call it, but at the time of Forbes' attempt it was deemed an impossible climb.

> Talking of it with an active forester in the service of Lord MacDonald named Duncan Macintyre [Forbes wrote], whom I engaged to guide me from Coruisk to Sligachan, he told me that he had attempted it repeatedly without success, both by himself and also with different strangers who had engaged him for the purpose; but he indicted a way different from those which he had already tried, which he thought might be more successful. I engaged him to accompany me and next day we succeeded in gaining the top; the extreme roughness of the rocks rendering the ascent safe, when, with any other formation, it might have been considerably perilous. Indeed I have never seen a rock so adapted for clambering.

Later in the century Professor Black, the geologist, was intoxicated by his ascent of the peak:

> I had lovely weather; not the clear cloudless sky which some tourists pray for, but a sky full of gleam, and gloom, and gust such as shows to the best advantage all those striking

lines of beauty in which the island of Skye is so pre-eminent. I ascended Sgurr-nan-Gillean. I shall never forget the sight; sombre black clouds, with long trailing skirts floating all above me and around; beneath a sheer descent of some two or three thousand feet, while the sun was shooting a sharp light through the long rugged ravines. Such ravines! Ravines that thousands and thousands of years had scooped out from the grim gritty grain of the hard hypersthene rocks. I beheld here with wonder the great grinding process by which the wind and the rain in these stormy regions pound the hard rock down into the soft green powder which is carried to the bottom and then spreads itself richly over the low ground; a Titanic natural machinery for the manufacture of soil; that most significant step in the mysterious process of Nature by which the hard is transmuted into the soft, as the soft is destined through various stages to be transmuted back into the hard. I never felt so awe-struck in my life. I clung to the rock happily of a gritty texture with both arms – feeling that a sudden whiff of the wind from the rugged tail of that surly cloud might lift me from my legs and hurl me into steep annihilation. Goethe's witches, and Byron's spirits of the mountains would look more native here than on the Brocken or the Alps. Looking with awe on that dark rampart of pinna-cled range, one cannot help wishing that the author of *Manfred* had been as true to the aesthetical worth of his country as Scott was. Had Byron composed his *Manfred* on Blaven or on Sgurr-nan-Gillean instead of the Jungfrau he would have been not less admired by foreigners, and much more esteemed by his countrymen.

Sgurr Na Stri (SKOOR na STREE) – peak of the conflict or fight. A. R. Forbes in his *Place-Names of Skye* suggests that the name may be derived from the contest between opposing winds, but this 1,623-ft. hill rising above Loch Scavaig is said to have been named so after a dispute between a Macleod and a Mackinnon for its possession. In 1730 the two chiefs agreed on a demarcation line and it was arranged that the new boundary between their lands should run north from the small bay of Port Sgailen where the Coruisk stream enters Scavaig. A poor boy was fetched from Soay, taken to Port Sgailen and thrashed to the point of extinction so that in time to come there should be at least one person around who would remember indelibly the spot from whence the boundary ran.

Sgurr Thearlaich (SKOOR HYALL-uch) (3,201 ft.) – Charles' Peak, named after the great climber Charles Pilkington.

Sgurr Thormaid (SKOOR HORR-a-mech (3,040 ft.) – Norman's Peak, named after the great Cuillin climber, Norman Collie.

-shader (SHUTT-er) – is a very common ending in place-names, particularly in the Staffin area. It probably has the same significance as *Saeter* (SAY-ter) in Scandinavia, meaning a place where the cattle are grazed in summer: Elishader, Marishader, Sulishader, Sheshader, Herishader all occur in Skye.

Sharks Commonest around Skye waters is the basking shark (*Cetorhinus maximus*) which can grow up to 30 ft. in length. The late Gavin Maxwell started a shark fishery in the isle of Soay after the last war, but it didn't prove economic (see his book *Harpoon at a Venture,* and *Hebridean Sharker* by Tex Geddes, who continued shark fishing from Soay and Mallaig in the early 1950s).

Sheep The stranger visiting Skye with a car should take the utmost care when approaching sheep. Sheep are inordinately stupid and are apt to rush on to a road with no warning. They have caused several accidents in recent years, at least one of them fatal. The most common sheep in Skye is the blackface which came out of Central Asia by way of the Pyrenees to England in the sixteenth century and on into Scotland in the eighteenth. Today the black-faced, the Cheviot and the Border-Leicester are all grazed in Skye. Skye mutton properly cooked is a rare gastronomic delight. There are about 100,000 sheep on the island and the annual wool clip of about 200,000 lb. goes to collecting centres in Central Scotland, except for a small amount retained for home weaving, particularly in the Portnalong area. The sheep are great destroyers of vegetation and before a young hazel, rowan, birch or willow tree or even a gorse bush has a chance to raise itself an inch from the ground the vacuous-faced sheep has nibbled it away. For the nibbling away of the nineteenth-century population of Skye by sheep *see* **Emigration.**

Sheilings (SHEE-lingz) – Before the young people of Skye took to going to Spain for their holidays they had to make do with a change of scene nearer home. In the summer they would take the cattle up to various moorland heather pastures. Each year they rebuilt the stone and turf bothies or sheilings which had been broken down by wandering animals and the winter storms. Butter and cheese were made and casks of *gruthim* were salted down for the winter. *Gruthim* was a mixture of curds and butter pounded together. Although not so warm as the Costa Brava the lone sheilings provided just as much opportunity for sexual experiment. In fact at one time the General Assembly of the Church of Scotland seriously debated the necessity of sending missionaries to the sheilings to try and persuade the misguided young that fornication was bad for them. A moor between Strath and Sleat is still marked on the Ordnance survey map as *Àraidh na suiridh* (the bothy of love-making). The sheilings are long deserted and only remembered in the sadness of poetry and song:

> From the lone sheiling of the misty island
>   Mountains divide us and the waste of the seas –
> Yet still the blood is strong, the heart is Highland,
>   And we in dreams behold the Hebrides.
>
> When the bold kindred, in the time long-vanish'd
>   Conquer'd the soil and fortified the keep –
> No seer foretold the children would be banish'd
>   That a degenerate lord might boast his sheep.
>
> Fair these broad meads, these hoary woods are grand;
>   But we are exiles from our fathers' land.

Shiant Isles (SHEE-unt) – the sacred or enchanted isles. These three islands lie about 14 miles out in the Minch. They contain columnar formations similar to Staffin and the Giant's Causeway, and were it not for their inaccessibility would no doubt have been the object of equal attention.

Shooting Around the middle of the nineteenth century a new industry hit the Highlands and spilled over into the Islands. Large fat men from the Midlands paid even larger and fatter sums of money to be allowed to slaughter anything which could be coaxed and beaten within gun range. The Rev. Canon MacLeod of MacLeod, when sorting through documents in the Muniment Room at Dunvegan Castle found that Lord Hill in 1850 paid £200 a year for the castle and all the adjacent shootings. At about the same time £100 was asked for Glendale and £50 for Grishornish. After 1860 prices rose steeply. In 1870 the forest of Harris was valued at £3,000 a year and around 1885 the shooting rents for Glen Drynoch, Borline and Ullinish in Skye brought in £1,100.

The annual migration of the *arrivistes* to the depopulated Highlands provided a full-dress field day for *Punch* cartoonists. Not only were they able to milk their favourite theme – the vulgar antics of the *nouveaux riches* – but they could also make fun of the Highlanders' comic accent; these four examples are fairly typical of a joke which lasted for years:

Keeper (on moor rented by the latest South African millionaire to guest): 'Never mind the birds, sir. For onny sake, lie down! The maister's gawn tae shoot!'

Cockney Sporting Gent: 'But I think it's a 'en!'
Sandy (his keeper): 'Shoot, man, shoot! She'll be no muckle the waur o' ye!!'

Our latest millionaire (to Gillie who has brought him within close range of the finest stag in the forest): 'I say, Mac, confound it all, which eye do you use?'

Financier (tenant of our forest, after a week's unsuccessful stalking): 'Now look here, my man. I bought and paid for the stags. If the brutes can't be shot, you'll have to trap them! I've promised the venison, and I mean to have it!'

Skeabost (SKAY-bust) – the sheltered house. In 1539 a bloody battle took place between the MacLeods and MacDonald and several heads cut off in the fray were later seen floating down the River Snizort. Skeabost, 5 miles north-west of Portree, was the birthplace in March 1821 of Mary MacPherson,

a Skye poetess, known in Gaelic as Mairi Nighean Iain Bhain.
Mary married an Inverness shoemaker who died in 1871, and in
that year she was sentenced, many people felt unjustly to a term
of imprisonment. Her feelings of outrage exploded in poetry and
when in 1882 she returned to Skeabost, where the laird provided
her with a rent-free cottage, she wrote a series of poems protest-
ing against the Clearances. Of her end Alexander Nicolson in his
History of Skye wrote: 'Always fond of company she degenerated
in her old age into a mere gadabout, and during her wanderings
she died suddenly in Portree in 1898.' In 1966 a plaque was
unveiled at Skeabost to her memory.

Skeabost is dominated by a late Victorian house rich in pine
panelling, large fireplaces, huge baths and an opulence 'redolent',
as the guide books say, 'of a more gracious past'. Skeabost House
is now a hotel but has lost none of its period flavour – the billiard-
room is still there with its Edwardian rules and the portraits in
oils, the library, the heavy silver, the big log fires complete the illu-
sion that one is staying as a guest in a private house.

Skudaborg (SKOO-da-borg) – a mile north of Uig, Skudaborg
(or Skudiburgh as the Ordnance Survey has it) is noted for a pile
of significant stones, remnants of an ancient *dun,* and its large
basaltic pillar known as the Skudiburgh Stack. It was a mile and
a quarter north of Skudaborg that Prince Charles and Flora
MacDonald landed on their arrival from Uist.

Skye oldest form of the name is *Scetis* or *Scitis,* as mentioned by
Ravenna. In Adamnan's *Life of St. Columba* it's referred to as
Scia. In the Dean of Lismore's book it appears as *Clar Sgith* –
the plain of the Scots. The Norse wrote variously about *Skyd,
Skyda* and *Scaia.* The Rev. Dr. John MacPherson of Sleat
always believed that it was derived from the Norse '*Sky*' (a
cloud) and *('Ey'* an island) hence 'The Misty Isle'. Another
possibility is that owing to its amoeba-like shape it derives from
Sgiath, a wing. Dean Monro, writing in 1549, first advanced
this theory.

Pennant and Jameson both thought it came from Norwegian
Ski, a mist. Pinkerton says that Skia, corruptly called Skye, is
named from Skua, one of the Faroes. James Buchanan in his
Defence of the Scots Highlanders claims that the origin is Celtic,

from '*Skia* a shield, skian, dirk, or a sword and *neach* a people, these arms making up part of the inhabitants of this isle, in hostile times, when arms and war were the daily employments of these warlike people and so might well be called *skian* and *neach* – the people with the dirks or swords'. Others reckon that the winged temple which Apollo had among the Hyperboreans lay in Skye – hence 'winged isle'. Ossian always referred to Skye as *Eilean a' Cheo* – the isle of mist.

Skye Agricultural Society holds its annual show in Portree every July. It's a great day and there's plenty for the visitor to see. On display are Skye's finest Blackface and Cheviot sheep, Highland ponies, horses, dairy cows and heifers, beef heifers and calves, stirks and working collies. There are trotting races, a fancy-dress parade, a dog show, exhibitions of sheep shearing, tweeds, handicrafts and fleeces, riding competitions and children's sports. The Pipe Band performs and with any luck the sun shines all day.

Skye Gatherings Two fairly formal balls are held in Portree at the end of every summer and have been held, wars permitting, since 1878. The dancers attend in full Highland evening dress and the *Oban Times* still prints each year a list of the house-parties organized by the gentry and the names of their guests. There is no danger that this exclusive Gathering will die, only that it may grow so large that it loses its traditional character. Never having attended such an occasion myself I'm very grateful to Otta Swire of Orbost, who sent me this account:

> The Skye Gathering was started by a group of Skye landowners who, egged on by Lady MacDonald of Sleat, decided to form a society to hold a Gathering once a year – two Balls and Games on the day between them. The rules made then still hold. The number of members was laid down as 50 and cannot be exceeded. The Balls are for dwellers in Skye or the adjacent mainland. £1,200 was subscribed with which to build the present hall with its supper room, sitting-out rooms, kitchens, cloakrooms and a public gallery. The number of dancers admitted at that time was 60 – they all knew each other and it was like a private dance; no one could then, or can now, get a ticket except by request of a member. After the gap caused by World War One it seemed doubtful if the Balls could be restarted as the Committee's savings were exhausted. But members rallied round and their wives volunteered to provide the supper and lend maids to serve it. Some provided grouse and salmon and others gave the drinks and a butler to serve them. By the 1930s interior alterations were made to allow 80 dancers. After the last war the Balls were restarted as soon as possible. The supper room was thrown into the ballroom and a new one built on. Our limit now is 260; even so, many are refused tickets each year, for it has succeeded in retaining its old status of a Highland Ball for Highlanders.
>
> We no longer all know each other, but almost every 'hostess' knows every other hostess or her mother or grandmother.

The Skye Games, no longer a part of the Gathering, still take place at the end of August and are held as always on the *Meall* beyond the Skye Gathering Hall.

Skye Week was started in 1950 as a tourist attraction, and held in May, in the hope that visitors might be charmed to the island earlier in the year than normal. A succession of fine Mays has made more and more people realize than an early holiday has many advantages. Dances, *ceilidhs*, exhibitions, Highland Games, shows and concerts are held, and each year the organizers try to cap the efforts of the year before. Skye Week having come of age in 1970 is now firmly established as a major tourist event in the Highland calendar.

Sligachan (SLIG-a-hun) – the shelly place. 'Sligachan is to Scotland,' stated an Edwardian Guide, 'what Wasdale Head is to England and Penygwryd was to Wales – the climber's paradise.' The Andersons in the *Guide Book* published in 1834 compared Glen Sligachan with Glencoe:

> In ranking this glen as a rival, in wildness and grandeur, to that of most established fame in the Highlands, we think we shall be justified by the observation of future travellers. The mountains are a great deal higher, bolder and not less savage than those of Glencoe; and in traversing this sequestered strath, we feel a constant and almost painful consciousness that no other form of mortal mould exists within its desert precincts. A solemn silence generally prevails, but is often and suddenly interrupted by the strife of the elements. The streams become quickly swollen, rendering the progress of the wayfaring stranger not a little hazardous; while fierce and fitful gusts issue from the bosom of the Cuchullins. The heaven-kissing peaks of this strange group never fail to attract a portion of the vapours, which rising from the Atlantic, are constantly floating eastward to water the continent of Europe; and fancy is kept on the stretch, to find resemblances for the quick succession of fantastic appearances which the spirits of the air are working on the weather-beaten brow of these hills of song.

There is little more at Sligachan than an inn but it was once one of the most famous climbing centres in Europe; from there the Cuillin peaks were first conquered, but today's climbers are more penurious than those of the nineteenth century and the centre of climbing has shifted from Sligachan's exceedingly comfortable inn to Glen Brittle, where most of today's climbers are quite happy to sleep in tents. But in the nineteenth century one of the morning sights at Sligachan was the organization of parties for the mountains. In the season of 1869 there were 400 names entered in the visitors' book. Not all of course climbed, many of them came to fish or just walk and sketch. But most people attempted to ascend into the Cuillins.

Sheriff Nicolson described one of these straggling parties ninety or so years ago:

A gay cavalcade might have been seen, accompanied by several sturdy pedestrians, starting in a southerly direction from the remote but well-frequented hostelry of Sligachan. The party consisted of five ladies and four gentlemen, the former, and one of the latter, being mounted on ponies. The sun is in our face, high in heaven and fills the glen with glory, making the rock crystals up the Sgurr-nan-Gillean glisten like water, and the pools in the marshes like sheets of silver. Marscowe is half in shadow, and its green sides contrast delightfully with the dry and scarred slopes of the Red Hills on the left. As we go on, the outlines of Sgurr-nan-Gillean and his attendant peaks change strangely, and presently his three graduate spires, seen from Sligachan as one, come into view, with their deep clefts between. As we clear Marscowe, there opens to us on the right the half-hidden grandeur of Harta Corrie with its girdling wall of rock, its towers and embrasures, clearly marked against the skyline. A little further on we come to Loch-nan-Uamh (Loch of the Caves) a shallow and uninteresting sheet of water, but now, in its best aspect, laughing brightly in the sun, and forming quite a beautiful foreground to the view, as we look back towards Sgurr-nan-Gillean. In front Blàveinn upheaves his high mass of precipice, crowned with his double head and long black ridge. His aspect from here is not unlike Eiger, as one looks up from Grindelwald. The scale is much reduced, but one doesn't think of that here, nor miss even the pine trees and the snow. At his base glitters the blue and beautiful Loch-na-Creathaich, the opposite side of which is overhung by a steep ridge with shelving rocks. The path goes by the margin of the bonnie loch, in which is a good store of trout not less bonnie;

and presently we come in comparatively high level ground to 'The Prince's Well', one of the numerous vestiges of poor Prince Charlie's wanderings.

For many years a cattle market was held at Sligachan, the first one being opened by Colonel MacLeod of MacLeod on Wednesday, 22 October 1794. About 4,000 people attended the tryst and 1,400 head of cattle and 200 horses and ponies changed hands. All the Skye ponies sold were taken to work in the Lanarkshire coalfields. One of the most colourful sights at the fair was the huge tinker camp set up at nearby Crossal where music and song and dance continued all through the night.

The Hotel at Sligachan has some splendid Victorian oil paintings of Skye, many of them by that minor master of Highland Cattle, Louis B. Hurt.

Sneosdal (SNEERS-dul) – Snow-dale. This loch lies a mile and a quarter due east from the township of Kilvaxter (on the Uig-Duntulm road). One of its claims to fame is its resident water-horse which frequently appeared dressed in immaculate black with a white linen shirt. A young woman up on a nearby sheiling met him disguised in this way and they sat down in the heather for a chat. She was very much surprised as she ran her hand through his hair (his head happened to be resting in her lap) to feel grains of sand among his jet-black locks. After a while the water-horse (whose libidinous drive must have been marginal) fell asleep. The woman managed to steal away and as she fled heard his infuriated neighing behind her. It is said the people of the hamlet, two miles away, heard it too.

Snizort (SNIZE-ort) – Sney's firth or snow-fjord. An island in the mouth of the River snizort holds the ruins of a large cathedral-like church which is supposed to have been the mother-church of Skye. Snizort has the distinction of possessing the longest river in Skye and the largest loch which runs 12 miles inland from Waternish Point.

Song was once a natural accompaniment to work in Skye. There were different songs for different occasions. Songs to row by, songs to spread muck in the field, songs for the grinding of corn in the quern, churning songs, milking songs, 'waulking' songs.

Souming (SOO-ming) – If you belonged to a Hebridean farming community you were entitled to graze your animals on the communal pasture land, but the number of animals you could put out to grass was strictly regulated. The scale was laid down depending on the size of the pasture and the number of farmers involved. The table of grazing was based on the consumption of different animals. A typical scale might be 1 horse equals 2 cows or 16 calves or 16 sheep or 16 goats or 32 hogs or 32 lambs or 32 geese. Farmers with more stock than others paid into a common pool which was divided among those with less than their entitled share. Today *souming* is either based on a certain proportion of stock to every croft or pound sterling of rent or may be based on a number of shares in the common grazing per croft.

Sowens appears in the *O.E.D.* as 'an article of diet formerly in common use in Scotland consisting of farinaceous matter extracted from the bran or husks of oats by steeping in water'.

In Gaelic it's known as *Sughan* and in Skye once formed a substantial addition to the daily diet. The bran was steeped in water in a crock for several days then strained and the juice allowed to settle in another dish. After the clear water was poured off the remainder was boiled for half an hour until it had a porridge-like consistency. This was known as *cabhruich*. *Cabhruich* was made during the siege of Mafeking and its sustaining powers enabled the author of *Scouting for Boys* to hold out until relief arrived.

Spar Cave If armed with a torch you take the Elgol road and from there the 2-mile track to Glasnakille, Mr. Neil Mackinnon who lives at No. 6 will point the way to the Spar cave 'for', as the Isle of Skye Tourist Association notes, 'a nominal charge'. This natural curiosity, long since defiled by nineteenth-century tourists was famed for its stalactites and was described in Scott's *Lord of the Isles:*

> Mermaid's alabaster grot,
> Who bathes her limbs in sunless well,
> Deep in Strathaird's enchanted cell . . .

> His foot is on the marble floor,
> And o'er his head the dazzling spars,
> Gleam like a firmament of stars.

It was on 25 August 1814 that Sir Walter visited the 'celebrated cavern'. A. M. Macallister who owned the land had built a 9-ft. wall round the cave with a stout door in it, to try and protect the stalactites which visitors were beginning to knock off. As the key was 3 miles away Scott and his friends scaled the wall with the aid of a rope. Late that night he recorded in his Journal:

> The floor forms a deep and difficult ascent, and might be fancifully compared to a sheet of water, which, while it rushed whitening and foaming down a declivity, had been suddenly arrested and consolidated by the spell of an enchanter. Upon attaining the summit of this ascent, the cave descends with equal rapidity to the brink of a pool of the most limpid water, about four or five yards broad. There opens beyond this pool a portal arch, with beautiful white chasing upon the sides, which promises a continuation of the cave. One of our sailors swam across, for there was no other mode of passing, and informed us (as indeed we partly saw by the light he carried), that the enchantment of Macallister's cave terminated with this portal, beyond which there was only a rude ordinary cavern speedily choked with stones and earth. But the pool on the brink of which we stood, surrounded by the most fanciful mouldings in a substance resembling white marble, and distinguished by the depth and purity of its waters, might be the bathing grotto of a Naiad. There is scarce a form or group that an active fancy may not trace amongst grotesque ornaments which have been gradually moulded in this cavern by the dropping of the calcareous water, and its hardening into petrifactions; many of these have been destroyed by the senseless rage of appropriation among recent tourists, and the grotto has lost (I am informed), through the smoke of torches, much of that vivid silver tint which was originally one of its chief distinctions.

Staffin the place of the upright pillars, a reference to the basaltic pillared rocks in the neighbourhood. It is 15 miles north of

Portree as the crow flies but slightly longer by road and has one
of the most beautiful bays in Skye. On a summer day it can look
Mediterranean; gale-lashed in the winter it can send ice into the
roots of your teeth. In such weather a seventeenth-century laird
of Raasay and his boat crew were drowned on the stormy
shores. The Dunvegan poetess Mairi Ni'n Alasdair Ruaidh
wrote an elegy on the occasion. Of the basaltic rocks which
surround Staffin an early nineteenth century note reads: 'They
produce a variety and sublimity of basaltic formations which
though surpassed in simplicity and beauty of detail is nowhere
in Britain equalled in extent or power. Had not Staffa made a
previous monopoly of fame, this spot would have been more
than a rival, and might have frowned the celebrious islet into
comparative insignificance.' Staffin today is one of the best
farming areas in the island and its people the most well off, but
it was here and at nearby Valtos that land agitation broke out in
1879 and spread like hillfire throughout the islands.

Stein (SHTAYN) – The name comes from Icelandic and means
'stone', but Stein is no stonier than other places. It was founded
in 1787 by the British Fisheries Society. They provided boats,
nets, lines, a pier and everything essential to promote a sound
fishing economy. The effort met with little success. There is a
theory that fishing was traditionally looked upon as an ignoble
activity, only fit for the deformed and weak, and for that reason
Skyemen refused to accept it as an honourable way of earning a
living. The Society, with the aid of a public subscription and
generous contributions from Scots abroad also bought land at
Ullapool and Tobermory. But the unpredictable movement of
the herring shoals meant that the harvests from the west coast
were too meagre and too intermittent to make a fishing industry permanently viable. The high cost of salt was another
contributing factor in the failure of Stein.

Emigration continued and the village was virtually abandoned
by 1837. Today the village has fallen into decay – an inn remains
and a post office and a bare handful of people. The house at the
top of the brae leading down into Stein was bought along with
island of Isay, the schoolhouse and some other properties in the
late 'sixties by the folk singer Donovan. He introduced a small
commune, initially numbering about ten, dedicated to living off

the land and getting away from the 'crap of city life' (as one of them expressed it on B.B.C. television) to the simpler pleasures of living off the land. When the members of the commune are not raising food from the soil, shooting rabbits and hares, looking after their livestock, or fishing, they devote themselves to writing poetry, composing, sculpting, painting and generally living The Good Life. Donovan frequently absents himself from the commune to give concerts in various parts of the world and it was reported in 1969 that his three-month autumnal tour of the United States would bring him in £1 million. Even if the crops should fail at Stein it seems unlikely that the commune will run disastrously short of bread. At a time when young people are leaving Skye to earn their living on the mainland it is encouraging to find that other young people see Skye as a place where they can live productively and peacefully and make the barren land fruitful. Even though they live under the golden umbrella of a showbiz singer the members of the commune at the time of writing do not appear to have been seduced from their stern purpose. What a succession of hard, wet winters might accomplish remains to be seen.

Storr a steep high cliff or pinnacle. The Storr rock rises to a height of 2,358 ft. 7 miles north of Portree along the Staffin road. The cliffs fall steeply away and in front of them rises the Old Man of Storr himself, a pinnacle 165 ft. high which can be seen from many miles away. 'Had this rock,' wrote the geologist MacCulloch in 1819, 'been on the plains of Hindostan instead of the mountains of Skye, it would have been an object of greater devotion than the Jaggernaut pagoda.' Perhaps the most exciting view of the Storr is the one from the Sligachan-Portree road; as one drives towards Portree it gradually begins to dominate the skyline 10 miles away to the north.

The Storr rock remained unconquered until 1955 when in the summer three climbers made the summit and descended on a rope suspended from a metal peg which they had hammered into the Old Man's crown.

On the shore below the rock in 1891 a hoard of silver and coins, perhaps hidden by one of the Norse invaders, was discovered. There were brooches, bracelet and rings, nearly a hundred tenth-century Anglo-Saxon silver pennies and eighteen coins minted in fabled Samarkand.

Strath means a low-lying level land between hills. Strath in Skye is centred on Broadford and includes the islands of Scalpay and Pabay. Strath was formerly in the possession of the ancient clan Fingan or MacKinnons who held the position of marshal to the MacDonalds of the Isles. Strath used to be noted for the large number of retired sea captains who lived there.

Strathaird the promontory in southern Skye, bounded by Lochs Scavaig and Slapin, was bought by one Alexander Macalister in the middle of last century, and when in 1851 he decided to put sheep on the slopes below Blaven his excuse was that the tenants owed him £450 in rent arrears. He would forget the debt, he said, and give them £1,200 as a *douceur* if they would pack up and leave for Canada or Australia. About 500 people were involved in eight townships and when they were 'cleared' the sheep came in.

Struanmore (STROO-un-MOR) – At the junction of the Dunvegan-Broadford road and the small side road leading to Ullinish Lodge Hotel lies one of the best preserved brochs in Skye – its unusually well preserved exterior walls can be seen from the road. Inside Dun Beag, as it's known, a staircase still exists, and the whole ruin is an eye-opener after the usual heap of rubble which marks the remains of most Skye *brochs*. When Pennant toured Skye in 1770 the walls were about 18ft. high, but removal of the stones for various domestic purposes over the years has reduced them to about 12 ft. or less. Excavations here have turned up stone implements, axes, hammers, arrowheads, combs and various articles made of bone, horn and pottery.

Stuart Charles Edward Louis Philip Casimir (1720-88), the eldest son of the Chevalier de St. George, the Old Pretender, was born in Rome. At the age of 25 he landed on the Isle of Eriskay with a few supporters to try and reclaim the throne of Scotland and England for his father, but from the start his expedition was inauspicious. Only a handful of Highlanders responded to his call and when he set out from Glenfinnan on 19 August 1745 it was at the head of a sadly small army of 1,200 men. Three days later a price of £30,000 was put on his head and in retaliation he, too, issued a proclamation promising a similar reward for the seizure of 'the person of the Elector of Hanover' as he liked to style George II. By the end of August the 'Rebell Army' had grown to over 2,000 and after routing the English at Prestonpans, Charles took up his headquarters in Holyrood, the old royal palace of the Scottish kings. He gave a ball in the picture gallery, held levees and it seemed as if the sun was shining on his crusade. By the end of October his army had swollen to 5,000 and in a buoyant mood the march south began.

Carlisle was taken in triumph, but there had been desertions on the way and the army began to shrink in size. The march continued south through Penrith, Kendal, Preston, Ormskirk, Manchester and Macclesfield until Derby was reached. Here, much against his instincts, Charles was persuaded to return north and a retreat began which was to culminate in the April defeat at Culloden before the superior forces of the Duke of Cumberland. Nine months after his landing, the disaster of Culloden settled his fortunes irreversibly – the only course left was an ignominious flight. On 26 April the Prince's party reached Loch nan Uamh, on the mainland just to the south of Skye, and they set off in a raging storm for the Outer Isles. Unable to get a boat back to France, Charles spent three weeks moving from sanctuary to sanctuary, his trail plotted to this day in the series of 'Prince Charles' Caves' sprinkled over the Ordnance survey maps of the Hebrides. Eventually he received a message from Hugh MacDonald of Armadale who suggested that he should be escorted to Skye by Hugh's stepdaughter Flora MacDonald. Clad in a flowered calico gown sprigged with purple, a quilted petticoat, a muslin cap, a hood, apron, dun-coloured mantle and a pair of cotton gloves, Charles, with a passport describing him as Betty Burke, an Irish maidservant, set out with Flora and a trusted follower for Skye. The follow-ing day they were off Waternish point, and two sentries of the MacLeod militia challenged them. They rowed off as fast as they could out of musket range and later in the day landed slightly north of Kilbride point, half a mile south-west of Monkstadt house. Here Sir Alexander MacDonald's factor, Alexander of Kingsburgh, agreed to take Charles to Kingsburgh house. It reveals the extent to which the rebellion had split the clans when one realizes that although Sir Alexander, head of the clan, was in attendance on the Prince's enemy, the Duke of

Cumberland, his wife Lady Margaret was more than willing to help the Prince.

At Kingsburgh Charles was given eggs, bread, butter, collops and ale and contrived to get slightly drunk on brandy. He slept until noon the following day and then cutting off a lock of his hair for Mrs MacDonald of Kingsburgh, he had dinner, several more glasses of wine, and set off in the company of a herdboy who led him through the drenching rain to Portree. At the inn, where the Royal Hotel now stands, Charles met Flora again, had a meal of fish, bread, butter and cheese sitting in his shirt sleeves, and finally in the small hours of the morning bade farewell to Flora. Armed with a bottle of brandy, a bottle of whisky, a cold roast chicken and four shirts he left for Raasay.

On the following day realizing that Raasay was too small an island for safety the party launched their boat and returned to Skye where they spent the night at Torvaig, north of Portree, sheltering in a cattle byre. From here they made their way over-land to Elgol. The Prince was by this time lice-infested and suffering from dysentery. He slept the night of 3 July in a cave near Elgol and about eight o'clock on the following morning left Skye for good.

It wasn't until 19 September that he finally embarked for France on the ironically named *L'Heureux* at Loch nan Uamh.

Charles never saw Flora again, never, as far as we know, even tried to communicate with her and there is still a little residual resentment in Skye at the offhand way in which he treated a woman who had done him a great service and suffered much subsequent inconvenience for her loyalty to the Stuart cause. As a great aunt of mine once said to me, 'Off he went and never so much as a postcard to Flora!'

Charles spent the remainder of his life in Europe and died as an alcoholic in Rome. He was buried in Frascati Cathedral and it wasn't until 1807 that his body was taken to lie in St. Peter's, Rome, alongside the bodies of his brother and the father whose fortunes he had tried so ineffectually to restore. When Boswell came to publish his *Journal* he went through profound agonies trying to work out how he should style the Young Pretender. Boswell had a great reverence for George III and was patholog-ically anxious to avoid offending him. The more he thought about the problem the more delicate it seemed: if he used the title 'Prince' it might sound as if in some way he recognized the man as a Prince. As for the word 'Pretender', that he found repugnant: 'A parliamentary expression but . . . not a gentlemanly expression.' On 6 June 1785 he wrote to the King and having received no reply he elbowed his way to the front of a levee nine days later and posed the problem directly to His Majesty. The King said that on the whole he thought as Boswell thought but didn't see the question as one really worthy of consideration. In the *Journal,* published in 1785, Charles is referred to by his title of 'Prince' throughout and Boswell added the following footnote to excuse what his reader might feel as over-reverence for a discredited traitor:

> I do not call him the Prince of Wales, or Prince, because I am quite satisfied that the right which the House of Stuart had to the throne is extinguished . . . I *know,* and I exult in having it in my power to tell, that THE ONLY PERSON in the world who is intitled to be offended at this delicacy, 'thinks and feels as I do'; and has liberality of mind and generosity of sentiment enough to approve of my tenderness for what even *has been* Blood Royal. That he is a *prince* by *courtesy,* cannot be denied; because his mother was the daughter of Sobiensky, king of Poland. I shall, therefore, *on that account alone,* distinguish him by the name of Prince Charles Edward.

Sudreyar the name applied by the Norseman to Skye and the other Hebridean islands to distinguish them from Orkney and Shetland which they called *Nordreyar,* the Northern Islands. Sudreyar exists only now in the ecclesiastical title of the Bishop of *Sodor* and Man. From the end of the eleventh century the Sudreys came under the mantle of the Norwegian kings as part of the kingdom of Man and the Isles.

Suicides It used to be believed in Skye that no herring could be netted in any part of the sea which could be spied from the grave of a suicide. Suicides were commonly buried along with unbaptized children outside the kirkyard walls.

Suishnish (SOO-ishnish) – a jutting stretch of land lying between Loch Slapin and Loch Eishort. Along with neighbouring Boreraig it was cleared in 1852 and 1853. As the people would not go voluntarily they were driven from their homes by a body of constables. Three men who resisted were imprisoned in Portree and then marched on foot to Inverness for their trial. Although a verdict of not guilty was returned, the families of the accused men were evicted the following Christmas. By the spring of 1854 the land was at last cleared and made free for sheep. Perhaps Suishnish will be remembered among all the Clearances in Skye as being accompanied by the greatest display of humbug and hypocrisy. The factor put out a circular defending his inhumanity on the grounds that Lord MacDonald had been 'prompted by motives of benevolence, piety, and humanity . . . because they (the people) were too far from the church'.

Swordale stands for Swardardale – grassy dale. There are three Swordales in Skye; for an account of how a dead Swordale man saved Dunvegan castle from being sacked *see* the entry under **Jones.**

T

Tacksmen were the most important men in the clan, second only to the Chief and indeed once known as 'chieftains'. They paid rent to the Chief for their farms, but they were also expected along with their men to serve the Chief in time of war. The tacksman held, as Johnson observed, 'a middle station, by which the highest and the lowest order were connected . . . if the tacksmen be banished, who will be left to impart knowledge or impress civility?' Many tacksmen departed with their tenants after the '45 to the New World, others left their tenants behind and moved to the greater comfort and convenience of the cities. The peculiar role of the tacksman was recognized by Robert Heron when he travelled round Skye in the 1790s:

> Till within these last 30 years the property belonged almost exclusively to the lairds and the tacksmen; the lands to the former, the animal stock chiefly to the latter. The want of varied industry and employment, necessarily left even moveable property, to remain long in those hands into which it had fallen: and the simplicity of the known modes of life, gave the great proprietors no choice of means to provide for their younger children, but that of making them tacksmen. Thus was formed a class of men, between the lairds and the peasants; of the blood of the former, and possessing almost all the moveable stock on the lands, while to the peasantry nothing remained but their hands and their labour.

Many tacksmen were men of substance and before the days of steam or regular inter-shipping services would have their own sailing smack or even a four-masted ship. These would be used to send cattle to the nearest point on the mainland from where they would be driven south to the Falkirk tryst. The

199

smack would go to Glasgow with the annual wool-clip, returning laden with a year's supply of meal, groceries and domestic
and farm supplies. Some of the larger schooners might even be
engaged in foreign trade. As John MacDonald recalled in his
fascinating book *Highland Ponies:*

> not very many years ago a lady – a descendant of a Skye
> tacksman – told me that a good deal of the furniture which
> I had admired in her drawing-room had been brought from
> France in the four-masted sailing ship of one of her ances-
> tors. Not only did those gentlemen furnish their drawing-
> rooms from France, but they also replenished their cellars
> with French wines – often duty free.

Talisker (TAL-iss-ker) – the house at the rock. Talisker has
given its name to the whisky produced six miles away at the
distillery in Carbost. The house lies in the shadow of Preshal
Mor (The Great Hill). A mile up Sleadale Burn is the remains
of a *broch* – it was about 40ft. broad with walls 9 ft. thick. Dun
Sleadale, as it's known, unlike most other forts in Skye doesn't
have a sea view. There is another *broch* about two miles north of
Talisker House on the lower slopes of Beinn nan Dubh-Lochan
(Mount of the Black Lochs). Here are the remains of a narrow
gallery, a roofless oval cell and a guard chamber.

Of Talisker Johnson wrote:

> The place beyond all that I have seen from which the gay and
> the jovial seem utterly excluded, and where the hermit might
> expect to grow old in meditation, without possibility of
> disturbance or interruption. It is situated very near the sea,
> but upon a coast where no vessel lands, but when it is driven
> by a tempest on the rocks. Towards the land are lofty hills
> streaming with waterfalls. The garden is sheltered by firs, or
> pines, which grow there so prosperously that some, which the
> present inhabitants planted are very high and thick.

The owner referred to was Colonel MacLeod – the house was
traditionally in possession of the son of the MacLeod Chief. The
present garden was laid out in the 1920s and although today more
overgrown than its creator visualized, it gives some indication of
what careful and intelligent planting can accomplish in Skye soil.

A thatched house in Skye in the 1880s.

Tarskavaig (TAAR-ska-vayg) – Skye terriers and bearded collies bred here on the shores of the bay are exported all over the world and have won championship prizes at Cruft's and most of the world's major dog shows.

Television didn't come to Skye until March 1966 when the V.H.F. relay mast perched on Skriaig, 1,288 ft. high and 22 miles south-west of Portree, was finally opened. The B.B.C. had at first hoped to have a relay station operating by 1962 but as the *Stornoway Gazette* recorded: 'Promises followed promises, and after being told that they would have the station in 1962, they were told that it would be built by the end of 1963, then March 1964, then the end of 1964 . . . the anger of the Skye people came to a head in 1963 when many Skyemen had to travel as far as Inverness and Fort Augustus to see the Real Madrid *v.* Rangers football match on television.' Commenting on the advent of T.V. the 1966 annual report on Religion and Morals issued by the Synod of Glenelg stated: 'A flood of lurid salacious matter emanates into our homes via a means which to date has resented and resisted all attempt at control and stricture. The Sabbath, for some unknown reason, seems to be the day when this medium excels in its foul moral oozings.'

Thatched houses are fast dying out. There are one or two carefully modernized and still lived in, but most crofters have preferred to build a new home (not always out of the most attractive materials) alongside the old one-storeyed cottage which is either used as a barn or store-room, or allowed to fall into decay. The museums at Kilmuir and Colbost are typical Skye thatched houses. Boswell described one of these houses in his *Journal:*

> The cottages in Skye are frequently built by having
> two stone walls at several feet distance filled up with earth,
> by which a thick and very warm wall is formed. The roof
> is generally bad. The couples such as they are, do not
> reach to the extremity of the wall, but only rise from the
> inner side of it; so that the circumference of the roof is a
> good deal less than that of the walls of the house, which has
> an odd appearance to strangers; and the storm finds
> a passage between the roof and the walls, as the roof does
> not advance so as to project over the wall. They are

thatched sometimes with straw, sometimes with heath, sometimes with ferns. The thatch is fixed on by ropes of straw or of heath, and to fix the ropes there is a stone tied in the end of each. These stones hang round the bottom of the roof and make it look like a lady's head in papers; but I think that when there is wind they would come down and knock people on the head.

A typical thatched house consisted of a kitchen on one side and a room on the other with a small apartment between large enough to accommodate a bed. A fireplace would be let into one or both of the end walls. The walls were constructed of undressed stones either lined inside with boarding or whitewashed. Light branches were laid over the rafters to carry the turf roof which, as Boswell noted, was anchored by stones. Sometimes rushes would be used or even straw brought in bales from Glasgow, and latterly many crofters have re-roofed with corrugated iron. The early thatched house had a fire in the middle and a hole in the roof through which some of the smoke escaped. Most of it rose to the thatch, where it settled and congealed into a sticky liquid which in damp weather would drip monotonously on to everyone underneath. When this eventually got too much on people's nerves they would take off the old roof, scrape the rafters clean and lay a new roof of turves or sedge or whatever was to hand. The old roof made excellent manure for the fields. Despite the dirt and discomfort (farm animals were often kept in one end of the cottage) Sheriff Nicolson was able to write:

Reared in those dwellings have brave ones been
Brave ones are still there.
Forth from their darkness on Sunday I've seen
Coming pure linen,
And, like the linen, the souls were clean
Of them that wore it.

Tir nan Òg (TYEER-nun-AWG) – the land of the ever-young, the legendary Celtic Shangri-La lies somewhere to the west of the Hebrides, where the sun sets in ultimate splendour.

Tobar (TOPER) – a well. Forbes in his *Place-Names of Skye* records at least 50 wells in Skye, most of them surrounded with superstitious stories of spectacular healing powers. Staffin still gets its mains water supply from two such wells – Tobar na Beatha (the Well of Life) and Tobar na Slainte (the Well of Health) which ought to make the people of Staffin the healthiest and longest lived in Skye.

Torrin the little hill. There is no better view of Blaven than to stand in Torrin and look across Loch Slapin to the majestic protuberance 'bearing his huge bulk on high' all 3,000 ft. of it.

Tote (ruin) here, 5 miles north-west of Portree on the shores of loch Snizort, a Viking grave was unearthed shortly after the first world war. The grave was contained in a round Bronze Age cairn. There was an iron axe, the wood and iron remnants of a shield, a bronze brooch, a whetstone and a bone bead. Half a mile north-east of Skeabost Bridge and 20 ft. from the north side of the road to Tote Lodge is a sculptured standing stone known as Clach Ard: $4^{1}/_{2}$ ft. high, it has three symbols cut into its face.

Trodday (TROD-a) – Troll's Isle. This large grassy island 2 miles north of Skye is now uninhabited but the *New Statistical Account of Scotland* published at the end of the eighteenth century records:

> Even so late as 1770 the dairymaids who attended a herd of cattle in the Island of Trodda were in the habit of pouring daily a quantity of milk on a hollow stone for the Gruagach. Should they neglect to do so they were sure of feeling the effect of Miss Brownie's wand next day.

This *Gruagach* was said to be armed with a pliable reed with which 'she switched any who would annoy her' (see **Gruagach**).

Trumpan said to be named from its resemblance to a *timpan*, a kind of harp. About a quarter of a mile to the east of the shores of Ardmore Bay are the rubbled ruins of Trumpan Church, or Kilconan Church as it was known long ago. In the graveyard are two late medieval grave slabs and a rough 4-sided pillar 4ft. high, called *Clach Deuchainn,* or the Trial stone. The stone contains a hole. An accused person was blindfolded and was then forced to aim for it. If he did so successfully he was innocent, if he failed, he was judged guilty.

What happened in this church on a Sunday in the beginning of May 1578 is one of the most sordid atrocities in a time distinguished for its sordid atrocities. The MacDonalds of Uist entered the bay of Ardmore in a fleet of eight ships and under cover of heavy mist landed without being seen; most of the inhabitants were worshipping inside the church. The MacDonalds climbed the slope above the shore, moved silently on the church and within moments had barred the door and set the thatched roof on fire. No one escaped alive except one girl, who although mortally wounded managed to give the alarm.

The Chief of the MacLeods on hearing the news in Dunvegan ordered the Fairy Flag to be taken out of its iron chest, and armed with this talisman the clan set off for Ardmore Bay where they were in time to capture the galleys of the MacDonalds and butcher them almost to a man. The corpses of the MacDonalds were dragged alongside a turf dyke and the dyke was tumbled over on top of them in a neat and effortless burial. The incident is known as the Battle of the Spoiling of the Dyke and is commemorated in a great pibroch.

Tweed According to the *O.E.D.* 'tweed' was a misreading of the Scottish name for twill – 'tweel', helped by association with the River Tweed.

$\mathcal{U}$

Uig (OO-ig) – a bay. One of the most beautiful bays in Skye, and apart from Armadale, the only place in Skye which has a daily (Sunday, of course, excepted) MacBrayne's sea service. The roll-on roll-off ferry makes daily journeys in less than two hours to Tarbert in Harris and Lochmaddy in North Uist. Viewed from the sea the town of Uig has an almost Norwegian aspect with its white houses dotted like playbricks on the green hills sweeping gently down to the shore. The round martello-shaped tower was a folly built by Captain Fraser, who owned part of Snizort and the whole of Kilmuir in the nineteenth century. Besides erecting the tower he also built himself a splendid villa overlooking the bay. Unfortunately in October 1877 a violent storm swelled the waters of the River Conon and the torrent carried away the house and part of the ancient Uig burial ground. Uig was probably the last place in Skye to have a publicly recognized witch. In 1880 an Elder of the Free Church preferred a charge of witchcraft against a mother and her five daughters. They took her before Captain Fraser and claimed that by exercising her evil arts she had taken milk from her neighbours' cows. She went unburnt.

The advent of the car-ferry to the Outer Isles in 1964 rescued Uig from its pastoral quiet and there are plans afoot to introduce industry in some form.

V

Varragill (VARR-a-gl) – Driving north through this glen most visitors to Skye get their first view of Portree and beyond, if it's a clear day, the rough finger of the Storr Rock. The river Varragill is the second longest in Skye, and salmon can still be taken out of it by those who are permitted – and often by those who are not.

Wadsetters were men who had the tenure of land, or *wadset*, from a superior – usually the Chief. The occupier of this kind of holding was under the obligation of paying Church dues to the Crown but was free to sub-let to anyone he liked. The wadsetters were so numerous in Skye in the eighteenth century that it was difficult to distinguish them from tacksmen. The system was encouraged by the departure of the clan Chiefs to the soft cities of the south and by their natural desire to take as much money with them as possible.

Water-Horse *Each Uisge* (E<u>ch</u> OOSHKUH) – In times past almost every freshwater loch in Skye was inhabited by a water-horse. Water-horses were often mistaken for ordinary horses as they looked not dissimilar. They had the ability to appear in any guise they chose, perhaps as a human, perhaps even as a tuft of wool. In Skye most water-horses were thought to have sharp bills or thin snouts like a ferret. Their main pastime was to lure people into the loch where they lived and then to eat them.

There was a determined attempt to catch a water-horse around the year 1870. A mile north of Teangue on the seaward side of the road lies Loch nan Dubhraichean in which a water-horse, 'more like a cow with a long mane' than anything else, had been seen so frequently that it was decided to trap it. Mary Donaldson, a Skye author, was told the story by an old man who took part in the fun as a boy:

> The occasion was made a regular holiday in the district, even the children being freed from school, and people in carts and traps came from far and wide to take part in the proceedings. My informant told me that a great supply of provisions was taken and that there was more whisky drunk there than at a funeral! Two boats had been brought, and when these were

launched out on to the loch a net was dragged between them. In the course of the dragging proceedings that followed, the net caught in a snag, and the majority of the spectators, thinking that the water-horse was indeed enmeshed, in terror rushed for their horses and carts or fled precipitately from the scene. Beside the snag, all that was caught on this occasion was two pike, so that the fisherman who aspires to a catch out of the common still has his chance of the water-horse.

If it strikes you as strange that the simple-minded folk of Skye should seriously waste their time searching for a water-horse in the 1870s pause and reflect. Less than a hundred miles to the east and a hundred years later research teams are using all the resources of modern technology to find an equally mythical monster.

Waterloo – South of Broadford - got its name from the large number of veterans of Wellington's army who once lived there; 1,600 Skyemen fought at the battle of Waterloo.

Waulking cloth was the final process after weaving. It was done to thicken the material and also to get rid of oil and grease from the wool. On his return from a walk to Kilchrist Church in 1772 Thomas Pennant, accompanied by his artist Moses Griffiths, watched a group of women waulking cloth:

a substitute for the fulling-mill: twelve or fourteen women, divided into two equal numbers, sit down on each side of a long board, ribbed lengthways, placing the cloth on it: first they begin to work it backwards and forwards with their hands, singing at the same time as at the *Quern*. When they have tired their hands, every female uses her feet for the same purpose, and six or seven pair of naked feet are in the most violent agitation, working one against the other: as by the time they grow very earnest in their labors, the fury of the song rises; at length it arrives to such a pitch, that without breach of charity you would imagine a troop of female *daemoniacs* to have been assembled. They sing in the same manner when they are cutting down the corn, when thirty or forty join in chorus. The subject of the songs at the *Luaghadh*, the *Quern*, and on this occasion, are sometimes love, sometimes panegyric, and often a rehearsal of the deeds of the antient heroes, but all the tunes slow and melancholy.

Whales Fairly common in Skye waters is the herring whale, the common rorqual, greyish in colour with a white underbelly. The killer whale or grampus (*Orchinus orca*) can grow to 20 ft. in length, and usually travels in packs of four or six. It is fairly aggressive and will attack not only seals and porpoises but also other whales. F. Fraser Darling and J. Morton Boyd in *The Highlands and Islands* write: 'We have occasionally seen grey seals jump right out of the water in obvious fear, not up and down, but in a low forward parabola, obviously trying to get away from something behind.' The whales do constitute a danger to small boats – if they surface under one they can overturn it. Fortunately such coincidences are rare.

About the middle of July 1871 a sperm whale entered Loch Scavaig and after floundering about, bellowing like a bull among the rocks, it expired two or three days later. The whale, which was 60 ft. long, proved of some benefit to the Elgol crofters, who removed most of its blubber and sold its teeth to tourists.

In the winter of 1950 two fishermen were on their morning lifting of lobster creels in Loch Brittle when suddenly they saw a long white creature break the surface about 50 yds. away. The British Museum, when informed of the details of this sighting, wrote: There is no doubt from the astonishingly correct description supplied by Mr. MacDonald, he witnessed something very rare in the British isles. He did see a White Whale, or Beluga (*Delphinapterus Leucas*), and there are less than a dozen records of its visiting the British Isles during the last 160 years.'

Whisky 'A man of the Hebrides,' noted Johnson when he was in Skye, 'as soon as he appears in the morning swallows a glass of whisky; yet they are not a drunken race, at least I was never present at much intemperance; but no man is so abstemious as to refuse the morning dram, which they call a *skalk*.' *(see* **Carbost**).

Witches A dying race; usually old women who relieved their poverty by making a few coppers out of the gullibility of their neighbours. Witches could magic milk from other people's cows, bring fish to their own shores, conjure up storms, drown their enemies, fly through the air, extend pregnancies, initiate disease. To do all these things they could assume the guise of mice, rats, whales, cats, black sheep – anything you liked. Their busy times were Beltane night, and the last night of every quarter. Witches married as frequently as other people, but their husbands were sometimes a bit of a nuisance. In Skye one man followed his witch-wife one evening and watched her turn into a cat. She went in the name of the Devil to sea in a sieve with seven other cats. The husband, by naming the Trinity, upset the sieve and the witches were drowned. In the nineteenth century three witches at Braes near Portree wrecked a boat coming from Raasay by floating a cockle-shell in a pool. Around the pool were placed black stones which began to bark like dogs as the witches made their incantations. When the barking rose to a crescendo the cockle-shell sank and with it the boat from Raasay. If you want to detect a witch get up early in the morning on the first Monday of each quarter and watch the smoke from your neighbour's chimney - witch's smoke goes *against* the wind. Not very long ago I was driving a very bright child of twelve through the township of —— in Trotternish, when she pointed to an unremarkable house and said: 'That's the house where the witch lives.' I was going to ask her more, but she changed the subject.

Perhaps it shouldn't be described as witchcraft but in the past there were some fairly thaumaturgic remedies for the highly infectious cattle disease known as murrain. Preventive measures involved pouring libations of milk into the local hollow stone *(see* **Gruagach***)* or encircling one's cattle with torches at least once a year and preferably at Whitsuntide. If the cattle succumbed to murrain the best thing to do was to collect 81 able-bodied men who when divided into nine teams of nine were encouraged to rub hazel sticks together until they caught fire. When, and presumably if, the sticks did catch fire, water was poured into a pot and boiled over the flames. The water was then sprinkled over the affected cattle and a Gaelic quatrain chanted. That relationship between this elaborate ceremony and a cure was purely coincidental was not fully appreciated until the end of the eighteenth century when the practice promptly died out.

Wolves were finally exterminated in Skye in 1743; until that time they had lived as predators on the deer population.

'Women in Skye,' said Martin Martin, 'observe that the Breasts contract to a lesser bulk when the Wind blows from the North, and that then they yield less Milk, than when it blows from any other Quarter; and they make the like observation in other Creatures that give Milk.'

Youth hostels The first activity of the Y.H.A. in Skye was to gain the use of the schoolhouse at Glen Brittle during the summer months. The Scottish Youth Hostels Association now has hostels at Glenbrittle (a specially designed Norwegian timber building at the foot of the Cuillins), Broadford (a stone villa on the south shore of the bay), Uig (the former John Martin Memorial Hospital) and Raasay (Creachan Cottage).

Anthology

There's no underlying theme in this anthology; only seven of the forty or so extracts were written by Skyemen and Skyewomen so it is very much a picture of Skye from the outside – Skye as seen by travellers, politicians, propagandists, mountaineers, poets, painters and tourists. It is not meant to be read straight through, but in fits and starts. It is, however, arranged chronologically for convenience and for the benefit of anyone who wants a perspective on how Skye has changed over the years, and perhaps more interestingly how the attitude of the outside observer has changed.

Send me some powder and lead	Dame Janet Mackenzie	1639
A very imperfect performance	Martin Martin	1703
My anxiety obliges me to Intreate	Lady Margaret MacDonald	1740
This mad rebellious attempt	Norman MacLeod	1745
The prince sung several songs	Dr. Burton	1746
The sure forerunner of Approaching Death	Theophilus Insulanus	1763
Migrations and depression of spirit	Thomas Pennant	1772
Their weather is not pleasing	Samuel Johnson	1773
A little woman of a genteel appearance	James Boswell	1773
The winter was a dreadful one	Abram	1784
A profusion of fish	John Knox	1786
Improvements humbly suggested	Robert Heron	1794
A Prophecy fulfilled	Dr Norman MacLeod	1799
Every faculty arrested	Robert Jameson	1800
The face in the chamber	John MacCulloch	18—
Black waves, bare crags	Walter Scott	1814
The ruinous system of rack-rent	Robert Southey	1819
Wanderings in an unknown country	Necker De Saussure	1820
Many of the Aborigines have been expelled	Allan Fullarton and Charles Baird	1838

The asylum of dreariness	Lord Cockburn	1841
The free Church yacht *Betsey*	Hugh Miller	184–
We succeeded in gaining the top	J. D. Forbes	1845
The MacLeod has established a Public store	Robert Somers	1847
Good-natured and anxious to oblige	Rev. Thomas Grierson	1849
Ingenuity and iniquity	Lady MacCaskill	1851
More cruel than banishment	*Dundas Warder*	1851
The lamentation became loud and long	Sir Archibald Geikie	1852
Many-tongued with foaming cataracts	Charles Weld	1859
Beasts of prey	John Colquhoun	1861
A remnant of the system of clanship	Alexander Smith	1865
Flaming in the morning light	Robert Buchanan	1873
Trusting in the barometer, we held on	Sheriff Nicolson	1874
A slight moistening in the eyes	MacIain Mor	18—
In capital trim for dinner	Malcolm Ferguson	1882
The eagles are not numerous	*Temple Bar*	1883
Rejoicing in the stillness	Mrs Gordon Cumming	1884
Warships in the bay	James Cameron	1884
Poverty, hunger and misery	J and E Pennell	1890
There is always something new	Norman Collie	1897
A calm, cold, snow-dazzling morning	D. T. Holmes	1904

Send me some powder and lead
Dame Janet Mackenzie

On 23 January 1639 Dame Janet Mackenzie sat down at her desk somewhere in Sleat, perhaps at Dunscaith or Castle Knock, and wrote to her uncle, Alexander Mackenzie of Kilcoy. Lady Janet was the wife of Sir Donald Macdonald, who had been knighted by James 1 in 1617. He was an ardent supporter of the Stuart cause, and in the year in which his wife wrote this letter he was made the King's Lieutenant in the Isles with authority to suppress anyone who rose up against the Crown. From the beginning of the Civil War, Charles I had been in touch with the Earl of Antrim (the 'good friend in Ireland'), who planned to raise a force of Irish soldiers to join up with the Highlanders on the west coast of Scotland under the command of Sir Donald. The plan came to nothing. Sir Donald was arraigned before the Scottish parliament on a charge of treason; was imprisoned, and died in 1643 shortly after his release. My Lord of Lorne was on the Covenanting side:

Loving Uncle, – My love being remembered to you, I thought meet to write these lines desiring you to send me a part of the surest news that you have for the present, and I hoped for a letter of yours with your best opinions and with news long ago, and since you have forgotten me, yet I cannot forget you nevertheless, and although my friends be offended at my husband for the present, yet I hope in God that is without deserving in him except to go to visit his good friend in Ireland. This is not to dishonour or to displease you his best friend in Scotland, which he will prove and testify to you all at his return by the Grace of God.

It is reported to me for certaintie that my Lord of Lorne is to send men to harry our lands. I desire you therefore earnestly to send me your best advice, with the consent of the rest of the friends thereanent, and to acquaint me what to do if the same come to pass, because my husband is afar off, and if my Lord my brother may get this helped, let him use his best endeavours to hold this abode, as I shall write to my Lord myself, because the best friend that I have under God.

As for that little monies you have of mine, I should fain, if you would spare it, have it, and send me sure word when I should send one to receive it. As for count and reckoning we need not, for we are friends and none of us will distress another. I would fain that you would speir at my Lord what should I do with my own personal goods if enemies come on, that his Lordship might send me his best opinion within your own letter. I rest and committing you to God, your loving brother's daughter.

[signed] Dame Janet Mackenzie, Lady of Sleat
From Sleat, January 23, 1639

Post Scriptum – You shall send me some powder and lead to keep me from my enemies, because I cannot get none to buy, or else grant me this favour as to buy it on my behalf, or send me it with this bearer.

A very imperfect performance
Martin Martin

Martin Martin (Gent) was for some years tutor to the Laird of MacLeod's children. In 1703 he wrote his *Description of the Western Islands,* containing among other things: 'A Full Account of the Situation, Extent, Souls, Products, Harbours, Bays, Tides, Anchoring Places and Fisheries', and he proudly pointed out that 'they have never been described till now by any Man that was a Native of the Country, or had travelled them'.

In the National Library in Edinburgh there is a copy of Martin's book in the front of which Boswell has written:

This very book accompanied me and Mr. Samuel Johnson in our Tour to the Hebrides in Autumn 1773. Mr. Johnson told me that he had read Martin when he was very young. Martin was a native of the Isle of Skye where a number of his relations still remain. His book is a very imperfect performance; and he is erroneous as to many particulars, even some concerning his own Island, yet as it is the only Book upon the subject, it is very generally known. I cannot but have a kindness for him, notwithstanding its defects. 16 April 1774.

The book is full of curious, sometimes inaccurate, information, founded all too often on hearsay. It's a kind of rag-bag of tittle-tattle and oral traditions, but it's strange how much of Martin's material turns up in different guises in later works. In the generous promiscuity of its contents it bears a remarkable resemblance to Aubrey's *Brief Lives.* These extracts, I hope may whet your appetite for more:

They have found out a strange Remedy for such as could never ease Nature at Sea by Stool, or Urine; there were three such Men in the Parish of *St. Maries in Trotterness,* two of them I knew, to wit, *John Mack Phade,* and *Finlay Mack Phade,* they liv'd on the Coast, and went often a Fishing, and after they had spent some nine or ten hours at Sea, their Bellies would swell; for after all their endeavours to get passage either ways, it was impracticable until they came to Land, and then they found no difficulty in the thing. This was a great inconvenience to any Boats-Crew in which either of these three Men had been Fishing, for it oblig'd them often to forbear when the Fishing was most plentiful, and to Row to the shoar with any of these Men that happened to become Sick, for Landing was the only Remedy. At length one of their Companions thought of an Experiment to remove this inconvenience; he considered that when any of these Men had got their feet on dry ground, they could then ease Nature with as much freedom as any other Person; and therefore he carried a large green Turff to the Boat, and placed the green side uppermost, without telling the reason. One of these Men who was subject to the Infirmity above-mentioned, perceiving an Earthen Turff in the Boat, was surpriz'd at the sight of it, and enquir'd for what purpose it was brought thither? He that laid it there answer'd that he had done it to serve him, and that when he was disposed to ease Nature, he might find himself on Land. The other took this as an Affront, so that from words they came to blows; their fellows with much ado did separate them, and blam'd him that brought the Turff into the Boat since such a Fancy could produce no other effect than a Quarrel. All of them employed their time eagerly in Fishing, until some hours after, that the angry Man who before was so much affronted at the Turff, was so ill of the swelling of his Belly as usual, that he begg'd of the Crew to row to the Shoar, but this was very disobliging to them all; he that intended to try the Experiment with the Turff, bid the Sick Man stand on it, and he might expect to have success by it; but he refus'd, and still resented the affront which he thought was intended upon him; but at last all the Boats Crew urg'd him to try what the Turff might produce, since it could not make him worse than he was. The Man being in great pain, was by their repeated Importunities prevail'd upon to stand with his Feet on the Turff, and it had the wished effect, for Nature became obedient both ways, and then the angry Man changed his note, for he thanked his Doctor, whom he had some hours before beat; and from that time none of these three men ever went to Sea without a green Turff in their Boat, which prov'd effectual. This is a matter of Fact sufficiently known and attested by the better part of the Parishoners still living upon the Place.

A *Ling-Fish* having brown spots on the Skin, causes such as eats of its Liver, to cast their Skin from head to foot. This happened to three children living in the Hamlet *Talisker*, after eating the Liver of a brown spotted *Ling*.

A Weaver in *Portrie* has a faculty of erecting and letting fall his Ears at pleasure, and opens and shuts his mouth on such occasions.

Some of the Natives are very dextrous in engraving Trees, Birds, Deer, Dogs &c. upon Bone, and Horn, or Wood, without any other Tool than a sharp pointed knife.

Several of both Sexes have a quick Vein of Posie, and in their Language (Which is very Emphatick) they compose Rhyme and Verse, both which powerfully affect the Fancy. And in my Judgement was as great a force as that of any Ancient or Modern Poet I ever yet read. They have generally very retentive Memories, they see things at a great distance. The unhappiness of their Education, and their want of Converse with Foreign Nations, deprives them of the opportunity to Cultivate and Beautify their Genius, which seems to have been form'd by Nature for great Attainments.

The Diet generally us'd by the Natives, consists of fresh Food, for they seldom taste any that is salted, except butter; the generality eat but little Flesh, and only Persons of distinction eat it every day, and make three Meals, for all the rest eat only two, and they eat more Boyl'd than Roasted. Their ordinary Diet is Butter, Cheese, Milk, Potatoes, Colworts, *Brochan*, i.e. Oatmeal and Water boyl'd; the latter taken with some Bread is the constant Food of several Thousands of both Sex in this and other isles, during the Winter, and Spring; yet they undergo many Fatigues both by Sea and Land, and are very healthful. This verifies what the Poet saith. *Populis sat est Lymphaque Ceresque.* Nature is satisafied with Bread and Water.

Some of the inhabitants of *Harries* Sailing round the Isle of *Skie* were strangely surpriz'd with an Apparition of two men hanging down by the Ropes that secur'd the Mast, but could not conjecture what it meant. They pursued their Voyage, but the Wind turn'd contrary, and so forc'd them into *Broadford* in the Isle of *Skie,* where they found Sir *Donald Mack Donald* keeping a Sheriffs Court, and two criminals receiving Sentence of death there, the Ropes and Mast of that very Boat were made use of to hang those Criminals. This was told me by several, who had this Instance from the Boats Crew.

My anxiety obliges me to Intreate
Lady Margaret MacDonald

Norman Macleod, who in later life succeeded his father as tacks-man of Berneray and died universally beloved and respected, was something of a tearaway in his youth. In 1739 he organized a kidnapping racket and started abducting Skye-folk of both sexes with the idea of transporting them to the Southern States of America to be sold into slavery. But the first ship was wrecked on the Irish coast and a few people found their way back.

Word got around that Sir Alexander MacDonald was responsible for the kidnapping, and the following letter was addressed to Lord Justice-Clerk Milton by his frantic wife, Lady Margaret, daughter of the ninth earl of Eglinton and a woman of such remarkable beauty that Mrs. Mackinnon of Coirechatachan told Boswell 'when she rode through the island, the people ran in crowds before her, and took the stones off the road, lest her horse should stumble and she be hurt'.

Sky, Jany 1, 1740

Dear Justice, – Being informed by different hands from Edr. that there is a currant Report of a Ship's haveing gon from thiss Country with a greate many people disignd for America, and that Sir Alexr. is thought to have concurred in forceing these people away. As I am positive of the falsehood of this, and quite acquainted with the danger of a Report of this kind, I begg leave to informe Your Lorp. of the real matter of fact. In Hervest last wee were pritty much alarmed with accounts from different corners of thiss and some neighbouring Islands, of persons being seized and carry'd aboard of a Ship which putt into differant places on thiss coast. Sir Alexr. was both angery and Concern'd at that time to hear that some of his oune people were taken in this manner; but cou'd not learn who were the Actors in thiss Wicked Scrape till the Ship was gon. One Norman M'Leod, with a number of Fellows that he had Pick'd up to execute his intentions, were the Real Actors of thiss affair. Sir Alexr. never made much noise about the thing in hopes that thiss Normand M'Leod might one time or other cast up; But he has never Yet appaired in thiss part of the World, and probably never will, as the thing has made so much noise; he's accom-

plices have betaken themselves to the Hills, and lately rob'd a
Servt. of ours comeing from Edr. out of pique to his master;
and one of them knock'd him doun and cutt him over the head
terribly. Sir Alexr. is just now bussy indeavouring to detect any of
these Rogues that may be Yet in Sky, and hopes soon to appre-
hend some of those who have left it. Tho' thiss is the real matter
of fact Sir Alexr. can't help being concerned that he shou'd be
any ways mentioned in the story, tho' quite inosent. This affair
has made so much noise with You because of the way it has been
represented from Irland that possibly there may be intention of
prosecuting Sir Alexr. If that shou'd go on, tho' it cannot be
dangerous to him, Yett it cannot faill of being both troublesome
and expensive; And therefore let me begg of Your Lorp. to write
to the people of poure above to prevent this impending Evell,
because a little time may bring the real Actors to tryall, which, I
dare say Your Lorp, Wou'd rather see in a pannel than imagenary
persones that had no hand in the matter. Tho' I have no reasone
to believe Your Lorp. will be remiss in any affair of such consequence to us both, my anxiety obliges me to intreate You'll take
this affair so much into consideration that You'll delay no time in
makeing applications where You judge it proper; amd trust me
Dr. Justice, thiss favour shall make me with more gratitude than
ever, Your most Obdt. and ever devoted Servt.

[Signed] Margtt. MacDonald

This mad rebellious attempt
Norman MacLeod

Although it is highly likely that the Young Pretender was encouraged in his plans to overthrow the Hanoverian régime by Sir
Alexander Macdonald of Sleat and Norman, the nineteenth Chief
of Macleod, when the moment of decision arrived both men
(although Jacobite at heart) turned their backs on the Prince. Had
Charles arrived with a larger army they might have fought with
him but weighing the chances, they declined to commit either their
lives or their fortunes to what was obviously going to be a fiasco.
Neither of the men ever lived down the shame of what most
Skyemen regarded as a betrayal. It was MacLeod who was the first
to inform the authorities of Prince Charles' arrival in the Western

Isles and the letter he wrote to Duncan Forbes of Culloden, Lord President of the Court of Session, even today seems an extraordinary breach of faith:

My dearest Lord,
To my no small surprise, it is certain that the pretended Prince of Wales is come into the coast of South Uist and Barra, and has since been hovering on parts of the coast of the Mainland; that is, between the point of Ardnamurchan and Glenelg. He has but one ship of which he is aboard; she mounts about 16 or 18 guns. He has about thirty Irish or French officers with him, and one Sheridan, who is called his governor. The Duke of Athole's brother is the only man of any sort of note (that once belonged to this country) that I can hear of that is along with him. His view, I need not tell you, was to raise the Highlands to assist him, etc. Sir Alex. Macdonald and I not only gave no sort of countenance to these people but we used all the interest we had with our neighbours to follow the same prudent method; and I am persuaded we have done it with such success that not one man of any consequence north of the Grampians will give any sort of assistance to this mad rebellious attempt. How far you think we acted properly, I shall long to know; but this is certain, we did it as our duty and for the best, for in the present situation of affairs in Europe, I should have been sorry to see anything like dissaffection to the Government appear, though ever so trivial; or that there was occasion to march a single company to quell it, which now I hope and dare say there is not.

As it can be of no use to the public to know whence you have this information it is, I fancy needless to mention either of us, but this we leave in your own breast, as you are a much better judge of what is or is not proper to be done. I have written to no one else; and as our friendship and confidence in you is without reserve, so we doubt not of your supplying our defects properly. Sir Alex. is here and has seen this scrawl – I ever am, most faithfully yours,

Norman MacLeod
Dunvegan 3rd August, 1745

P.S. Last night I had the pleasure of yours of the 25th. A thousand thanks for your advice; but I am in good health by the very means you mention, moderate exercise and regularity, without starving. Young Clanranald has been here with us, and, has given us all assurances of his prudence, etc.

The Prince sung several songs
Dr. Burton

If Sir Alexander Macdonald was not prepared to help the Cause his wife, Lady Margaret, was ready to risk all. It was to the Macdonald house at Monkstadt that Prince Charles was brought by Flora Macdonald. She had gone from Skye to Milton in South Uist to visit a relative at the time that the defeated Prince was being hunted by the government militia. Flora was asked to help and, as we know, she did. There is no extant account by Flora herself of the part she played in the Prince's escape, but she told her adventures to Dr. Burton of York and they appeared in print in a collection of 'speeches, letters and journals relative to the affairs of Prince Charles Edward Stuart' edited by the Rev. Robert Forbes, Bishop of Ross and Caithness. *The Lyon in Mourning,* as the collection was called, is the major source book of the rebellion. It was on the morning of 28 June 1746 that Flora heard of the arrival in Benbecula of General Campbell, who was leading the hunt. She herself was questioned by his men, but they got nothing from her:

When all were gone who were not to accompany the Prince in his voyage to the isle of Sky, Miss Macdonald desired him to dress himself in his new attire, which was soon done, and at a proper time they removed their quarters and went near the water with their boat afloat, nigh at hand for readiness to embark in case of an alarm from the shore.

At eight o'clock, June 28th Saturday 1746 the Prince, Miss Flora Macdonald, Neil Mackechan etc, set sail in a very clear evening from Benbecula to the Isle of Sky. They had not rowed from the shore above a league till the sea became rough, and at last tempestuous, and to entertain the company the Prince sung several songs and seemed to be in good spirits.

Next morning the boatmen knew not where they were, having no compass and the wind varying several times, it being then again calm. However, at last they made to the point of

Waternish, in the west corner of Sky, where they thought to
have landed, but found the place possessed by a body of forces
who had three boats or yawls near the shore. One on board one
of the boats fired at them to make them bring-to; but they
rowed away as fast as they could.

From hence they rowed on and landed at Kilbride, in
Trotternish in the Isle of Sky, about twelve miles north from the
above-mentioned points. There were also several parties of militia in the neighbourhood of Kilbride. Miss left the Prince in the
boat and went with her servant, Neil Mackechan, to Mougstot,
Sir Alexander Macdonald's house, and desired one of the
servants to let Lady Margaret Macdonald know she was come
to see her ladyship on her way to her mother's house. Lady
Margaret knew her errand well enough by one Mrs. Macdonald,
who had gone a little before to apprize her of it.

As Mr. Alexander Macdonald of Kingsburgh was accidently
there, Lady Margaret desired him to conduct the Prince to his
house; for it is to be remarked that Lady Margaret did not see
the Prince in any shape. Then Kingsburgh took some wine, etc.
to refresh the Prince with, and set forwards for the place of
rendezvous, leaving Miss Macdonald with Lady Margaret at
Mougstot where the commanding officer of the parties in search
of the Prince was, and who asked Miss whence she came,
whither she was going, what news? etc., all which Miss
answered as she thought most proper, and so as to prevent any
discovery of what she had been engaged in.

The Prince and Kingsburgh went over the hills till they
arrived at Kingsburgh house, which was about twelve o'clock at
night, and they were very wet.

Here the Prince got his most material refreshment, and was
very much fatigued. Yet he was very merry till the company
parted to go to rest. Morning being come and pretty far
advanced, Miss Macdonald was in pain about the Prince's lying
so long in bed lest he should be overtaken by his enemies, and
therefore she entreated Kingsburgh to go and call him up, which
with much ado he was prevailed upon to comply with, he being
desirous that the Prince should take as long a rest as he could.
Though the Prince was determined to cast off his disguise, yet it
was necessary he should leave the house in the female dress he
came in, which would, if enquiry happened to be made, prevent

the servants telling the particular dress he had put on when he stripped himself of the gown, petticoats etc., and therefore in Kingsburgh's house Miss put on his cap for him.

The day was far advanced before he set out, and when he arrived at a wood side not far from Kingsburgh, he changed his apparel once more and put on the Highland dress Kingsburgh had furnished him with. Then Kingsburgh sent a guide with him to Portree, thro' all byways, while Miss Macdonald went thither on horseback by another road, thereby the better to gain intelligence and at the same time to prevent a discovery. They were very wet, it having rained very much. Here he only dried his clothes, took some little refreshment, and staid about two hours. Hither Kingsburgh had sent to prepare a boat, and to have it ready to convey the Prince to the place where he wanted to be at, not allowing the people about Portree in the meantime to know anything about the person's being the Prince whom they were to receive and to take care of. Young Macleod of Raaza came with Malcolm Macleod to conduct the Prince over to the Island of Raaza. The Prince was very uneasy he had not a Macdonald to conduct him still. He left Portree on Tuesday 1st July, and landed that very same day at a place called Glam in Raaza. Miss Macdonald took leave of the Prince at Portree, and from thence went to her mother, after a fatiguing journey cross the country. She never told her mother, or indeed anybody else, what she had done.

The sure forerunner of approaching death
Theophilus Insulanus

Dr. Johnson when he was in Skye was much taken with the idea of Second Sight. Because few people in Skye were able to give Johnson first-hand information in his own tongue his inquiries were inconclusive, but he was certainly intrigued. 'I never could advance my curiosity to conviction,' he wrote, 'but came away at last only willing to believe.'

The sort of stories which Johnson heard about this 'involuntary affection' were reported at length in a book published in 1763 just before Johnson came to the Hebrides. Its author was 'Theophilus Insulanus', the Rev. Donald Macleod of Hamera in Glendale. These five instances of second sight, all from Skye, are typical of Highland precognition. Whether people who are accustomed to the idea of foreknowledge are granted it more often than those who aren't is one of those circular arguments which don't get anywhere. There is no denying the innate Celtic predisposition to believe in Second Sight. When you are in Skye you may, if you are not sceptical, hear stories similar to these but at *first hand*.

John Martin and Donald Macleod

On the twelfth of November, at even, 1755, Lieut. Keith, Lieut. Habden, with several others of the country gentlemen, went from the castle of Dunvegan, to the change-house of that place, where they diverted themselves for some time, with a moderate glass of wine; and as they were to return to the castle, all on a sudden, Mr. Keith dropt in his chair, with all the symptoms of death; the company suspecting him only in a trance, employed in vain all the ordinary means for his recovery. John Martin the change-keeper, whose office obliged him to give close attendance, imagined to have seen him fall dead in his chair, about three hours before he expired. Which he told me, as well as several others; and this was the first time he had the Second Sight. The said night Donald Macleod, merchant in Feorlig, being of the same company, saw the said Mr. Keith shrunk to the bigness of a young boy, and in the twinkling of an eye, resume his former size and posture; which he told me once and again: and that both he and John Martin, are still willing to make oath to the premises.

John Macleod

tacksman of Feorlig, informed me, that as he and a servant were employed about their labouring, they saw the deceased Mr. John Macleod, late minister of Durinish, passing by; and having followed him a piece on his way, after they returned to their work, he inquired of his servant, if he observed any remarkable circumstance about the minister? who answered he did, and that he seemed to him, to dwindle away to the bigness of a boy of six or seven years old, and then recover his former size: which my informer having likewise observed, moved him to put the question to his servant. The minister some short time thereafter sickened, of which he died. And I am told that this kind of Second Sight, is commonly the sure forerunner of approaching death.

Major Donald Macleod

who had been an officer in the Dutch service, having visited Roderick MacLeod of Hammer, who went along with him to visit William MacLeod of Watersteine, where having passed most of the day, as they were on their way to return, towards the evening, an old woman that lived in a cottage close to the road they passed by, had a view of them; and having met Watersteine as he came back from giving the convoy, inquired who was he that passed by with him and his brother? He told her it was a Dutch officer; upon which she said, they would never see him again, as she saw him shrouded up in his winding sheet, to the crown of his head, which she said was a sure sign of his approaching end. The Major soon thereafter went south, and waiting for a ship at Leith, to transport himself and recruits to Holland, was seized with a fever of which he died. I had this relation from Watersteine himself, who was a person of unquestionable veracity, and remarkable pious.

Jack Macleod

tacksman of Bay in the Isle of Sky, a gentleman not in the least tinctured with enthusiasm, declared to me, and several others, that in a morning before he awaked, he dreamed, that a person whom he intimately knew came into the room where he lay, and told him, with much concern, that his late Majesty, George the Second of glorious memory, was departed this life, which he told directly to his spouse in bed with him; that same day the post having come on before he had well dressed, he got the public news, in which he found his dream verified: which is the more remarkable, that the King's death was so sudden, the account of his ailment could not have travelled to many parts in England, much less have time to circulate to the most remote parts of Scotland.

Allan MacDonald, the younger of Kingsburgh, writing to the author of this treatise on 22 December 1756 gave him further instances of Second Sight including this:

In the end of the year 1744, fourteen persons saw a large vessel coming in below Kingsborough, in the dusk of the evening, and drop anchor in the entrance of Loch Snisort, a very uncommon harbour which surprised us all. This sight we had till night deprived us of it; but next morning there was no vessel to be found, so that we all agreed it to be the Second Sight, which was soon accomplished; for Captain Ferguson being in search of the young Pretender, with the Furnace sloop of war, anchored exactly in the dusk of the evening, in that unusual place above-mentioned half a mile below the house of Kingsborough.

Migrations and depression of spirit
Thomas Pennant

In the summers of 1770 and 1772 the traveller Thomas Pennant undertook a voyage to the Hebrides and the results of his observations, illustrated by the work of the artist Moses Griffiths, was published in 1774. Pennant is a much more reliable guide than Martin Martin, even though the really authentic eighteenth-century portrait of Skye was still to emerge from Johnson's pen. After commenting on the lateness of the spring, the heavy rainfall and the unusually difficult climate, Pennant volunteered some general thoughts:

The quantity of corn raised in tolerable seasons in this island is esteemed to be about nine thousand bolls. The number of mouths to consume them near thirteen thousand: migrations and depression of spirit, the last a common cause of depopulation, having since the year 1750 reduced the number from fifteen thousand to between twelve and thirteen: one thousand having crossed the *Atlantic,* others sunk beneath poverty, or in despair, ceased to obey the first great command, ENCREASE and MULTIPLY. In that year the whole rent of *Skie* was three thousand five hundred pounds. By an unnatural force some of the rents are now doubled and trebled. People long out of all habit of industry, and used to the convivial tables of their chieftain, were unable instantly to support so new a burden: in time not very long preceding that, they felt the return of some of their rents: they were enabled to keep hospitality; to receive their chieftain with a well covered board, and to feed a multitude of poor. Many of the greater tacksmen were of the same blood with their chieftains; they were attached to them by the ties of consanguinity as well as affection: they felt from them the first act of oppression, as *Caesar* did the wound from his beloved *Brutus.*

The high advance of the price of cattle is a plea for the high advance of rents; but the situation of the tacksman here is particular: he is a gentleman, and boasts the same blood with his laird: (of five hundred fighting men that followed *Macleod* in 1745 in his Majesty's army, four hundred were of his kindred) has been cherished by him for a series of years often with paternal affection: has been used to such luxuries as the place affords; and cannot instantly sink from a good board to the hard fare of the common farmer. When the chieftain riots in all the luxuries of *South Britain,* he thinks himself entitled to share a due degree of the good things of this life, and not to be forever confined to the diet of *Brochan* or the compotation of *Whisky.* During the feudal reign their love for their chieftain induced them to bear many things, at present intolerable. He was their pride and their glory: they strained every nerve in support of him, in the same manner as the *French* through vanity, refuse nothing to aggrandize their *Grand Monarque.*

Resentment drove many to seek a retreat beyond the *Atlantic:* they sold their stock, and in numbers made their first essay. They found, or thought they found, while their passions were warm, an happy change of situation: they wrote in terms favouring of romance, an account of their situation: their friends caught the contagion: and numbers followed; and others were preparing to follow their example. The tacksmen from a motive of independency: the poor from attachment; and from excess of misery. Policy and humanity, as I am informed, have of late checked this spirit so detrimental to the public. The wisdom of legislation may perhaps fall on some methods to conciliate the affections of a valuable part of the community: it is unbecoming my little knowledge of the country to presume to point out the methods. It is to be hoped the head will, while time permits, recollect the use of the most distant members.

Their weather is not pleasing
Samuel Johnson

Johnson's discovery of the Hebrides must rank in importance
with Cook's sighting of the islands named after him. Strangely,
both journeys were made in the same year, 1773. Although
other travellers from the south had penetrated to the islands
before, never had anyone so eminently head and shoulders
above his contemporaries made the slengthy pilgrimage. For a
man of sixty-four, overweight and of sedentary disposition, this
visit over storm-tossed waters at the time of the autumn
equinoctial gales was every bit as daunting a feat as Captain
Cook's voyage to the South Seas.

Nobody named any islands after Johnson, indeed his stric-
tures on some of the less admirable characteristics of the natives
roused a certain amount of resentment, but he certainly put
Skye on the tourist map. As he said himself: 'To the southern
inhabitants of Scotland, the state of the mountains and the
islands is equally unknown with that of Borneo and Sumatra: of
both they have have only heard a little, and guess the rest.'
Johnson's account of his journey and the publication of
Boswell's *Journal* put an end to much ignorant speculation
about life in the islands even though they brought back a fairly
bleak report. Johnson suffered a great deal, was several times in
danger of his life and endured the kind of discomfort that he
could never have envisaged when he set out from the comparative luxury of London on his 94-day journey. His account when
placed alongside Boswell's, is restrained and prosaic – no host-
esses sit on his knee, no toasts are drunk, there is no merry
laughter; Johnson emerges as a dull dog indeed and Skye as not
perhaps the first place in Europe to rush off to for a high time.
Johnson was not the last visitor to assume that just because it
was wet and windy while he was there the weather was disas-
trous all the year round. But Johnson was royally entertained
both in Corriechatachan and in Raasay, and from there he and
Boswell moved on to Dunvegan:

Raasay has a stout boat, built in Norway, in which, with six
oars, he conveyed us back to Skye. We landed at Port Re, so
called because James the Fifth of Scotland, who had curiosity to
visit the islands, came into it. The port is made by an inlet of

the sea, deep and narrow, where a ship lay waiting to dispeople Skye, by carrying the natives away to America.

In coasting Skye, we passed by the cavern in which it was the custom, as Martin relates, to catch birds in the night, by making a fire at the entrance. This practice is disused, for the birds, as is known often to happen, have changed their haunts.

Here we dined at a public-house, I believe the only inn of the island, and having mounted our horses, travelled in the manner already described, till we came to Kingsborough, a place distinguished by that name, because the king lodged here when he landed at Port Re. We were entertained with the usual hospitality by Mr. Macdonald and his lady Flora Macdonald, a name that will be mentioned in history, and if courage and fidelity be virtues, mentioned with honour. She is a woman of middle stature, soft features, gentle manners, and elegant presence.

In the morning we sent our horses round a promontory to meet us, and spared ourselves part of the day's fatigue, by crossing an arm of the sea. We had at last some difficulty in coming to Dunvegan; for our way led over an extensive moor, where every step was to be taken with caution, and we were often obliged to alight, because the ground could not be trusted. In travelling this watery flat, I perceived that it had a visible declivity, and might without much expense or difficulty be drained. But difficulty and expense are relative terms, which have different meanings in different places.

To Dunvegan we came, very willing to be at rest, and found our fatigue amply recompensed by our reception. Lady Macleod, who had lived many years in England, was newly come hither with her son and four daughters, who knew all the arts of southern elegance, and all the modes of English economy. Here therefore we settled, and did not spoil the present hour with thoughts of departure.

We had here more wind than waves, and suffered the severity of a tempest, without enjoying its magnificence. The sea being broken by the multitude of the islands, does not roar with so much noise, nor beat the storm with such foamy violence as I have remarked on the coast of Sussex. Though, while I was in the Hebrides, the wind was extremely turbulent, I never saw very high billows.

The country about Dunvegan is rough and barren. There are no trees, except in the orchard, which is a low sheltered spot, surrounded with a wall.

Johnson found the people a bit rough too and his inventory of their miseries is a further catalogue of gloom:

The inhabitants of Skye, and of the other islands which I have seen, are commonly of the middle stature, with fewer among them very tall or very short than are seen in England; or perhaps, as their numbers are small, the chances of any deviation from the common measure are necessarily few. The tallest men that I saw are among those of higher rank. In regions of barrenness and scarcity, the human race is hindered in its growth by the same causes as other animals.

The ladies have as much beauty here as in other places, but bloom and softness are not to be expected among the lower classes, whose faces are exposed to the rudeness of the climate, and whose features are sometimes contracted by want, and sometimes hardened by the blasts. Supreme beauty is seldom found in cottages or workshops, even where no real hardships are suffered. To expand the human face to its full perfection, it seems necessary that the mind should co-operate by placidness of content, or consciousness of superiority.

Their strength is proportionate to their size, but they are accustomed to run upon rough ground, and therefore can with great agility skip over the bog, or clamber the mountain. For a campaign in the wastes of America, soldiers better qualified could not have been found. Having little work to do, they are not willing, nor perhaps able, to endure a long continuance of manual labour, and are therefore considered as habitually idle. Having never been supplied with those accommodations, which life extensively diversified with trades affords, they supply their wants by very insufficient shifts, and endure many inconveniences, which a little attention would easily relieve. I have seen a horse carrying home the harvest on a crate. Under his tail was a stick for a crupper, held at the two ends by twists of straw. Hemp will grow in their islands, and therefore ropes may be had. If they wanted hemp, they might make better cordage of rushes, or perhaps of nettles, than of straw.

Their method of life neither secures them perpetual health

nor exposes them to any particular diseases. There are physicians in the islands, who, I believe, all practise chirurgery, and all compound their own medicines. It is generally supposed that life is longer in places where there are few opportunities of luxury; but I found no instance here of extraordinary longevity. A cottager grows old over his oaten cakes, like a citizen at a turtle feast. He is indeed seldom incommoded by corpulence. Poverty preserves him from sinking under the burden of himself, but he escapes no other injury of time. Instances of long life are often related, which those who hear them are more willing to credit than examine. To be told that any man has attained a hundred years gives hope and comfort to him who stands trembling on the brink of his own climacteric.

A little woman of a genteel appearance
James Boswell

Boswell's *journal of a Tour to the Hebrides* was not published until 1785, twelve years after the event and just nine months after Johnson died. Where Johnson is heavy with judicious information and prosaic observation, Boswell presents the gossipy story of what actually happened. The only time the *Journal* sags is when Boswell exercises his unfortunate gift of total recall and sets down great chunks of Johnsoniana – the Doctor on death, the importance of chastity in women, Ossian, Goldsmith's *Traveller* and Dr. Macpherson's *Dissertations,* all like so much English porridge, grey, stodgy and not worth the warming up.

But a remarkable picture emerges not only of the rigours of the pilgrimage but the happier moments: the dancing at Raasay, the hospitality in Skye. There were some memorable encounters, none more than that between the high Tory literary dictator and the romantic embodiment of Jacobite disillusion, Flora Macdonald. Johnson, as we've seen, dismisses the meeting in a few lines; Boswell, a man of greater imagination, made a monumental meal of it:

We had a dish of tea at Dr. Macleod's, who had a pretty good house, where was his brother, a half-pay officer. His lady was a polite, agreeable woman. Dr. Johnson said, he was glad to see that he was so well married, for he had an esteem for physicians. The doctor accompanied us to Kingsburgh, which is called a mile farther; but the computation of Sky has no connection whatever with real distance.

I was highly pleased to see Dr. Johnson safely arrived at Kingsburgh, and received by the hospitable Mr. Macdonald, who, with a most respectful attention, supported him into the house. Kingsburgh was completely the figure of a gallant Highlander, – exhibiting 'the graceful mien and manly looks' which our popular Scotch song has justly attributed to that character. He had his Tartan plaid thrown about him, a large blue bonnet with a knot of black ribband like a cockade, a brown short coat of a kind of duffil, a Tartan waistcoat with gold buttons and gold button-holes, a bluish philibeg, and Tartan hose. He had jet black hair tied behind, and was a large stately man, with a steady sensible countenance.

There was a comfortable parlour with a good fire, and a dram went round. By and by, supper was served, at which there appeared the lady of the house, the celebrated Miss Flora Macdonald. She is a little woman, of a genteel appearance, and uncommonly mild and well bred. To see Dr. Samuel Johnson, the great champion of the English Tories salute Miss Flora Macdonald in the Isle of Sky, was a striking sight; for though somewhat congenial in their notions, it was very improbable they should meet here.

Miss Flora Macdonald (for so I shall call her) told me, she heard upon the main land, as she was returning home about a fortnight before, that Mr. Boswell was coming to Sky, and one Mr. Johnson, a young English buck, with him. He was highly entertained with this fancy. Giving an account of the afternoon which we passed at Anoch, he said, 'I, being a buck, had miss in to make tea.' – He was rather quiescent to-night, and went early to bed. I was in a cordial humour, and promoted a cheerful glass. The punch was excellent. Honest Mr. M'Queen observed that I was in high glee, 'my governour being gone to bed'. Yet in reality my heart was grieved, when I recollected that Kingsburgh was embarrassed in his affairs, and intended to go to America. However, nothing but what was good was present, and I pleased myself in thinking that so spirited a man would be well every where. I slept in the same room with Dr. Johnson. Each had a neat bed, with Tartan curtains, in an upper chamber.

Monday, 13th September

The room where we lay was a celebrated one. Dr. Johnson's bed was the very bed in which the grandson of the unfortunate King James the Second lay, on one of the nights after the failure of his rash attempt in 1745-6, while he was eluding the pursuit of the emissaries of government, which had offered thirty thousand pounds as a reward for apprehending him. To see Dr. Samuel Johnson lying in that bed, in the Isle of Sky, in the house of Miss Flora Macdonald, struck me with such a group of ideas as it is not easy for words to describe, as they passed through the mind. He smiled, and said, 'I have had no ambitious thoughts in it.'

From Kingsburgh the travellers moved on to Dunvegan where the company 'listened with wonder and pleasure' as the Doctor harangued his captive audience of lairds and gentle-folk. Saturday 18 September was Johnson's sixty-fifth birthday and the fifth day of their stay in the castle:

Before breakfast, Dr. Johnson came up to my room, to forbid me to mention that this was his birth-day; but I told him I had done it already; at which he was displeased; I suppose from wishing to have nothing particular done on his account. Lady M'Leod and I got into a warm dispute. She wanted to build a house upon a farm which she has taken about five miles from the castle, and to make gardens and other ornaments there; all of which I approved of; but insisted that the seat of the family should always be upon the rock of Dunvegan. – Johnson: 'Ay, in time we'll build all round this rock. You may make a very good house at the farm, but it must not be such as to tempt the Laird of M'Leod to go thither to reside. Most of the great families of England have a secondary residence, which is called a jointure-house: let the new house be of that kind.' – The lady insisted that the rock was very inconvenient; that there was no place near it where a good garden could be made; that it must always be a rude place; that it was a Herculean labour to make a dinner here. I was vexed to find the alloy of modern refinement in a lady who had so much old family spirit. – 'Madam, (said I), if once you quit this rock, there is no knowing where you may settle. You move five miles first; – then to St. Andrews, as the late Laird did; – then to Edinburgh; – and so on till you end at Hampstead, or in France. No, no; keep to the rock; it is the

very jewel of the estate. It looks as if it had been let down from
heaven by the four corners, to be the residence of a Chief. Have
all the comforts and conveniences of life upon it, but never leave
Rorie More's cascade.' – 'But, (said she), is it not enough if we
keep it? Must we never have more convenience than Rorie More
had? He had his beef brought to dinner in one basket, and his
bread in another. Why not as well be Rorie More all over, as live
upon his rock? And should not we tire, in looking perpetually
on this rock? It is very well for you, who have a fine place, and
everything easy, to talk thus, and think of chaining honest folks
to a rock. You would not live upon it yourself.' – 'Yes, madam,
(said I), I would live upon it, were I Laird of M'Leod, and
should be unhappy if I were not upon it.' – Johnson (with a
strong voice, and most determined manner), 'Madam, rather
than quit the old rock, Boswell would live in the pit; he would
make his bed in the dungeon.' – I felt a degree of elation, at
finding my resolute feudal enthusiasm thus confirmed by such a
sanction. The lady was puzzled a little. She still returned to her
pretty farm, – rich ground, – fine garden. – 'Madam (said Dr.
Johnson), were they in Asia, I would not leave the rock.' – My
opinion on this subject is still the same. An ancient family residence ought to be a primary object; and though the situation of
Dunvegan be such that little can be done here in gardening, or
pleasure-ground, yet, in addition to the veneration acquired by
the lapse of time, it has many circumstances of natural
grandeur, suited to the seat of a Highland Chief: it has the sea,
– islands, – rocks, – hills, – a noble cascade; and when the
family is again in opulence, something may be done by art.

The winter was a dreadful one
Abram

In 1781 an English servant called Abram came to the Highlands
with his master, a Captain Macleod, with whom he had served
in America. Macleod died at Fort George in 1782, and it was his
dying wish that Abram should remain with the widow and family.
It was arranged that for a time they should all go and live with
relatives at Arnisdale in Glenelg. Abram kept a journal which was
published in the *Inverness Courier* in 1854. He had a pretty bleak
stay in the West; the widow was not well off and times were lean:

In December we went to the Island of Skye, to the house that young Mr. Macleod of Gesto had provided for us. It had been the residence of the Dowager Lady Macleod, but was sadly out of repair. There were no windows in the lower rooms, and the rain came in at the roof. But there was a middling good room and a closet above stairs, and there was no family but our own in the house. My mistress got a servant maid that could speak English. Provisions were dear and scarce almost to a famine, and I had great distances to go for everything, acting the part of both man and horse.

I used to go for butter and cheese to a place called Boreland which was seventeen miles from our house. I once made this journey and back again the same day with 75 lbs. of butter and cheese on my back, but the creel blistered me severely. I have several times, when meal was to be sold at Dunvegan, brought a boll, or 160 lbs. weight, home on my back, a distance of five miles. I often used to cross the mountains to Portree to buy tea and sugar, with any other articles I could get, and this journey would be betwixt thirty and forty miles for me. There are no bridges over the many rivulets in the island, and there was no other way of crossing but by fording them, yet though I was thus continually on my feet and out in everlasting rains, I cannot say that I ever had colds. The Highland gentry are fond of going about from place to place to visit one another, sometimes being a fortnight or three weeks from home; and when they return they perhaps carry along with them those they have been staying with. This they call hospitality, but it is only paying them in their own way by killing time together.

A stranger such as I was, and in a humble situation, need not go to the Highlands and Islands. If the Highland servant's master rides anywhere, the man must run after him on foot, be it ever so far; and when they come to the place they are going to, he may be for hours without getting anything to eat or drink, although he is melting with heat and wet with running through bogs and fording streams.

In the summer of 1784 we began to live better. We got two cows to milk, and we began to provide for ourselves. We cut peats and dried them. We also commissioned a barrel of flour and a barrel of biscuit from Liverpool. In November we bought a cow and killed it for winter keep. Oatmeal was very dear, being at the rate of £1 8s. the boll. I went in a boat and bought six sheep, giving 4s. 6d. a-piece for them, afterwards killing and salting them. We also laid in our stock of butter and cheese for the winter; and fortunate it was for us that we were so provident, for the winter of 1784 was a dreadful one in the Highlands. The crops were poor, and the snow was so deep and lay so long on the ground that numbers of the cattle died, some of the farmers losing eighty and a hundred each. Everything was so scarce that the people eat the meat of those cattle that died, many of them without any salt to it. It was a distressing sight to see in every place you came nigh the men skinning the dead cattle, and cutting off the fleshy parts for food.

When snow lies long in the Highlands a great many cattle are always lost. No provision is made for them in the summer, the farmers depending entirely on the openness of the winter in that part of the country from its proximity to the sea. They have a great deal of rain, and though the oats and barley may grow well enough, it is often spoiled in the getting in, owing to the winds and rains at that season. For this reason the gentlemen farmers, instead of raising corn, breed droves of black cattle, which they sell every year. The drovers come and purchase them, and drive them to the south country. There is a great want of method in their management, and it keeps a number of idle fellows about a farm-house who could be dispensed with, but then the system in time of war gives the gentlemen more consequence. The heads of clans obtain leave to raise regiments, and are successful, though many of the men are taken sorely against their will.

A profusion of fish
John Knox

There are two facts worth noting about travel in Scotland before the advent of steam. Few foreign travellers crossing the border ever steeled themselves to the hardship of a journey to the Western Isles and those who did visit islands like Skye inevitably wound up on the same hospitality circuit, staying with the same five or six men of substance. In the eighteenth century there was only a handful of houses in Skye worthy of receiving a cultivated guest; this accounts for the frequency with which the names of their owners crop up in successive narratives. Thus John Knox visiting Skye in 1786, met the same few lairds that Boswell and Johnson met and no doubt heard the same prejudices and attitudes aired. It is consequently not surprising that the eighteenth-century reports brought back from Skye tended to reflect the views of the 'superior classes' and not the great mass of the people – none of whom could communicate in any language other than Gaelic. Knox's tour through the Hebrides was undertaken on behalf of the British Society for Extending the Fisheries. He landed at Portree procured horses and rode west:

At Brackadale, I was introduced to Mr. Macleod of Ulinish, who, from his great probity, and the respect in which he is held, has, in some cases, the duty of a sheriff imposed upon him by the inhabitants, to whom he is a father. Here also Mr. Pennant and Dr. Johnson were lodged and accommodated. The Lady of the family had not forgot the quantity of tea, which she filled out to the latter, amounting to twenty-two dishes. I had intended to proceed to Dunvegan, on the west side of the island; but Mr. Macleod, and other gentlemen, strongly urged a short cruise to the seat of Colonel Macleod of Talisker, which stands upon the coast, some miles eastward. We had a pleasant voyage, along a lofty romantic shore, abounding in beautiful cascades, from one ledge of rocks to another, till they were lost in the sea immediately below.

Before we could land at the Bay of Talisker, Mr Macleod, though extremely corpulent, had, with his usual politeness reached the beach, from whence we were conducted, through a small, but rich valley, to the seat of plenty, hospitality, and good nature.

The mountains abound in deer, hare, and wild fowl; the fields in grain, hay, and pasturage; the gardens in fruits and vegetables; the rivers in trout and salmon; the sea in herrings and white fish. Such, with the additional circumstance of a well stocked cellar, are the felicities of this very remote and almost inaccessible corner.

While these furnish many of the choicest luxuries in life, Talisker and his lady enjoy the good will of the people around, of which we had a specimen, in their readiness to convey us back to Brackadale, on a wet day, and against a head wind, that would have required the utmost exertion of six or eight men alternately at the oars.

After a short ride, we reached Dunvegan, the seat of Macleod, the chief of that ancient clan, and proprietor of the south-west part of Sky, with the lands which lie between Loch Urn and Loch Duich, on the continent. This estate has been greatly diminished of late years, on account of debts; and much remains to be discharged. Not withstanding this circumstance, the proprietor raised no rents, turned out no tenants, used no man with severity, and in all respects, and under the most pressing exigencies, maintained the character of a liberal and human friend of mankind. Here Dr. Johnson, who met with the utmost civility from the family, made a *faux pas*. Lady Macleod, who had repeatedly helped him to sixteen dishes, or upwards, of tea, asked him if a small bason would not save him trouble, and be more agreeable. 'I wonder, madam,' answered he roughly, 'why all the ladies ask me such impertinent questions? It is to save youselves trouble, madam, and not me.' The lady was silent, and went on with her task.

Knox's final report on Skye, which led to the establishment of a fishing station at Stein, was ripe with expectations which were never fully realized:

The great wealth of Sky consists in its marine productions. Here are at least twenty bays or lochs, which are occasionally frequented by herrings, and where many cargoes have been procured by vessels from the ports of the Clyde, but none by the natives, because they have no vessels wherein to cure them.

The lakes are frequented by salmon, mackarel, white and shell fish. Without, in the ocean, there are many excellent banks, of which the natives, from the want of stout wherries or decked vessels, are not able to avail themselves. Amidst this profusion of fish, in all their varieties, the utmost exertion of the people seems only to procure supplies for their own families, and a small quantity of cod, of inferior size and indifferently cured; which, as before observed, they sell or exchange for necessaries. When foundations shall be laid for the growth of three or four towns, and when the period arrives which will facilitate fisheries around this great island, by means of decked vessels, well provided in salt, cask, and experienced curers, the value of Sky will be found to exceed belief. To the navy it will be able to spare 1,000 seamen in every war, which, at the rate of 200 seamen for every ship of the line, will be sufficient to navigate a little squadron, with men inured to hardships, and fearless of dangers.

Improvements humbly suggested
Robert Heron

In 1794 Robert Heron drew up for the consideration of the Board of Agriculture and Internal Improvement a document outlining conditions in the Hebrides. Although based on personal observation it leaned heavily on the observations of early travellers, Johnson, Buchanan, Campbell's Survey and the old *Statistical Account.* He also proposed some suggestions to improve the conditions in the islands. 'Agriculture,' he wrote, 'is the nursing mother of all the *mechanic arts,* and they are all her handmaids: among the *fine arts, architecture* and *gardening* are in particular connected with Agriculture. Of such extensive importance are agricultural inquiries to the improvement of Science and Art.' Of Skye, or Sky, as he called it, he had this to say:

This island is deeply intersected round its whole circumference, by arms of the sea. The bay of Portree, Loch-Snizort, and Loch-Braccadale are the largest of its bays. The *aspect* of its *surface* is irregular as its *figure.* Its mountains tower up in different places, into the lofty summits of Cullinn, Scornifrey, Bein-Store, Bein-vore-scowe, Bein-cro, Bein-nin Kaillich, the two Hallivails, and others. Below are vales, here and there divided by streams of various magnitudes; wide morasses moistened by stagnant water; slowly sloping declivities, and level fields. The bare crags often appear without vegetation towards the summit of the hills; brown heath spreads over their declivities, and around their bases; the morasses are covered with grey mosses, inter-mingled with bog-grasses of a dark green hue; spots of a livelier verdure are thinly scattered here and there among the heaths and morasses; and fair green pastures and cultivated grounds skirt the bays and rivers; and are continually incroaching upon the wilder country. Here is little wood; yet, at Armidel, on the east coast, the garden is shaded by some stately ashes, of a species uncommonly valuable. Sea-weeds grow in great plenty around the shores. The climate of Sky is not the most genial or benignant. The Spring is backward; Summer indeed warm, yet not torrid; but about the dog-days, the rains usually begin, and with few intervals of any length, continue to fall till the end of Autumn. Winter seldom or never brings severe frosts or heavy falls of snow; but the rains still continue till the return of Spring, and are often accompanied with loud tempestuous winds.

The number of the inhabitants of Sky, is about 16,000. Lord Macdonald, Colonel Macleod, and Mackinnon, three chief of clans, with Macalister of Strathaird, are the proprietors of the lands of the islands. In it are seven parochial clergymen. It has two *grammar-schools*. The tacksmen are gradually dwindling into simple farmers.

All the more necessary mechanic arts are practised by artisans in Sky. Here are taylors, shoemakers, weavers, carpenters, masons. The old Highland dress is still worn partially by the labouring class. The houses are huts, with walls of mud or of heath; buildings having walls of stones and mortar, with a single row of windows, and equally covered with turf over the rafters, and upon the turfs, straw with ferns, or heath.

At Sconser is a post-office. Kelp is made on the shores. Liverpool, and some trading towns in Ireland, are the markets to which the greater part is sent. Fishing for immediate home-consumption, or for curing and exportation, is practised round all the coasts of the island. Men servants receive for yearly wages, from £2 10s. to £5, with four pairs of shoes; women servants from 8s. to £1 with three pairs of shoes in the year. Men servants who are married are allowed each man for wages, as much arable ground as he can cultivate; pasture for two milk-cows, twelve sheep, and two horses; two days in the week for his own work; and his food when he works for his master.

Goats, sheep, black-cattle, and horses, feed upon the open hills and moors. Of the black-cattle especially, which are the staple commodity of the island, very large numbers are annually exported. Out of the returns from the exported cattle are the landlord's rents chiefly paid. The sheep are not numerous in proportion to the extent of the island. Cheese, butter or wool are not exported.

The inclosed and cultivated ground consists of gardens, meadows and fields of corn, flax and potatoes. The gardens of the poor afford only the most common pot-herbs; those of the farmers produce these in greater variety and abundance, with perhaps a fruit-tree or shrub. The gardens of the gentlemen which are surrounded with good walls, and carefully dressed, afford all the various fruits, flowers, roots and herbs that are raised in Scottish gardens. Even in the best years, no grain can be exported from Sky; in unfavourable years, a considerable importation is required. Roads begin to be very industriously made through the island. New fields and farms are now annually inclosed. The price of labour is rising.

A Prophecy fulfilled
Dr. Norman MacLeod

Coinneach Odhar, or Kenneth Ouir, who lived at Ness in Lewis in the sixteenth century, was undoubtedly the most famous prophet or seer to live in the Islands. He foretold the fate of individuals, of families and dynasties and, like his successor the Brahan Seer, appeared to predict events which came true many years after his own death. One of these concerned the MacLeods of Dunvegan. The story is told by Dr. Norman MacLeod, known in his life-time as the *Caraid nan Gaidheal,* or Friend of the Gaels, who in 1799 was on a visit to Dunvegan:

One circumstance took place at the castle on this occasion which I think worth recording, especially as I am the only person now living who can attest the truth of it. There had been a traditionary prophecy, couched in Gaelic verse, regarding the family of MacLeod, which on this occasion received a most extraordinary fulfilment. Such prophecies were current regarding almost all old families in the Highlands. Of the MacLeod family, it was prophesied at least a hundred years prior to the circumstance which I am about to relate.

In the prophecy to which I allude it was foretold that when Norman the son of the hard, slender English lady would perish by an accidental death; that when the 'Maidens' of MacLeod (certain well known rocks on the coast of MacLeod's country) became the property of a Campbell;

when a fox had young ones in one of the turrets of the castle, and particularly when the fairy-enchanted banner should be for the last time exhibited, then the glory of the MacLeod family should depart – a great part of the estate should be sold to others; so that a small *curragh* (a boat) would carry all the gentlemen of the name of MacLeod across Loch Dunvegan; but that in times far distant a chief named Ian Breac should arise, who should redeem those estates, and raise the powers and honour of the house to a higher pitch than ever. And now as to the curious coincidence of its fulfilment.

There was, at the time, at Dunvegan, an English smith, with whom I became a favourite, and who told me, in solemn secrecy, that the iron chest which contained the 'Fairy Flag' was to be forced open next morning; that he had arranged with Mr. Hector MacDonald Buchanan to be there with his tools for that purpose. I was most anxious to be present, and I asked permission to that effect of Mr. Buchanan (MacLeod's man of business), who granted me leave on condition that I should not inform any one of the name of MacLeod that such was intended, and should keep it a profound secret from the Chief. This I promised, and most faithfully acted on. Next morning we proceeded to the chamber in the east turret, where was the iron chest that contained the famous flag, about which there is an interesting tradition. With great violence the smith tore open the lid of this iron chest; but in doing so, a key was found under part of the covering, which would have opened the chest, had it been found in time. There was an inner case, in which was found the flag, enclosed in a wooden box of strongly-scented wood. The flag consisted of a square piece of very rich silk, with crosses wrought with gold thread, and several elf-spots stitched with great care on different parts of it.

On this occasion the melancholy news of the death of a young and promising heir of MacLeod reached the castle, 'Norman, the fourth Norman' was a lieutenant of H.M.S. *Queen Charlotte*, which was blown up at sea, and he and the rest perished. At the same time, the rocks called 'MacLeod's Maidens' were sold, in the course of that very week, to Angus Campbell of Ensay, and they are still in possession of his grandson. A fox in possession of a Lieutenant MacLean, residing in the west turret of the castle had young ones, which I handled, and thus all that was said in the prophecy alluded to was literally fulfilled.

Every faculty arrested
Robert Jameson

In the late eighteenth century, the first serious geologist arrived in the Islands. He was Robert Jameson, a distinguished fellow of the Royal and Antiquarian Societies of Edinburgh. In 1800 he published a two-volume work, *Mineralogy of the Scottish Isles.* Like all these early authors, Jameson was very conscious that he was exploring an area that had in the past been infrequently written about and he naturally took great pains to record his impressions of the place and the people.

At a little distance from Loch-Staffin we observed a beautiful fresh-water lake, called Shiant, or The Sacred Lake. Its banks are covered with natural wood, and it is filled by numerous springs; so that its water is cool, clear, and refreshing. It has not escaped the particular regard of the inhabitants, who formerly frequented it in great numbers, as it was reckoned sacred, and capable of healing all diseases. From this loch we walked for a short way through cornfields, and then along a dreary moor, which was bounded, upon one side, by the range of hills which extended to Portree, and, upon the other, by the ocean, and the distant mountains of the mainland of Scotland.

The silence of the scene was broken only by sounds which rendered it more dismal – the mournful whistle of the plover, or the wild notes of the curlew; while the sullen roar of the ocean came at intervals upon the ear as it heaved its mighty surges on the shore. The day, which was for some time extremely delightful, began to lour, the wind arose, and we saw the clouds gathering upon the neighbouring mountains. To avoid the coming storm, we hastened to pass the muir, that we might reach the path which leads across the mountains. After a journey of several hours, we came to the bottom of the mountains; they were enveloped in clouds and the rain was falling in torrents. Fatigued by a long march, and with our clothes wet and clinging about us, we had still the steep ascent of the mountains, which divide the northern part of the island, before us.

We began to ascend, and persevered in climbing against the blast; the long heather, and the wetness of the ground, increased our toil; but at last we gained a considerable plain.

As we continued to ascend, the thickness of the mist was terrible. Our guide began to talk seriously of his doubts and fears; assuring us that frequently people, going in search of cattle among the mountains were overtaken by these mists, and forced to sit quietly down, and wait for the morning. The situation forcibly impressed us with the truth of what he related; and we entered with a lively sympathy into the anxiety and despair, and vain struggles of those who are left thus to wander alone. While we went musing on our situation, and indulging in imaginary distresses, our guide pointed to the cairn of a poor shepherd who had perished in the snow.

The travellers passed a few days at Kingsburgh, where they were entertained with 'extreme kindness and hospitality', and then walked on to Portree where they obviously got a poor welcome at the Inn: 'There are in the Highlands, as in other countries, places where strangers find bad accommodation; but certainly the inn of Portree has seldom been equalled for dirtiness: a traveller from among the Hottentots might well recognize the Kraal, although so far removed from its customary situation.' On their way to Broadford to stay with Mackinnon of Corriechatachan they climbed Beinn na Caillich, the highest of the Red Hills.

We now hastened with eager step towards the summit, and soon reached the cairn, which is upon the most elevated part of the mountain. Here, our most sanguine expectations were more than realized, every faculty for a while seemed arrested, until we could burst into an exclamation on the vastness of the scene, and on the mighty and eternal power of Him who framed so great a work. Before us were many great valleys bounded by lofty mountains, whose steep sides were furrowed by the many torrents which collect during the dreadful storms that often reign in these wilds. At a great distance, the dark, lurid and terrible summits of the Cuillin mountains retiring in majesty among the clouds; thus dimly seen, adding much to the sublimity of the scene. To the north, we observed below us the low part of the island, with the isles of Rona, Raasay,

Scalpa and Fladda: towards the east and south, the rugged
mountains of the mainland appeared stretching in all the
grandeur of Alpine wildness to the point of Ardnamurch; and
nearer the isles of Eigg and Rum added to the variety of this
interesting scene but the darkening of the sky admonished us
to shorten our stay, and hasten again to the valley. The clouds
were now seen driving through the glens, and covering the
mountains with a dark veil; soon all was lost in grand confusion; what a few minutes before was clear and distinct, was
now a troubled scene of tremendous mountainous peaks,
shooting above the dark clouds, and reddened valleys dimly
seen through the driving mist and rain. We took the lea side of
the mountain, and soon reached the house of Cory.

The face in the chamber
John MacCulloch

John MacCulloch was born the year after Boswell and Johnson
made their voyage of discovery to the West. He interested
himself in geology but for some strange reason he never, in his
lifetime, reaped the rewards to which he felt his years of travel
and study in the Highlands and Islands entitled him. He was an
outspoken man. Referring to his four-volume work *The
Highlands and Western Isles of Scotland*, published in 1824, the
Dictionary of National Biography says: 'Some pungent remarks in
the first and fourth of these works on the procrastination,
slovenly habits and other defects of the sea-coast Celts excited
vehement indignation.' At least one fellow-Scot lunged into
print to attack the mildly misanthropic MacCulloch. But it was
Mackinnon of Corry who devised a crude and fundamental
comment on MacCulloch's *magnum opus*. He ordered a large
number of chamber pots as gifts for his friends – inside each one
was a portrait of MacCulloch.

Despite his faults MacCulloch was a careful and enthusiastic geologist and he was the first man ever to provide a literate
description of Loch Coruisk. This account was written in the
form of a letter to his lifelong friend Walter Scott:

So suddenly and unexpectedly does this strange scene
break on the view, so unlike it is to the sea bay without, so

dissimilar to all other scenery, and so little to be foreseen in a narrow insulated spot like Sky, that I felt as if transported by some magician into the enchanted wilds of an Arabian tale, carried to the habitations of Genii among the mysterious recesses of Caucasus. I could almost have imagined that it had suggested the idea of the happy valley in Rasselas; but in Johnson's day, even its existence was not suspected.

It is a rugged walk round this valley. The bottom is itself a mixture of heath and bog, with huge insulated rocks, which, in any other place, might be thought hills. A thousand streams, incessantly rushing down the mountains, traverse it in all directions to discharge themselves into the lake; and, at every step, some enormous fragment tumbled down from the precipice, obstructs the way; while many are poised in such a manner on the very edges of the precipitous rocks on which they have fallen, as to render it difficult to imagine how they could have rested in such places. It was a lovely day when first I found this place; which, excepting the shepherds of Strathaird, mortal foot had scarce ever trod. I was alone. The day was calm, and the water, glassy and dark, reflecting one solitary birch that, unmoved by the slightest air, hung over it from the margin of the green island on which it grew. Not a billow curled on the shore of the black lake, which like Acheron, seemed as if dead, and fixed in eternal silence. Not even a bird was to be seen – no fish dimpled the water, not a bee nor a fly was on the wing; it appeared as if all living beings had abandoned this spot to the spirit of solitude. The white torrents were foaming down the precipices; but so remote that they seemed not to move; they thundered as they fell, but they were inaudible.

At the upper extremity, where we at length rounded the lake, the scene became somewhat changed. Still the western barrier was grey, and misty and distant. Here the sun had never shone since the creation; and a thousand reflected lights, mingling with the aerial tints, gave a singular solemnity to the huge irregular masses which now rose over head, deeply cleft by the torrents, that were now at length audibly foaming down the black precipices, and which gradually diminishing till they were lost in the misty mountain summit, seemed to have their sources in the invisible regions of the clouds.

In spite of all my patriotic attempts, I suspect that the

knowledge of this place is still limited to half a dozen persons exclusive of yourself and me. But as travellers become more adventurous, and as Englishmen discover that the people of Sky have the usual proportion of legs and arms, it will become known. Then the loungers and the what thens will return angry and disappointed, dinnerless, per chance, and dry within, and wet without; grumbling at their guide, complaining that it is nothing like what they expected, with much more such matter as I have often heard and expect again to hear. Then I may answer, but not in my own words, 'Since you decry my account, why did you not write it yourself.'

The Lord Macdonald of MacCulloch's day had conceived a grandiose scheme for converting the small village of Kyleakin into a sizeable town. The old drove road off the island using the narrows of Kyle Rhea had almost been superseded by the new ferry carrying road passengers from Inverness across from Kyle of Lochalsh to Kyleakin:

The air of life given by the ferry houses, and by the boats and vessels perpetually navigating this strait, adds much to the natural beauty of the scenery; which is also further enhanced by the ruins of Kyle Haken, or Moil Castle, as it is sometimes called.

The town of Kyle Haken, though but just founded, and therefore containing but the mere germs of Lord Macdonald's intention, is, notwithstanding, a very interesting object here; its crowded and commodious anchorage, compensating, in life and bustle, for the defects of the city itself. After solitary days or weeks spent in the wild and deserted harbours of these seas, the sights of this place is like a return to life and civilisation. The situation is beautiful as well as commodious; for the buildings at least; since they have abundance of room, on an extended gravelly and dry beach: nor is it less so for the shipping which can lie close in shore, in excellent holding ground, and with perfect security against all weather and winds. The design also appears convenient and good judging from the drawings; and being in the form of a single crescent, it is picturesque and neat. The policy is another question. If an agricultural town were not, in itself, an useless, as well as an impolitic contrivance, Kyle Haken is, at any rate, unfit for one, because it has not access to a sufficient tract of good land. It is impossible to discover any use for it as a town simply. Of the usual business of towns, it can have none; because there is no demand. It is not a very good fishing station; far from it; and if it were, there can be no fishing, on the present system, to furnish such a town with sufficient employment; while the houses or feus, are far too expensive for the population of this country; or any population that it is ever likely to possess. If it be meant like Tobermory, to combine fishing with agriculture, bad fishing with bad agriculture, its fate will be that of Tobermory, and of all similar projects. It then becomes what, virtually, such towns must generally be in the Highlands; a congregation of crofters living by agriculture and fishing united, and not likely to be more prosperous because they are forced into a village; nor more likely to pay the landlord a high rent, when it is all which they can do to pay any rent at all, even when they build their own houses at no expense, either to their landlords or to themselves. But these are tender points. Where good is intended, it is painful to be obliged to think that it is not likely to be attained.

Black waves, bare crags
Walter Scott

Walter Scott paid two visits to the Hebrides. He was there in 1810 and again in 1814. *The Lady of the Lake*, which sold 20,000 copies within a few months of publication, had secured Scott's reputation and, casting around for another best-selling subject, he made up his mind to penetrate further into the Highlands. On his first visit he didn't keep a journal, but four years later, when he set off on a cruise in the Lighthouse Yacht, he did. The voyage, which lasted five weeks, took Scott right round the north of Scotland. One of the islands he visited was Skye.

The impressions he gathered here and elsewhere in the Hebrides provided a rich background for *The Lord of the Isles*. The poem was not a failure, but it was never a success. The *Quarterly Review* put it very tactfully: 'Although *The Lord of the Isles* is not likely to add very much to the reputation of Mr. Scott, yet this must be imputed rather to the greatness of his previous reputation, than to the absolute inferiority of the poem itself.' It can still be bought in a small tartan-bound pocket edition, more as a souvenir of Skye than a poem to be read and enjoyed. Scott and his party set sail from Harris at five in the evening. There was a splendid sunset and they sat up until ten at night admiring the scenery. When they awoke in the morning their yacht was anchored in Loch Dunvegan.

23rd August 1814. I had sent a card to the Laird of Macleod in the morning, who came off before we were dressed, and carried us to his castle to breakfast.

The whole castle occupies a precipitous mass of rock over-hanging the lake, divided by two or three islands in that place, which forms a snug little harbour under the walls. There is a court-yard looking out upon the sea, protected by a battery, at least a succession of embrasures, for only two guns are pointed, and these unfit for service. The ancient entrance rose up a flight of steps cut in the rock, and passed into this court-yard through a portal, but this is now demolished. You land under the castle, and walking round, find yourself in front of it. This was originally inaccessible, for a brook coming down on the one side, a chasm of the rocks on the other, and a ditch in front, made it impervious. But the late Macleod built a bridge over the stream, and the present laird is executing an entrance suitable to the character of this remarkable fortalice, by making a portal between two advanced towers and an outer court, from which he proposes to throw a drawbridge over to the high rock in front of the castle. This, if well executed, cannot fail to have a good and characteristic effect. We were most kindly and hospitably received by the chieftain, his lady, and his sister; the two last are pretty and accomplished young women, a sort of person whom we have not seen for some time; and I was quite as much pleased with renewing my acquaintance with them as with the sight of a good field of barley just cut (the first harvest we have seen), not to mention an extensive young plantation and some middle-aged trees, though all had been strangers to mine eyes since I left Leith. In the garden – or rather the orchard which was formerly the garden – is a pretty cascade, divided into two branches, and called Rorie More's Nurse, because he loved to be lulled to sleep by the sound of it. The day was rainy, or at least inconstant, so we could not walk far from the castle.

24th August 1814. This morning resist with difficulty MacLeod's kind and pressing entreaty to send round the ship, and go to the cave at Airds by land; but our party is too large to be accommodated without inconvenience and divisions are always awkward. Walk and see MacLeod's farm. The plantations seem to thrive admirably, although I think he hazards planting his trees greatly too tall. MacLeod is a spirited and judicious improver, and if he does not hurry too fast, cannot fail to be of service to his people. He seems to think and act much as a chief, without the fanfaronade of the character. See a female school patronised by Mrs. M. There are about twenty girls, who learn reading, writing, and spinning; and being compelled to observe habits of cleanliness and neatness when at school, will probably be the means of introducing them by degrees at home. The roads around the castle are, generally speaking, very good; some are old, some made under the operation of the late act. Macleod says almost all the contractors for these last roads have failed, being tightly looked after by Government, which I confess I think very right. If Government is to give relief where a disadvantageous contract has been engaged in, it is plain it cannot be refused in similar instances, so that all calculations of expenses in such operations are at an end. The day being delightfully fair and warm, we walk up to the Church of Kilmore. In a cottage, at no great distance, we heard the women singing as they waulked the cloth, by rubbing it with their hands and feet, and screaming all the while in a sort of chorus. At a distance, the sound was wild and sweet enough, but rather discordant when you approach too near the performers.

Return to the castle, take our luncheon, and go aboard at three – Macleod accompanying us in proper style with his piper. We take leave of the castle, where we have been so kindly entertained with a salute of seven guns. The chief returns ashore, with his piper playing 'The Macleod's Gathering', heard to advantage along the calm and placid loch, and dying as it retreated from us.

The towers of Dunvegan, with the banner which floated over them in honour of their guests, now showed to great advantage. On the right were a succession of three remarkable hills, with round flat tops, popularly called Macleod's Dining-

Tables. Far behind these, in the interior of the island, arise
the much higher and more romantic mountains, called
Quillen, or Cuillin, a name which they have been said to owe
to no less a person that Cuthullin, or Cuchillin, celebrated by
Ossian.

The party left the hospitality of Dunvegan on 25 August
and sailed round to Loch Scavaig, in order to visit Coruisk, a
description of which Scott had already received from the
geologist John MacCulloch. They landed and went ashore.

We found ourselves in a most extraordinary scene: we were
surrounded by hills of the boldest and most precipitous character, and on the margin of a lake which seemed to have
sustained the constant ravages of torrents from those rude
neighbours. The shores consisted of huge layers of naked
granite, here and there intermixed with bogs, and heaps of
gravel and sand marking the course of torrents. Vegetation
there was little or none, and the mountains rose so perpendic-
ularly from the water's edge, that Borrowdale is a jest to them.
We proceeded about one mile and a half up this deep, dark,
and solitary lake, which is about two miles long, half a mile
broad, and, as we learned, of extreme depth. The vapour
which enveloped the mountain ridges obliged us by assuming
a thousand shapes, varying its veil in all sorts of forms, but
sometimes clearing off altogether. It is true, it made us pay
the penalty by some heavy and downright showers, from the
frequency of which, a Highland boy, whom we brought from
the farm, told us the lake was popularly called the Water
Kettle. The proper name is Loch Corriskin, from the deep
corrie or hollow in the mountains of Cuillin, which affords
the basin for this wonderful sheet of water. It is an exquisite
savage scene, as Loch Katrine is as a scene of stern beauty.
After having penetrated so far as distinctly to observe the
termination of the lake, under an immense mountain which
rises abruptly from the head of the waters, we returned, and
often stopped to admire the ravages which storms must have
made in these recesses when all human witnesses were driven
to places of more shelter and security. Stones, or rather large
massive fragments of rock of a composite kind, perfectly
different from the granite barriers of the lake, lay upon the

rocky beach in the strangest and most precarious situations, as, if abandoned by the torrents which had borne them down from above; some lay loose and tottering upon the ledges of the natural rock, with so little security that the slightest push moved them, though their weight exceeded many tons. The opposite side of the lake seemed quite pathless, as a huge mountain, one of the detached ridges of the Quillen, sinks in a profound and almost perpendicular precipice down to the water. On the left-hand side, which we traversed, rose a higher and equally inaccessible mountain, the top of which seemed to contain the crater of an exhausted volcano. I never saw a spot on which there was less appearance of vegetation of any kind; the eye rested on nothing but brown and naked crags, and the rocks on which we walked by the side of the loch were as bare as the pavements of Cheapside. There are one or two spots of islets in the loch which seem to bear juniper, or some such low bushy shrub.

Scott and his friend returned on board the yacht and after visiting Mr. Macallister's famous cave stood off for Eigg. That was the last Scott ever saw of Skye but that visit on 24 August to Coruisk made a profound impression, one which provided the following lines in *The Lord of the Isles*.

Rarely human eye has known
A scene so stern as that dread lake,
With its dark ledge of barren stone
Seems that primeval earthquake's sway
Hath rent a strange and shatter'd way
Through the rude bosom of the hill,
And that each naked precipice,
Sable ravine, and dark abyss,
Tells of the outrage still,
The wildest glen, but this, can show
Some touch of Nature's genial glow;
On high Benmore green mosses grow,
And heath-bells bud in deep Glencroe,
And copse on Cruchan-Ben;
But here – above, around, below,
On mountain or in glen,
Nor tree, nor shrub, nor plant, nor flower,

Nor aught of vegetative power,
The weary eye may ken.
For all is rocks at random thrown,
Black waves, bare crags, and banks of stone,
As if were here denied
The summer sun, the spring's sweet dew,
That clothe with many a varied hue
The bleakest mountain-side.

The ruinous system of rack-rent
Robert Southey

It is surprising that none of the English Romantic poets ever ventured to the Hebrides – Coruisk would certainly have afforded them the ultimate in natural sublimity. Perhaps being a Lake poet is not the same thing as being a Loch poet. Robert Southey, whose reputation has declined more rapidly than Coleridge's or Wordsworth's, did, however, see Skye when in the autumn of 1819 he undertook a tour of Scotland in company with the great engineer Thomas Telford. This was the same year that his contemporary Byron started to write *Don Juan* with its offhand dismissal of all that the Wordsworthians represented:

Thou shalt believe in Milton, Dryden, Pope,
Thou shalt not set up Wordsworth, Coleridge, Southey;
Because the first is crazed beyond all hope,
The second drunk, the third so quaint and mouthy.

Mouthy mabye, but Southey was now at the height of his career, having just become Poet Laureate: Telford had recently been installed as president of the Instution of Civil Engineers. The couple spent nearly three months on their Highland tour and eventually arrived at their most western limit on the shores of Loch Carron:

Loch Carron is a beautiful inlet. A tongue of land runs out on the north side and forms a natural pier, protecting the bay where Jean-Town stands. The pier at Strome Ferry is sheltered by a smaller neck of land. The loch is enclosed by mountains on three sides, and on the fourth the mountains in the Isle of Skye are seen at no great distance. Ours was the first carriage which had ever reached the ferry, and the road on the southern shore, up which we walked, had never yet been travelled by one. We went up the hill so as to command the descent along which it inclines towards Loch-Alsh – a district, not a Lake – and communicates by Kyle Haken Ferry with the Isle of Skye, where an hundred miles of road have been made by the Commisioners. To hear of such roads in such a country, and to find them in the wild western Highlands is so surprising, everything else being in such a rude state, that their utility, or at least their necessity, might be doubted if half the expence were not raised by voluntary taxation. The Lairds indeed have one inducement for entering largely into the scheme, which explains what might otherwise seem on their part, a lavish expenditure on such improvements. Large arrears of rent were due to them, which there was no chance of their ever recovering in money; but the tenants were willing to work for them, to discharge the debt. When therefore the estimated expence of a road was about £5,000, they received from the Government £2,500, and the tenants did for them £5,000 worth of labour; thus they were clear gainers by all which they received, and by the improved value of the estates.

Some years ago a villainous adventurer by name Brown, made his appearance in these parts, professing that he had a 'capability' of improving estates – not in their appearance but in their rents. His simple secret consisted in looking at the rent-roll, and doubling, trebling, or even quadrupling the rent, according to the supposed capability of the tenant, without regard to any local circumstances, or any priciple of common justice. Some Lairds allowed this fellow to make the experiment upon their estates, and it succeeded at first, owing to accidental causes. The war occasioned a great demand for black cattle; and the importation of barilla being prevented by the state of affairs in Spain, kelp rose to such a price that it enabled the tenants to pay the increased rent without difficulty. This brought Brown into fashion, and whole districts where brought under the ruinous system of rack-rent in some instances even to a sixfold augmentation. The war at length was brought to an end; cattle and kelp fell to their former price; the tenants were unable to pay; and some of the Lairds were at once unthinking and unfeeling enough to go thro' with their extortionate system, and seize their goods by distress. They suffered doubly by this: first by the entire ruin which was brought upon their poor tenants; secondly by the direct consequences of the process. For according to the forms of their law, they took the cattle at a valuation, in part payment of arrears; the valuation was made at the then market price, and before the cattle could be driven to market, there was a very considerable fall; so that both causes operating, those grasping and griping Landlords have gone far towards ruining themselves.

There is good marble in the Isle of Skye. The Laird upon whose estate it was discovered was persuaded that the quarries might be made up of great immediate value; he determined therefore to work them upon a great scale and to expend £20,000 in constructing piers, laying rail-roads and other works. But Mr. Telford advised him to proceed cautiously, select a few specimens, and those good ones, send them in carts to the shore to be shipt, and not involve himself in any serious expence till the marble had obtained reputation in London. The Laird followed this judicious advice in part, and the ruinous cost in which he would have engaged was spared; but he sent off a shipload of seventy tons without selection, and of course it was disregarded, and perhaps undervalued.

Wandering in an unknown country
Necker De Saussure

Shortly after Walter Scott's visit Skye received its first Swiss tourist. He was L. A. Necker De Saussure, Honorary Professor of Mineralogy and Geology in the Academy of Geneva. Although he came mainly on a scientific visit he found time to write a travel book, which was published in 1822 and contained observations on 'the manners and customs of the Highlanders'. From Benbecula in the Outer Hebrides, Necker De Saussure sailed across the Minch to Talisker Bay, arriving there on 23 September, probably in the year 1820.

The isle to which we were going is classic ground; the name of each rock, mountain and lake, being connected with some fact related in the traditions of which the poems of Ossian form a part. On our arrival at a lone house in Talisker, we sent our guide before us to solicit hospitality for strangers overtaken by the night, and wandering in an unknown country. We anticipated the reply: in fact we were invited in the politest manner into a small neat parlour, where three aged persons, and a young man, were seated round a good fire. They hastened to offer us seats; they next brought in tea, wine, and liquors; and, in truth, supplied us with everything necessary for our comfort.

At supper, we had the pleasure of hearing some very interesting conversation; they gave us all the information requisite for our journey, entertained us with an account of the Isle of Skye, the antiquities and natural curiosities contained in this wild and poetic country, and the traditionary poems recited by the inhabitants; they likewise entertained us with some amusing anecdotes respecting Dr. Johnson, whom they very well recollected to have seen at the time of his Travels in the Hebrides. The anecdotes which we heard, fully justified the reputation for rusticity which that great lexicographer had acquired. Thus we separated for the night, without their knowing who were the strangers whom they lodged under their roof, and without our having once thought of telling them.

We found excellent beds, and after blessing our generous hosts, we retired to rest.

September 24th At breakfast this morning, we hastened to repair our omission of the preceeding evening, and to introduce ourselves to our hosts. The moment I said that I came from Switzerland, Mrs. Macleod (our hostess) testified the joy which she felt on seeing a native of that country. 'For', said she to me, 'I lived for a long time in Holland with my husband, who was colonel of a Scottish regiment in the service of that Republic; and I knew many officers of Swiss regiments, with whom those of our regiment were always so intimate that they used to call each other brother mountaineers.'

September 26th Mr. Macleod of Talisker, being informed of our arrival in the Isle of Skye, sent horses and a guide to conduct us to his house, and after two hours route on wretched roads, we arrived at Talisker House, where we were received, (thanks to Mr Maclean of Coll, and thanks, above all, to Scottish hospitality,) as ancient friends. This fine house, surrounded with trees, is situated at the bottom of a little valley, which opens on the south upon the sea; the environs are fertile, and well cultivated; a small rivulet, which takes its rise in the rocky and basaltic hills in the neighbourhood, runs, winding around the house, after forming a beautiful cascade, at the foot of which the road passes. During dinner, the piper played, in the hall, on the bag-pipes, the Pibrochs, or marches of the tribe of Macleods; and these romantic airs, for a long time resounded in the vaults of the castle of Talisker.

After taking leave of the amiable family of Talisker, and my fellow-travellers, I proceeded as far as the *Cullen Mountains,* a name which is derived from the King Cuchullin, sung by Ossian, who reigned over the inhabitants of the Isle of Sky. I amused myself in the association of these sites with the ancient heroes who had once inhabited them, and of the bards who sung their exploits. I figured to myself, these inspired poets, walking through the obscure and deep valleys, their imagination revelling amidst these imposing scenes, and thinking they saw in the mists and light clouds which fly around these high mountains, the departed spirits of their forefathers and heroes, still wandering near the places where they had long dwelt. It was an interesting task for me, to trace, in a country which presents such striking and sublime traits, the germs of poetry so strongly characteristic of its finest features.

Many of the aborigines have been expelled
Allan Fullarton and Charles Baird

The seasons of 1835 and 1836 were cold, wet and stormy in the Highlands and Islands. The crops failed and a simultaneous failure took place in the fishing industry. So great was the distress that a nationwide appeal was launched which eventually produced £50,000. The Chairman and the Secretary of the Glasgow Committee which distributed the fund were Allan Fullarton and Charles Baird. Not unnaturally, their charitable work brought them in a vast amount of information about the area and this they published in 1838. Like the majority of thinking men at the time they were convinced that the only solution to the acute problems of poverty in Skye and the other islands was – emigration:

Unquestionably nature designed Skye for a grazing country; and on this account, as well as because the effect of a change in the Corn Laws would inevitably be to throw the inferior soils out of cultivation, after great expense had been incurred in improving them, the proprietors of Skye have wisely devoted their chief attention to the improvement of their stocks of black cattle and sheep, and to the enlargement of their farms, of which they have latterly, in many places, given leases. Here, as elswhere, these operations have, in the first instance, been attended with very distressing effects. Many of the aborigines have been expelled from the possessions which they and their fore-fathers have held for successive ages, and turned adrift to struggle for subsistence, for themselves and their familes, in a world to which almost all of them were utter strangers. While we admit the necessity of such changes in the Highlands as shall occasion the expatriation of many of her best sons, we deprecate the least precipitancy or harshness in the completion of a measure so lamentable in its immediate consequences, and one, the necessity for which is as much to be attributed to the carelessness and folly of the landlords, as to the ignorance and stubbornness of their tenants and vassals.

The present population of Skye is 24,485, being an increase since 1798, of 10,015 – a rate of increase, which if continued, as it cannot fail to be, unless the crofting and cotter system be destroyed, will, at no very distant period of time, land the country in irretrievable ruin – in utter and incurable pauperism. As it is, the population, with the limited means they enjoy, cannot well exist. Without any kind of manufacture, that of kelp being nearly annihilated – without fisheries, which in Skye were never much in repute, and are now hardly worth following – and without even the means of transporting themselves to any country more suitable to their circumstances, the great mass of the people is reduced to such a state of wretchedness as could not fail, in almost any other country, to produce acts of lawless violence. Yet these poor people remain quiet and peaceable. Wishing and praying for, rather than expecting, better times. Comparing the number of schools and scholars in Skye with those in some of the other Islands, it appears evident that neither the landlords, nor the other resident gentry – no, nor even the clergy – have made any very peculiar or energetic

effort to forward the education or improvement of the people –
although it is upon this alone that the prosperity and ultimate
happiness must depend on the country and of its inhabitants of
every description. As an exemplification of the ignorance which
has, till within these few years, been suffered, without obstruc-
tion of any kind, to prevail in Skye, we mention that, in the
year 1831, the General Assembly's Report states no less than
10,478 – nearly a half of the whole population – as being
unable to read in any language. We trust their number has
greatly diminished, although we have good reason to fear the
very reverse.

The asylum of dreariness
Lord Cockburn

On 30 August 1841 Henry Thomas, Lord Cockburn, a man of
great wit and a Lord Commissioner of Judiciary set off on an
Autumn circuit of the north. The 62-year-old judge was accompanied by his wife, his daughter Jane, his son Frank and his
niece. They reached Corry, near Broadford, on the evening of
Sunday, 5 September. On the following day the Lord confided
these thoughts to his journal:

The cold cheerless rocks, the treeless desolation, the
perpetual tendency of the clouds to rest, as if it was their home,
on the tops of the hills, the great corries into which the weather
has hollowed one side of most of the mountains, the utter want
of natural verdure, the grey, benty colour of the always drenched
pasture, the absence of villages and of all human appearance –
these things mark Skye as the asylum of dreariness.

Corry, Sunday
We Saxons went into the English part of the service, which
closed with Gaelic prayers and psalmody. I never saw a more
respectable country congregation. There were about 350
present, all except Corry's party in the humblest rank. The men
had almost all strong, blue fishermen's jackets. The women,
with only one exception, so far as I could observe, had all on red
tartan cloaks or shawls and clean mutches of snowy whiteness,
with borders of many piles. I can't comprehend how such purity
can come out of such smoky hovels. There was not one child or

very young person. This was perhaps the reason that there was no beauty. The reverse. Some of them had walked eight miles, and some sailed three.

While at Broadford the party made an expedition to Coruisk. They left Mackinnon's house at seven in the morning and drove for miles until the road stopped at the sea. Awaiting them was a boat with a crew of three men and a boy which had been carted overland from Broadford.

So we went on, till, almost palpitating with anxiety, we were landed on a rock at the head of the loch (Scavaig). I found an oar lying in some heather, and on looking round saw a boat seemingly deserted, on the beach, and eight barrels at a little distance. These, I learned, were the still ungathered store of a poor fisherman, who was drowned three days before, in trying to cross the stream which flows out of Coruisk, when it was in flood.

I bade the boatmen remain with the boat to rest and refresh themselves, and went forward and in a few minutes stood on the side of Coruisk. I was foolish enough, considering what I knew, to feel a moment's disappointment at the smallness of the cupful of water. But it was only for a moment. And then I stood entranced by the scene before me. The sunless darkness of the water, the precipitousness of the two sides and of the upper end, the hardness of their material, consisting almost entirely of large plates of smooth rock, from which all turf, if there ever was any, has been torn with the torrents; the dark pinnacles, the silence, deepened rather than diminished by the sound of a solitary stream – above all, the solitude, – inspired a feeling of awe rather than solemnity. No mind can resist this impression. Every prospect and every object is excluded, except what are held within that short and narrow valley; and within that there is nothing except the little loch, towered over by the high and grisly forms of these storm-defying and man-despising mountains.

After lingering over the solitude for above an hour, it being now three and another four hours rowing in front of us, I withdrew from a scene which far less than an hour was sufficient to comprehend, and which once comprehended, there was no danger of forgetting.

As our bark receded from the shore, the Cuillins stood out
again, and the increased brilliancy of the sun cast a thousand
lights over Scavaig, and over all its associated islands and
promontories, and bays.

As we sailed close by the shore of Scavaig and near the
point of Slapin, the rowers stopped to point out five huts. It
was there they said, that the drowned fisherman had lived, and
where his remains were lying, preparatory to their being
interred, in a burying-place (not a churchyard) about two
miles off next day . . .

We passed close by the Spar Cave, which I did not know we
were to do, and so yielded to the rowers, who seemed to think it
ominous that any stranger should pass their wonder without
entering. Not thinking of this as a part of the day's work, we had
brought no lights, and had to send for candles to a house not far
off, but which I never saw. We wasted an hour on this piece of
nonsense. It is not worth describing; even MacCulloch, who
saw it when its stalactites were unbroken, thought it insignifi-
cant. Now that *not one* remains, the whole charm, which was in
its sparriness, is gone, for in its mere dimensions it is nothing.
There is no dirt in it, I mean no mud, but it is very wet, a pool
of about thirty feet has to be crossed on a Celt's back, a steep
and slippery inclined plane of about 40 feet has to be scrambled
up on one side, and down on another, a feat requiring skill even
from the guide; and after all this splashing and straining, and
wetting of hands and feet, there is nothing whatever, absolutely
nothing to be seen. The only way to deal with it would be to
shut it up for a century or two, and to let the dropping recon-
struct the white figures, which alone can ever give it interest. At
present the only reward for going in consists in getting out.

How difficult travel was in those days, even for a judge going
about his business, can be gathered from Cockburn's testy stric-
tures on the Kylerhea ferry:

This ferry, though boasted as the best in Skye, is detestable
at least for carriages, and is ill-conducted as possible. But what
can a ferry be for carriages, where ours is only the third that
has passed this year, and the object of the landlord of the
ferry-house on each side is to detain instead of advancing the
passenger, and where, when at last it is seen that they can

carry it on no longer, the only machinery for putting the vehicle on board consists of dozens of lazy and very awkward Highlanders, all scolding in Erse, who almost lift it and throw it into the groaning boat.

The Free Church yacht Betsey
Hugh Miller

Hugh Miller describes in his *Cruise of the* Betsey *or a Summer Holiday in the Hebrides* how clad 'in a gray maud over a coat of rough russet, with waistcoat and trowsers of plaid' and looking rather like a shepherd, he took his place on the mail-gig at Loch Carron for the long drive to the East Coast of Scotland. One of his fellow passengers was a minister of the Established Church, but it wasn't until they reached the inn at Garve that Miller found occasion to reveal his identity. He tells it this way: 'The minister stopped short in the middle of a discussion. "We are not on equal terms," he said, "You know who I am, and I don't know you: we did not start fair at the beginning, but let us start fair now." "Ah, we have agreed hitherto," I replied, "but I know not how we are to agree when you know who I am: are you sure you will not be frightened?" "Frightened! said the minister sturdily, "no, by no man." "Then I am the editor of the *Witness*." There was a momentary pause.' And well there might have been. The time was the 'forties when the Disruption was at its height. Hugh Miller was well known for his opposition to the Established Church and his editorship of the Free Church paper, and Christians in Scotland carried their religious differences more aggressively than they do now.

But Miller was also an amateur naturalist and geologist. He was on his way home after a holiday in the Hebrides with an old friend the Rev. Mr. Swanson, minister of the Small Isles. Mr. Swanson had been thrown out of his Church and had taken up floating quarters on the small yacht *Betsey,* 'beyond the reach of man's intolerance'. Miller writes at length of the geological formations of Skye and in his extract we find him with his friend the Rev. Swanson in Broadford Bay:

Friday made amends for the rains and fogs of its disagreeable predecessor: the morning rose bright and beautiful, with just wind enough to fill, and barely fill, the sail, hoisted high, with miser economy, that not a breath might be lost; and, weighing anchor, and shaking out all our canvass, we bore down on Pabba to explore. This island, so soft in outline and colour, is formidably fenced round by dangerous reefs; and leaving the *Betsey* in charge of John Stewart and his companion, to dodge on in the offing, I set out with the minister in our little boat, and landed on the north-eastern side of the island, beside a trap-dyke that served us as a pier. He would be a happy geologist who, with a few thousands to spare, could call Pabba his own. It contains less than a square mile of surface; and a walk of a little more than three miles and a half along the line where the waves break at high water brings the traveller back to his starting point; and yet, though thus limited in area, the petrifications of its shores might of themselves fill a museum. They rise by thousands and tens of thousands on the exposed planes of its sea-washed strata, standing out in bold relief, like sculpturings on ancient tombstones, at once mummies and monuments,– the dead, and the carved memorials of the dead. Every rock is a tablet of hieroglyphics, with an ascertained alphabet; every rolled pebble casket, with old pictorial records locked up within. Trap-dykes, beyond comparison finer than those of the Water of Leith, which first suggested to Hutton his theory, stand up like fences over the sedimentary strata, or run like moles far into the sea. The entire island, too, so green, rich, and level, is itself a specimen illustrative of the effect of geologic formation on scenery.

The tide began to flow, and we had to quit our explorations, and return to the *Betsey*. The little wind had become less, and all the canvas we could hand out enabled us to draw but a sluggish furrow. The stern of the *Betsey* 'wrought no buttons' on this occasion; but she had a good tide under her keel, and ere the dinner-hour we had passed through the narrows of Kyle Akin. The village of this name was designed by the late Lord M'Donald for a great sea-port town; but it refused to grow; and it has since become a gentleman in a small way, and does nothing. It forms, however, a handsome group of houses, pleasantly situated on a flat green tongue of land, on the Skye side, just within the opening of the Kyle; and there rises on an eminence beyond it, a fine old tower, rent open, as if by an earthquake, from top to bottom, which forms one of the most picturesque objects I have almost ever seen in a landscape. There are bold

hills all around, and rocky islands, with the ceaseless rush of
tides in front; while the cloven tower, rising high over the shore,
is seen, in threading the Kyles, whether from the south or north,
relieved dark against the sky, as the central object in the vista.

The ebb-tide set in about half an hour after sunset; and in
weighing anchor to float down the Kyle,– for we still lacked
wind to sail down it,– we brought up from below, on one of the
anchor-flukes, an immense bunch of deep-sea tangle, with huge
soft fronds and long slender stems, that had lain on the rocky
bottom, and had here and there thrown out roots along its
length of stalk, to attain itself to the rock, in the way the ivy
attaches itself to the wall. Among the intricacies of the true
roots of the bunch, if one may speak of the true roots of an
algae, I reckoned up from eighteen to twenty different forms of
animal life, – *Flustrae, Sertulariae, Serpulae, Anomiae, Modiolae,
Astarte, Annelida, Crustacea* and *Radiata.* Among the
Crustaceans I found a female crab of a reddish-brown colour,
considerably smaller than the nail of my small finger, but fully
grown apparently, for the abdominal flap was loaded with
spawn; and among the Echinoderms, a brownish-yellow sea-
urchin about the size of a pistol-bullet, furnished with comparatively large but thinly-set spines. There is a dangerous rock in
the Kyle Rhea, the Cailleach stone, on which the
Commissioners for the Northern Lighthouses have stuck a bit of
board, about the size of a pot-lid, which, as it is known to be
there, and as no one ever sees it after sunset, is really very effec-
tive, considering how little it must have cost the country, in
wrecking vessels. I saw one of its victims, the sloop of an honest
Methodist, in whose bottom the Cailleach had knocked out a
hole, repairing at Isle Ornsay; and I was told, that if I wished to
see more, I had only just to wait a little. The honest Methodist,
after looking out in vain for the bit of board, was just stepping
into the shrouds, to try whether he could not see the rock on
which the bit of board is placed, when all at once his vessel
found out both board and rock for herself. We also had anxious
looking out this evening for the bit of board; one of us thought
he saw it right a-head; and when some of the others were trying
to see it too, John Stewart succeeded in discovering it half a
pistol-shot astern. The evening was one of the loveliest. The
moon rose in a cloudy majesty over the mountains of Glenelg,

brightening as it rose, till the boiling eddies around us curled on the darker surface in pale circlets of light, and the shadow of the *Betsey* lay as sharply defined on the brown patch of calm to the larboard as if it were her portrait taken in black. Immediately at the water-edge, under a tall dark hill, there were two smoulder-ing fires, that now shot up a sudden tongue of bright flame, and now dimmed into blood-red specks, and sent thick strongly-scented trails of smoke athwart the surface of the Kyle. We could hear, in the calm, voices from beside them, apparently those of children; and I learned that they indicated the places of two kelp-furnaces,– things which have now become compara-tively rare along the coasts of the Hebrides. There was the low rush of tides all around, and the distant voices from the shore, but no other sounds; and, dim in the moonshine, we could see behind us several spectral-looking sails threading their silent way through the narrows, like twilight ghosts traversing some haunted corridor.

We succeeded in gaining the top
J.D. Forbes

Although by no means the first climber to scramble among the Cuillins, J. D. Forbes, the geologist, was the most serious and successful. When Forbes went to Skye there was no proper map of the Cuillins; the one he drew was remarkably accurate and served for a good many years. His description of the Cuillins must have daunted any potential climber thinking of packing a rucksack for the north: "Their distance from countries usually visited is the least obstacle to their examination; their tops pene-trating an almost ever stormy atmosphere, their bases bathed by a wild and ever-chafing ocean, and their sides and peaks presenting more appearance of inaccessibility than perhaps any other mountains in Britain.' Here, in his own words, is a description of how he became the first man to climb Sgurr nan Gillean. Its height, by the way, is 3,167 ft.

The ascent of Scuir-na-Gillean was deemed impossible at the time of my first visit in 1836. Talking of it with an active forester in the service of Lord MacDonald, named Duncan Macintyre, whom I engaged to guide me to Coruisk from

Sligachan, he told me that he had attempted it repeatedly without success, both by himself and also with different strangers, who had engaged him for the purpose; but he indicated a way different from those which he had tried, which he thought might be more successful. I engaged him to accompany me, and the next day (July 7) we succeeded in gaining the top; the extreme roughness of the rocks (all hypersthene) rendering the ascent safe, where, with any other formation, it might have been considerably perilous. Indeed, I have never seen a rock so adapted for clambering. At the time I erected a cairn and temporary flag, which stood, I was informed, a whole year; but having no barometer, I could not ascertain the height, which I estimated at 3,000 feet. In 1843, I was in Skye with a barometer, but had not an opportunity of revisiting the Cuchullins; but in May 1845, I ascended the lower summit, nearly adjoining, marked Bruch-na-Fray in the map, and wishing to ascertain the difference of height of Scuir-na-Gillean, I proposed to Macintyre to try to ascend it from the west side. It was no sooner proposed than attempted. It was impossible to do otherwise than descend deep into the rugged ravine of Loat-e-Corry, which separates them, which cost us a severe scramble, and then face an ascent, which from a distance appeared almost perpendicular; but aided by the quality of the rocks already mentioned, we gained the Scuir-na-Gillean from the west side, although, on reaching the top, and looking back, it appeared like a dizzy precipice. My barometrical observations were unfortunately rendered somewhat unsatisfactory by the comparison of the height of the mercury at starting and returning to our fundamental station at Sligachan Inn. There appeared to have been a great fall during the ten hours that I had been absent; and in such circumstances, interpolation for the height of the barometer at the lower station is always undertain and inconclusive. A very rigorous comparison which I have made of all the readings of the barometer before, at the time of, and after, the observations, do not allow me to attribute any probable error to the observations themselves, nor any probable injury to the barometer which seemed to have as good a vacuum after my return as before; but another check remained. My friend, Mr. Necker, foreign member of this Society, being then resident at Portree, and having a barometer similar to mine (on Bunten's construction) which he observed from time to time, and with which mine was compared some days after, and found to agree to within .012 inch, kindly allowed me to make use of his observations. Though the barometer was falling at Portree (ten mile distant) at the time, there did not appear to have been the great and sudden change which I observed. Nevertheless, fully acknowledging the difficulty, I am disposed to think that some local rarefaction, not unfrequent in climates so agitated, and in localities so mountainous as Skye, produced the fall in the barometer which I observed. But to make the best use of my opportunities, I have computed the height of the Cuchullin hills on two suppositions: first, by an interpolation of the apparent change in the height of the mercury at Sligachan; and, secondly, by direct comparison of my observation on the summit of the Scuir-na-Gillean with Mr. Necker's almost simultaneious observation at Portree. The first computation gives 3,193 feet for the height above Sligachan Inn; the second 3,115 feet above Mr. Necker's house at Portree. But the first is 30 or 40 feet above the sea-level, the latter 80 or 90: the result, therefore is nearly coincident, and it is probable that the true height of Scuirr-na-Gillean is between 3,200 and 3,220 feet. Bruch-na-Fray is probably about 40 feet lower.

The MacLeod has established a public store
Robert Somers

In October 1847 Robert Somers made a *Tour of Inquiry in the Highlands*. His articles were published in the *North British Daily Mail* and they painted a grim picture of life in the Islands.

Somers took the stage coach run thrice weekly by MacLeod of MacLeod from Dingwall to the gates of his castle at Dunvegan. The journey of 144½ miles was accomplished 'in little more than twenty hours'. Somers' tour was an important one for he was the first person to state clearly and unequivocally that there was no prospect of tenants in Skye being offered any security of tenure – what was expected of them was a decent and speedy withdrawal to some other part part of the globe:

When the croft system was introduced, it was never intended that the people should prosper on the soil. The object nearest the landlords' hearts was to clear them from the soil, and if possible to sweep them from the country. If their purses had been as capacious as their hostility to the people, they would never have stayed their hand till every man, woman, and child was shipped to a foreign shore. But the expense of emigration was too much for their slender means and the project had to be abandoned. The croft system was then introduced as a temporary expedient to facilitate the clearances, and to afford a refuge to the outcasts until an opportunity should arise of transporting them to their allotted homes in Australian or Canadian wildernesses. From that day to this the idea of emigration has never been relinquished by the Highland lairds. There is a lurking expectation in the minds of all of them that they will yet be able by the help of government public money to ship away the miserable population which swarms along their shores. In order that the favourable moment may be seized when it comes, it is necessary that the people hang loosely upon the soil. Leases would be very awkward barriers. The people must not be permitted to forget that the Highlands are not their home – that they are only pilgrims – pilgrims from the interior glens of their native country to the wilds of foreign lands and that they are merely camping for a little while on the shore till the ships come and the winds blow that are to carry than to their destined places of abode. They must keep their lamps trimmed, and be ready on an hour's warning to set out on a long journey to the other side of the world. Why attempt to ward off the evil tendency of a system which is already doomed? Why make any effort to improve the condition of a people on the march to another hemisphere, and from whom we have nothing either to hope or fear? Leave them to themselves. Let them marry, subdivide and multiply till they are ready to eat each other up in the struggle for existence. When things are at their worst they will mend. The more deplorable and hopeless the extremity to which matters come, the more cogent the reasons for wholesale expatriation, and the more urgent the necessity for government to interfere so that when the night is darkest then will come the dawn. These are the silent cogitations and the secret hankerings in the minds of the Highland lairds, which paralyse improvement, which withers up the soul of enterprise, and which undermine every humane and patriotic resolution. The chiefs do not believe in the improveability of the people, they suspect, they distrust, and throw contempt upon their own blood. They want faith – faith which is the mainspring of all success – faith in that God who has made of one blood all the nations of the earth, and who has infused into our common nature the inextinguishable elements of improvement and progression. The refusal of leases is the sign of neglect, and not of control. When a landlord wishes to improve and to bind down his tenants to a course of improvement he grants leases and give expression and effect to his principles through their conditions, Bur when a landlord is indifferent and reckless he refuses leases, and stands up for tenancy-at-will and this is the course which has found favour with the Highland lairds.

In point of subdivision of the crofts and what is commonly called over-population, the Isle of Skye is in a still worse condition than any of the districts of the mainland which I have visited. The MacLeod has established at Dunvegan a public store for retailing groceries and articles of general consumption. This practice is not uncommon in the Highlands on the part of the landed proprietors; and it is worthy of consideration how far so unusual a step is becoming or advisable. In remote Highland districts there is necessarily great difficulty in establishing good retail shops; and the want of them proves a very serious obstacle to the comfort and even the improvement of the population. In this light the introduction of shops is well worthy of the attention of a landlord, but shops established and carried on by proprietors and necessarily dealing with their own tenants and labourers bear a strong resemblance to the truck system; and we should not be surprised to find them attended with some of its evils. Complaints are made at

Dunvegan of the high prices charged at the laird's store and upon inquiry they seem to me to be considerably above the prices common in rural villages. But it does not follow that MacLeod is making inordinate gains by his shopkeeping. He requires to commit the management of his store to paid servants, whose wages must come off the first of the profits and who cannot be expected to apply the same care and economy to the business which a man usually devotes to his own concerns. A gentleman moreover of MacLeod's standing is not likely to buy his goods so cheaply in the wholesale market as a tradesman with perhaps equal command of cash, but much humbler pretensions; and I should also suppose that he will sell at equal disadvantage. Had MacLeod selected a man out of the common walks of life in whom he had confidence, and assisted him by his credit in procuring a supply of goods until he was able to stand upon his own footing, he would have done all the good which he intends, without incurring any of the evil.

Good-natured and anxious to oblige
Rev. Thomas Grierson

In the autumn of 1849, the year in which David Livingstone began his exploration of Central Africa, another Scottish Christian undertook a gentler exploration – of Skye. He was the Rev. Thomas Grierson, minister of Kirkbean on the shores of the Solway Firth. Like Livingstone, Mr. Grierson made his safari on foot. It was a short visit, only a week, but he covered a lot of ground. Like Livingstone, Mr. Grierson found the natives mildly exasperating: 'The people, generally speaking,' he complained, 'have no idea of the value of time. Many of them, unfortunately, have little to do themselves, conceive all others similarly circumstanced, and their great object seems to be to spin out every little job that occurs.' These extracts give some idea of the sense of 'foreign-ness' that visitors still felt about Skye even in the mid-nineteenth century.

The inhabitants of this island, in so far as we saw, are inoffensive and civil, not given to quarrelling nor drinking; and though there are evidently a great many of them oppressed with poverty, I do not think we met with a beggar all the time we were there; so that greediness is not one of their besetting sins. Between Stenchol and Uig we saw women spinning on the distaff while walking along the road, a pretty good proof of their being industriously disposed. The want of English on their part, and of Gaelic on ours, prevented the intercourse of speech, but they always looked good-natured, and anxious to oblige. Owing to the soil and climate, agriculture makes but little progress. The rearing of black cattle and horses is their chief dependence.

Among the rocks we observed miserable patches of potatoes and oats, some of which were not above four or five yards square; and as the potatoes were diseased and the oats would never ripen, it may readily be conceived they had bad prospects for the winter. The Highland Destitution Society has given a good deal of encouragement in road-making, and at Uig we were privileged by being admitted to a committee room, where wool was given out for stocking-making and other purposes. The entrance to this most primitive emporium of fashion was through a byre. It was full of women, young and old, who were receiving wool from a shop-keeper in Portree, and money for the stockings they had wrought. Like the Irish, the Highlanders are idolent and inactive at home, but in almost all cases are industrious and excellent workers abroad. Emigration therefore seems the only effectual remedy for the evil; and, in such an emergency, there is much to reconcile them to the prospect, provided whole families remove from the same district, and are not separated beyond seas. . . .

Next morning, the Sabbath, was very gloomy and wet; and as there happened to be no public worship in Portree. we were confined to the house till mid-day when it faired, so that we resolved to walk seven miles to be present at the Free Church sacrament at Snizort. In defiance of the heavy rain, Portree seemed emptied of its inhabitants. Every kind of vehicle was in requisition, and many were on foot. The Country towards Snizort is heathy and uninteresting; but the river there, being much swollen, and having a very rocky channel was well worth seeing. The Free Church is neat enough, but the manse is one of the largest and finest I have seen. The place of meeting on this great Occasion was an open heath, about a mile farther on than the church, and near a large fir plantation. The assemblage was immense, surrounded by numberless carts, gigs etc., and the horses either running loose, or having two legs tied together. The tent was placed with its back to the wood, nearly surrounded by the strangest looking group we ever witnessed. The number present was estimated at about 7,000; and when it is considered that many had come from Lewis, Harris, Uist and many other islands, as well as from the mainland, it may readily be conceived that this was by no means above the mark.

We regretted much being too late for the sermon by the talented Mr. Roderic M'Leod, who, I believe, is the only Free Church ordained minister in the island, and whose sway is despotic. He is much liked and respected, not only by his own people, but by the people and ministers of the Establishment. The whole of the service was in Gaelic, and it is questionable if there were one hundred who could have been edified by any other language. We heard two tables served; and, if power of lungs, and extravagant gesticulation constitute eloquence, there was no lack of it here. To do the people justice, it must be allowed they were all calm, and seemingly attentive. There was none of that agitation and screaming which were too common in such meetings a few years ago. This it seems instead of being connived at by their ministers as formerly, has of late been discouraged and suppressed, as it was bringing their religious assemblies into disrepute among the judicious and intelligent.

When we returned at night to Portree, I expressed surprise to the company in the inn that several of the elders assisting at the tables wore red and striped worsted night-caps, even the precentor wearing one of the former flaming complexion. A gentleman, particularly conversant with everything connected with the Highlands assured me that this was no mark of disrespect, but a badge of distinction; that none wore these articles but such as had great spiritual attainments, and that they wore red, striped, or blue head gear, according to their various gradations in sanctity.

Ingenuity and Iniquity
Lady MacCaskill

In 1851, Lady MacCaskill, a well-known philanthropist, spent twelve days in Skye and was overwhelmed by the tragic destitution which she saw wherever she went. Many families who had been ejected from their homes were living in tents – the sheep were as fat as the people thin. A succession of poor harvests from 1846 onwards had reduced thousands to starvation level. Many were clad only in rags and ate perhaps only once a day and then only meal and potatoes with the occasional luxury of a herring. Queen Victoria on reading Lady MacCaskill's account of conditions in the island sent a donation of £100. But in Victorian times philanthropy was often regarded as nothing more than a direct encouragement to laziness and apathy; God was believed to help only those who helped themselves. Hence the building of a woollen mill in Portree. Today in the summer months tourists flock inside to buy tweed lengths and tartan souvenirs; for Lady MacCaskill in October 1851 it was a seamy sweatshop designed for the exploitation of the destitute:

By the side of the school stands Hogg's Woollen Manufactory – a water-mill sets the machinery in motion – towards the end of one endless room, lie the skins of sheep in a heap, dirty and daubed with tar; on a bench beside them sat two strong-looking girls, (they were fed!) who with their shears cut off the tarred points of the wool which was used up for coarse purposes; at the extreme end of this long room lay in heaps, the progress of human industry, *ingenuity and* INIQUITY! – stockings, socks, gloves, shirts, comforters, and drawers – all from the sheep's back! The articles were all arranged, paired, tied and bound together, as if for the London market!

'*Beautiful* stockings,' said I, 'and *beautiful* socks! How closely knitted, how even, how warm! How good the form and ribbed toe! What a blessing this manufactory exists to benefit the starving poor! No doubt the knitters are well paid, for they knit along the road, ofttimes with their creels full of peats on their backs; these creels are large wicker baskets which reach from the back of their necks to below the middle of their backs – they are secured by rough coarse ropes across their *bare* chests. Slightly bending beneath their load, blow high or blow

low, through wind and rain, and mud and mire, bare headed
and bare legged they wend their way *and they knit as they go!!'*

This Woollen Manufactory I learnt, was built with the
remains of a fund collected for the destitute Highlanders, and
with the special aim of benefitting and employing the destitute
poor of the island! Now then, the poor knitters are paid thus:-
Two pence halfpenny for each pair of stockings, full men's
size; gloves and comforter and waistcoats and all other things
in the same proportion. Thus a good knitter may earn with
diligence and industry something less than a penny a day!
Ample remuneration! – great profits – but in what quarter?
Into whose pockets does the money flow?

More cruel than banishment
Dundas Warder

If conditions in Skye were dire they were relatively comfortable
compared with the reception which awaited emigrants in Canada.
Little was heard of what happened to the thousands of men,
women and children who were forcibly ejected from their homes
in Skye and marshalled on to the emigrant transports. This report
from an Ontario paper, the *Dundas Warder*, dated October 1851,
reveals not only the great burden which was placed on the receiving community, but the often helpless position in which a family
might find themselves on arriving in what they had been led to
believe was a land of promise and opportunity:

We have been pained beyond measure for some time past
to witness in our streets so many unfortunate Highland
emigrants, apparently destitute of any means of subsistence,
and many of them sick from want and other attendant causes.
It was pitiful the other day to view a funeral of one of these
wretched people. It was, indeed, a sad procession. The coffin
was constructed of the rudest material; a few rough boards
nailed together was all that could be afforded to convey to its
last resting-place the body of the homeless immigrant.
Children followed in the mournful rain; perchance they
followed a brother's bier, one with whom they had sported and
played for many a healthful day among their native glens.
Theirs were looks of indescribable sorrow. They were in rags;
their mourning weeds were the shapeless fragments of what

had once been clothes. There was a mother, too, among the mourners, one who had tended the departed with anxious care in infancy, and had doubtless looked forward to a happier future in this land of plenty. The anguish of her countenance told too plainly these hopes were blasted and she was about to bury them in the grave of her child.

There will be many to sound the fulsome noise of flattery in the ear of the generous landlord, who had spent so much to assist the emigration of his poor tenants. They will give him the misnomer of a *benefactor*, and for what? Because he has rid his estates of the encumbrance of a pauper population. Emigrants of the poor class who arrive here from the Western Highlands of Scotland are often so situated that their emigration is more cruel than banishment. Their last shilling is spent probably before they reach the upper province – they are reduced to the necessity of begging. But again, the case of those emigrants of whom we speak is rendered more deplorable from their ignorance of the English tongue. Of the hundreds of Highlanders in and around Dundas at present, perhaps not half-a-dozen understand anything but Gaelic.

In looking at these matters, we are impressed with the conviction that, so far from emigration being a panacea for Highland destitution, it is fraught with disasters of no ordinary magnitude to the emigrant whose previous habits, under the most favourable circumstance, render him unable to take advantage of the industry of Canada, even when brought hither free of expense. We may assist these poor creatures for a time, but charity will scarcely bide the hungry cravings of so many for a very long period. Winter is approaching, and then – but we leave this painful subject for the present.

The lamentation became loud and long
Sir Archibald Geikie

Sir Archibald Geikie was one of the most eminent geologists that Scotland has produced, and it has produced a great many. He became Professor of Geology at Edinburgh and eventually Director-General of the Geological Survey of the United Kingdom. He wrote many books on geology but this extract is from a book published in 1904, *Scottish Reminiscences*. Geikie spent many of his holidays in Skye, staying with John Mackinnon, minister of Strath. In the summer of 1852, Geikie then in his late twenties, was living with the Mackinnons in the manse at Kilbride when he saw at first hand the work of Lord Macdonald's notorious factor, Ballingall:

One of the most vivid recollections which I retain of Kilbride is that of the eviction or clearance of the crofts of Suishnish. The corner of Strath between the two sea-inlets of Loch Slapin and Loch Eishort had been for ages occupied by a community that cultivated the lower ground where their huts formed a kind of scattered village. The land belonged to the wide domain of Lord Macdonald, whose affairs were in such a state that he had to place himself in the hands of trustees. These men had little local knowledge of the estate, and though they doubtless administered it to the best of their ability, their main object was to make as much money as possible out of the rents, so as on the one hand, to satisfy the creditors, and on the other, to hasten the time when the proprietor might be able to resume possession. The interests of the crofters formed a very secondary consideration. With these aims, the trustees determined to clear out the whole population of Suishnish and convert the ground into one large sheep-farm, to be placed in the hands of a responsible grazier, if possible, from the south country.

I had heard some rumours of these intentions, but did not realize that they were in process of being carried into effect, until one afternoon, as I was returning from my ramble, a strange wailing sound reached my ears at intervals on the breeze from the west. On gaining the top of one of the hills on the south side of the valley, I could see a long and motley procession winding along the road that led north from Suishnish. It halted at the point of the road opposite Kilbride and there the lamentation became loud and long. As I drew nearer I could see that the minister with his wife and daughters had come out to meet the people and bid them farewell. It was a miscellaneous gathering of at least three generations of crofters. There were old men and women, too feeble to walk, who were placed in carts; the younger members of the community on foot were carrying their bundles of clothes and household effects, while the children, with looks of alarm,

277

walked alongside. There was a pause in the notes of woe as the last words were exchanged with the family of Kilbride.

Everyone was in tears; each wished to clasp the hands that had so often befriended them, and it seemed as if they could not tear themselves away. When they set forth once more, a cry of grief went up to heaven, the long plaintive wail, like a funeral *coronach*, was resumed, and after the last of the emigrants had disappeared behind the hill, the sound seemed to re-echo through the whole wide valley of Strath in one prolonged note of desolation. The people were on their way to be shipped to Canada. I have often wandered since then over the solitary ground of Suishnish. Not a soul is to be seen there now, but the greener patches of field and the crumbling walls mark where an active and happy community once lived.

Many-tongued with foaming cataracts
Charles Weld

Charles Richard Weld was not only a writer of guide books but also a member of the Alpine Club. He was a pioneer climber on the Cuillins and did a great deal to spread the news that here in the far north-west was climbing well worth attention. Weld made the ascent of Sgurr na Strith, the Peak of Conflict, fourteen years before Sheriff Nicolson climbed Sgurr Alasdair. It was in July 1859 when London lay sweltering in a heat-wave that Weld was invited by five 'genial companions' to join them in a fishing and shooting expedition in the wild Highlands. Packing a Gladstone bag and sending on his heavy baggage by sea, he was soon hurtling to Peebles by fast steam train. Those were the days when gentlemen of means could set off on prolonged holidays without a second thought. Weld's *Two Months in the Highlands, Orcadia, and Skye* was published in 1860 and although he may have been enthusiastic about the Cuillins he was depressed by the lack of comfort that Skye afforded: 'It would be well for the tourist in Skye,' wrote Weld, 'if Lord Macdonald were as wealthy as the Duke of Sutherland. In this case his Lordship would perhaps provide good inns for visitors to his romantic island. Now, with the exception of those at Portree and Broadford, all the other inns in Skye are sorry taverns, where you must be prepared to rough it in bed and board.'

After three days of appalling weather in Sligachan there was a promise of a fine day:

... Accordingly, after a hurried breakfast, I mounted a pony, and accompanied by a guide started for Camasunary from whence I purposed taking a boat to Loch Scavaig. The ride through Glen Sligachan is one of the roughest I ever saw. Path in any definite sense of the word does not exist, the way lying amidst a wilderness of rocks which have fallen from the riven peaks on either side of the glen. The gloomy grandeur of this defile is almost overpowering. Nowhere is the influence of mountains greater; for the Cuchillins are not only lofty, attaining in some instances an elevation of upwards of 3,000 feet, but their forms are particularly solemn and impressive, while their dark grim sides torn, furrowed, and honeycombed by the tempests of ages, awe the beholder. Nor are they generally silent. Every mountain is many-tongued with foaming cataracts, which dash down their sides, making a murmur as rills on high, swelling to thunder tones when, the innumerable water-courses uniting, form the raging torrent which sweeps down the glen.

No dwelling of any kind breaks the spell of savage sterility, the sole occupants of the wastes being deer and a few goats. The first mountain on the right, after passing Sligachan, is Scuir-na-Gillian, and that on the left is Marscow. The first has the reputation of being the highest of the Cuchullins, its height according to Professor James Forbes, being 3,216 feet. We are now fairly in the midst of a congregation of splintered peaks of wonderfully wild forms, some standing clearly out, backed by deep blue sky, others steeped in ever-changing mist which curls round their heads. Half-way to Camasunary you come to the entrance of Hart o'Corrie, a dark purple glen. The jaws of this gloomy gorge are set round with huge rocks; one, which is much larger than the rest, is called the Bloody Stone, from a shepherd having lost his life there. The view up Hart o'Corrie is considered one of the finest of its kind in the Cuchullins, and certainly it would be difficult to find a combination of wilder scenery than it presents. Two miles more, and the gloomy sterility is somewhat relieved by two tiny lakes gleaming in the glen, Loch na Aanan, the Lake of the Ford, and Loch na Crioch, the Lake of the Wooded Valley: a strange misnomer this, you think, when you look around upon the treeless waste; but if you examine the mosses, you will find that the name was not inappropriate, for they are full of the roots and stumps of trees, showing that this now sterile and storm-vexed island was once covered with wood. Indeed, the word Cuchullin is said to be derived from culin, Gaelic for holly which was once abundant in this part of Skye.

Beyond the lakes the glen again contracts and you pass through a grim gorge, Blabhein on the east, not strictly one of the Cuchullins, and Sgor-na-strith – the Hill of Dispute on the west, an outlier of the Cuchullins separating Camasunary from Loch Coruisk. At the mouth of this gorge you come upon Camasunary, a little oasis in the desert, where the storm-stricken traveller will find shelter and a shake-down in a farmhouse at the head of a sandy bay. Not far from the farm is an establishment for reclaiming drunkards, where it is to be presumed the total abstinence system can be enforced with complete success. The farmer is proprietor of one small boat, which fortunately I found disengaged, and hiring it and four men, I left my pony in charge of the guide and embarked for Loch Scavaig. The wind, which was blowing from the west, swept in fitful gusts through the Sound of Soa and the gorges of the Cuchullins, which tower in grisly grandeur round the head of Scavaig Bay. No amateur boating will do here, and it was easy to see that my men, experienced as they were in the navigation of these stormy waters, were frequently perplexed by the furious blasts which often blew at the same moment from every point of the compass.

My boatmen landed me near the mouth of the river that dashes brawling into the bay, and assuring me that I could not miss the way to Loch Coruisk, I started for the famous Lake. No indeed, you cannot miss the way, for you have but to scramble about 300 yards over rocks to see the gloomy lake. The distance between this and Loch Scavaig is about three-quarters of a mile, and the whole way lies amidst huge rocks tossed about in wild disorder. At length I stood on the shores of Loch Coruisk, and it needed but a glance to see that its wonders have not been exaggerated.

It is rather an arduous undertaking to go round Loch Coruisk. The circuit is between two and three miles, and with the exception of a little grassy plateau at the head of the lake, the

sides consist of great rocks, among and over which you have to
worm your way. The circuit occupied me more than two hours,
but I was in no hurry to accomplish the undertaking. For,
besides the succession of wonderful scenes that present themselves as you advance – now passing beneath tremendous
precipices dipping into the lake, and now climbing over rocks
out of which houses might be fashioned, you cannot fail to be
struck by the remarkable character and forms of the rocks.
These are very peculiar, so much so, indeed, that although you
may hold all the 'ologies in supreme contempt, do not, I pray
you, think of visiting the Cuchullins without making yourself, to
some degree, acquainted with the geological features of those
mountains, which will greatly enhance the pleasure of your visit.
For you are not only in the presence of some of the most
sublime scenery in this varied world, but also of wonderful
phenomena.

Beasts of Prey
John Colquhoun

At one time *the* eagle of Skye was the White-tailed Sea Eagle but
systematic slaughter culminated towards the end of the nineteenth century in its complete extermination in the island. This
account by the keen sportsman and student of natural history,
John Colquhoun (1805–85) appeared in *Blackwood's Magazine*
in 1862. Just as the modern tourist takes his car, so Colquhoun
took a horse and a dog-cart to Skye. He embarked on the
paddle steamer at Oban and, landing at Portree, drove all round
the island until eventually he arrived in the north end:

The mists were sweeping across the mountain-range of
Quirang when we summoned our guide to ascend what he
called 'an awfu' strynge place'. We had hoped that the high
wind would dispel the vapour, but the higher we climbed the
thicker it gathered. On every side terrible ragged pillars sprang
from the gloomy abyss, which yawned with fearful blackness
below. As we crept cautiously up the cliff a small stone slipped
from its bed, and, falling into the mist, we heard it bounding
from point to point, the sound growing fainter and fainter
among the caves below. The receding echoes alone made one
feel dizzy. At length we stood nearly on a level with some of

these needles, as they are called in Gaelic, where the fierce cry of the raven was heard so near as to be almost unnatural, and the reverberating sound of his croak gave us much the same sensation as the fall of the pebble. A detached boulder of one of these rocks looked strangely like a ruined cathedral, where several starlings, quite in character, were rearing their young.

The Quirang range, from its lonely ruggedness, is a favourite resort of the wilder birds and beasts of prey for the purpose of rearing their young. In addition to the peregrine, the raven and the fox there are always several eagles' eyries among the remoter crags. I therefore begged the old keeper, if possible to find me a nest of the sea-eagle, still a deficit in my collection. On his return in the evening he told me that there were three couples on the beat, but that their eyries were not yet discovered. These sea-eagles are neither so rare nor so savage as the golden, but, although more vulture-like in their spirits and tastes, are still destructive and ferocious birds. Their liking for fish and water-fowl makes them choose a range in the neighbourhood of the sea or of a fresh-water loch. They will not scruple to attack a full-grown goose, although I have never been able to prove their power to lift one. Macleod's former gamekeeper lately asked me if I had ever heard of an eagle attacking a goose. Macleod had sent two very fine specimens of a rare kind of goose down to Dunvegan. One of them escaped shortly after, and flew out upon the bay. A large sea-eagle soon attacked it, when the goose resorted to the usual ruse of plunging below water. The eagle, according to custom, circled round awaiting its re-appearance. At length the goose was so completely tired out as to be unable to dive, when it immersed its body in water up to the neck, keeping the head nearly on a level with the sea. As soon as the eagle swooped down, the goose struck straight up with its bill, exactly like a boxer, delivering his blow. This unexpected defence so disconcerted the enemy, that after several attacks he fairly quitted the field, or rather the water. The keeper looked on from the shore, and soon after getting a boat he easily captured the goose, now completely exhausted.

The time for the sea-eagle's fishing is when the warm weather brings its prey to the surface. I have known a shepherd lad secure a good breakfast every day while the eaglets were rearing, simply by watching the feeding hour and robbing the eyrie. Now and then the eagle is foiled in its fishing by striking too deep in the water. In that case the wings flap on the sea, and the heavy body of course comes down on the surface. The bird is unable to rise again, until it swims ashore. This it does very rapidly, for, by using the wings as well as the legs, it appears, like the stormy petrel, almost to run upon the face of the deep. When there are many sea-eagles it is not uncommon to find them in this predicament.

A remnant of the system of clanship
Alexander Smith

What Scott did for the Trossachs was done for Skye by a man modestly named Smith. The son of an artist who designed patterns to be printed on calico, he was of Highland descent and at the age of 28 he married a Highland woman, Miss Flora Macdonald of Ord, a descendant of *the* Flora. In 1865 his book *A Summer in Skye* was published. Based on three holidays in the island, it was part fact, part fiction. Mr. M'Ian, the patriarchal landlord in the book, is a portrait of his own father-in-law. Alexander Smith, poet and essayist, is unremembered now for his Victorian effusions, *Alfred Hagart's Household* or his volume of essays, *Dreamthorp*. But *A Summer in Skye,* even after more than a century, remains a remarkable and memorable book. Smith was a poet (when an early work, *A Life Drama* appeared, at least one critic compared him to Keats) and he relished to the full the poetry that he found lying all around him. He certainly glossed over the bleaker sides of mid-nineteenth century life in Skye, but his portrait of the island is both creative and highly readable. Nobody before or since has succeeded quite so well in evoking the spirit of the place. Smith accepted the contemporary *status quo* in Skye, indeed he saw merit in the traditional relationships of landlord, tacksman and cottar. For him a turf hut, however leaky and insanitary, was preferable to an Edinburgh or Glasgow slum. This is Ord house on the southern shore of Loch Eishort in all its feudal splendour:

The house of my friend Mr M'Ian is set down on the shore of one of the great Lochs that intersect the island; and as it was built in smuggling times, its windows look straight down the Loch towards the open sea. Consequently at night, when lighted up, it served all the purposes of a lighthouse: and the candle in the porch window, I am told, has often been anxiously watched by the rough crew engaged in running a cargo of claret or brandy from Bordeaux. Right opposite, on the other side of the loch, is the great rugged fringe of the Cuchullin hills; and lying on the dry summer grass you can see it, under the influence of light and shade, change almost as the expression of a human face changes. Behind the house the ground is rough and broken, every hollow filled, every knoll plumaged with birches, and between the leafy islands, during the day, rabbits scud continually, and in the evening they sit in the glades and wash their innocent faces, A mile or two back from the house a glen opens into soft green meadows, through which a stream flows; and on these meadows Mr M'Ian, when the weather permits, cuts and secures his hay.

When, nearly half-a-century ago, Mr M'Ian left the army and became a tacksman, he found cotters on his farm, and thought their presence as much a matter of course as that limpets should be found upon his rocks. They had their huts, for which they paid no rent; they had their patches of corn and potato ground, for which they paid no rent. There they had always been, and there, so far as Mr M'Ian was concerned, they would remain. He had his own code of generous old-fashioned ethics, to which he steadily adhered; and the man who was hard on the poor, who would dream of driving them from their places in which they were born, seemed to him to break the entire round of the Commandments. Consequently the huts still smoked on the hem of the shore and among the clumps of birch-wood. The children who played on the green when he first became tacksman grew up in a process of time, and married; and on these occasions he not only sent them something on which to make merry withal, but he gave them – what they valued more – his personal presence; and he made it a point of honour, when the ceremony was over, to dance the first reel with the bride. When old men or children were sick, cordials and medicines were sent from the house; when old man or child died, Mr M'Ian never failed to attend the funeral. He was a Justice of the Peace; and when disputes arose amongst his own cotters, or amongst the cotters of others – when, for instance, Katy M'Lure accused Effie M'Kean of stealing potatoes; when

Red Donald raged against Black Peter on some matter relating
to the sale of a dozen lambs; when Mary, in her anger at the
loss of her sweetheart, accused Betty (to whom said sweetheart
had transferred his allegiance) of the most flagrant breaches of
morality – the contending parties were sure to come before my
friend; and many a rude court of justice I have seen him hold at
the door of his porch. Arguments were heard pro and con,
witnesses were examined, evidence was duly sifted and weighed,
judgement was made, and the case dismissed; and I believe
these decisions gave in the long run as much satisfaction as
those delivered in Westminster or the Edinburgh Parliament-
House. Occasionally, too, a single girl or shepherd, with whose
character liberties were being taken, would be found standing at
the porch-door anxious to make oath that they were innocent of
the guilt or the impropriety laid to their charge. Mr M'Ian
would come out and hear the story, make the party assert his
or her innocence on oath, and deliver a written certificate to
the effect that in his presence, on such and such a day, so and
so had sworn that certain charges were unfounded, false, and
malicious. Armed with this certificate, the aspersed girl or
shepherd would depart in triumph. He or she had passed
through the ordeal by oath, and nothing could touch them
farther.

Mr M'Ian paid rent for the entire farm; but to him the
cotters paid no rent, either for their huts or for their patches of
corn and potato ground. But the cotters were by no means
merely pensioners – taking, and giving nothing in return. The
most active of the girls were maids of various degree in Mr
M'Ian's house; the cleverest and strongest of the lads acted as
shepherds, &c.; and these of course received wages. The grown
men amongst the cotters were generally at work in the south, or
engaged in fishing expeditions, during the summer; so that the
permanent residents on the farm were chiefly composed of old
men, women, and children. When required, Mr M'Ian
demands the services of these people just as he would the
services of his household servants, and they comply quite as
readily. If the crows are to be kept out of the corn, or the cows
out of the turnip-field, an urchin is remorselessly reft away
from his games and companions. If a boat is out of repair, old
Dugald is deputed to the job, and when his task is completed,

he is rewarded with ten minutes' chat and a glass of spirits up at the house. When fine weather comes, every man, woman and child is ordered to the hay-field, and Mr M'Ian potters amongst them the whole day, and takes care that no one shirks his duty. When his corn or barley is ripe the cotters cut it, and when the harvest operations are completed, he gives the entire cotter population a dance and harvest-home. But between Mr M'Ian and his cotters no money passes; by a tacit understanding he is to give them house, corn-ground, potato-ground, and they are to remunerate him with labour.

Mr M'Ian, it will be seen, is a conservative, and hates change; and the social system by which he is surrounded wears an ancient and patriarchal aspect to a modern eye. It is a remnant of the system of clanship. The relation of cotter and tacksman, which I have described, is a bit of antiquity quite as interesting as the old castle on the crag – nay, more interesting, because we value the old castle mainly in virtue of its representing an ancient form of life, and here is yet lingering a fragment of the ancient form of life itself. You dig up an ancient tool or weapon in a moor, and place it carefully in a museum: here, as it were, is the ancient tool or weapon in actual use. No doubt Mr M'Ian's system has grave defects: it perpetuates comparative wretchedness on the part of the cotters, it paralyses personal exertion, it begets an ignoble contentment: but on the other hand it sweetens sordid conditions, so far as they can be sweetened, by kindliness and good services. If Mr. M'Ian's system is bad, he makes the best of it, and draws as much comfort and satisfaction out of it, both for himself and for the others, as is perhaps possible.

Flaming in the morning light
Robert Buchanan

In the field of mellifluous verbiage Robert Buchanan had few peers. Poet of nature and romantic novelist (his *St. Abe and His Seven Wives – A Tale of Salt Lake City,* was a Victorian best-seller), Buchanan's every patch was purple, and he rained clichés over Skye with joyous abandon. If a place didn't strike a poetic chord it was dismissed out of hand: 'Portree is the capital of Skye, and like all Highland capitals is dreary beyond endurance and without single feature of interest.' On the other hand something as awe-inspiring as Loch Coruisk was greeted without reservation: 'Shakespeare with his faultless vision would not have failed to see Coruisk as it is, and to picture it in true emotional colours, but perhaps only Shelley, of all our poets, could have felt it to the true spiritual height, and blended it into music, thought and dream.'

In 1873 Buchanan published a book called *The Hebrid Isles*. It was ripe with hyperbole and beautiful hand-crafted prose.

The British lover of beauty wanders far, but we question if he finds anywhere a picture more exquisite than opens out, vista after vista, among these wondrous Isles. Here year after year they lie almost neglected, seen only by the hard-eyed trader and the drifting seaman; for that mosaic being, the typical tourist, seldom quits the inner chain of mainland lakes, save, perhaps, when a solitary Saturday Reviewer oozes dull and bored out of the mist at Broadford or Portree, takes a rapid glare at the chilly Cuchullins, and, shivering with enthusiasm, hurries back to the South. When day broke, red and sombre, we were off Hunish Point, and saw on every side of us the basaltic columns of the coast flaming in the morning light, and behind us, in a dark hollow of a bay, the ruins of Duntulm Castle, grey and forlorn. The coast views here were beyond expression magnificent. Tinted red with dawn, the fantastic cliffs formed themselves into shapes of the wildest beauty, rain-stained and purpled with shadow, and relieved at intervals by slopes of emerald, where the sheep crawled. . . . The whole coast from Aird point to Portree forms a panorama of cliff-scenery quite unmatched in Scotland. Layers of limestone dip into the sea, which washes them into horizontal forms, resembling gigantic slabs of white and grey masonry, rising sometimes stair above stair, water-stained, and hung with many-coloured weed; and on these slabs stand the dark cliffs and spiral columns: towering into the air like the fretwork of some Gothic temple, roofless to the sky; clustered sometimes together in black masses of eternal shadow; torn open here and there to show glimpses of shining rowans sown in the heart of the stone, or flashes of torrents rushing in silver veins through the darkness; crowned in some places by a green patch on which the goats feed small as mice and twisting frequently into towers of most fantastic device, that lie dark and spectral against the grey background of the air.

All our facilities were soon engaged in contemplating the Storr, the highest part of the northern ridge of Skye, terminating in a mighty insulated rock or monolith which points solitary to heaven, two thousand three hundred feet above the sea, while at its base rock and crag have been torn into the wildest forms by the teeth of earthquakes, and a great torrent leaps foaming into the Sound. As we shot past, a dense white vapour enveloped the lower part of the Storr, and towers, pyramids, turrets, monoliths were shooting out above it like a supernatural city in the clouds. At every hundred yards the coast presented some new form of perfect loveliness.

We were now in smooth water. The red dawn had grown into a dull grey day, and the wind was coming so sharp off the land that we found it necessary to take in a reef. We had scarcely beaten into Portree, in the teeth of most severe squalls, when the bad weather began in earnest with some clouds from the north-west, charged like mighty artillery with wind and rain. Snug at our anchorage, we smiled at the storm, and heartily congratulated ourselves that it had not caught us off the perilous heads of Skye.

And here is the ultimate hyperbole. After a long walk from Sligachan, Buchanan stood looking down on the great romantic heart of the Cuchullins, Coruisk:

Below there was a glimpse of the Lone Water, glassy calm and black as ebony. A few steps downward, still downward, and the golden day was dimming into shadow. Coming suddenly on Loch Coruisk, I seemed in a moment surrounded with twilight. I paused close to the corry, on a rocky knoll, with the hot sun in my eyes; but before me the shadows lay moveless – not a glimmer of sunlight touched the solemn Mere – everywhere the place brooded in its own mystery, silent, beautiful and dark. Coming abruptly on the shores of this loneliest of lakes, I had passed instantaneously from sunlight to twilight, from brightness to mystery, from the gladsome stir of the day to a silence unbroken by the movement of any created thing. Every feature of the scene was familiar to me – I had seen it in all weathers, under all aspects – yet my spirit was possessed as completely, as awe-stricken, as solemnized, as when I came thither out of the world's stir for the first time. The brooding desolation is there for ever. There was no sign to show that it had ever been broken by a human foot since my last visit. Perpetual twilight, perfect silence, terribly brooding desolation. Though there are a thousand voices on all sides – the voices of winds, of wild waters, of shifting crags – they die away here into a heart-beat. See! down the torn cheeks of all those precipices tear headlong torrents white in foam, and each is crying, though you cannot hear it. Only one low murmur, deeper than silence, fills the dead air. The black water laps silently on the dark claystone shingle of the shore. The cloud passes silently, far away over the melancholy peaks.

As one paces up the aisle of some vast temple, I walked thither, threading my way among gigantic boulders, which in some wild hour have been torn loose and dashed down from the heights, I felt dwarfed to the utter insignificence of a pigmy, small as a mouse crawling on the pavement of the great cathedral at Cologne.

Trusting in the barometer, we held on
Sheriff Nicolson

On 6 September 1874 Alexander Nicolson, the famous Sheriff Nicolson of Skye, became the first man to climb Sgurr Dubh na Da-Bheinn, 3,069 ft. high, and one of the two peaks of Sgurr a Mhadaidh-Ruaidh. Nicolson was pushing fifty at the time and this was undoubtedly his most daunting mountaineering feat. He described the experience in Dickens's magazine *Good Words*, in 1875:

Sgurr Dubh is one of the most formidable of the Coolin peaks, and was reputed 'inaccessible'. The ascent of it, or rather the descent, was, on the whole, the hardest adventure I have had among these hills. I came over with a friend from Sligachan to Coruisk, and, after visiting the young artists in their curious habitation, we commenced the ascent about four in the afternoon from the rocks above Scavaig. Considering that the sun was to set that evening about seven o'clock, it would have been extreme folly to have attempted such an excursion so late in the day, had not the barometer 'set fair', and the night been that of full moon, of which we wished to take advantage for a full moonlight view of Coruisk.

The ascent is a very rough one, up the corrie between Sgurr Dubh and Garsveinn, and partly along the banks of the 'Mad Stream'. This corrie, well named the 'Rough Corrie' (Garbh Choire), is full of enormous blocks of stone of a very volcanic appearance, many of them of a reddish colour and cindery surface. About half-way up we were overtaken by a shower of rain and took shelter for a while under a ledge of rock. When it cleared a little we saw that the ridge above was covered with mist, but trusting in the barometer, we held on, expecting that by the time we got to the top the mist would have passed away, as it did. The last quarter of the ascent was very hard work and not quite free of danger. It was about seven when we found ourselves on the summit, a very narrow rocky ridge, but covered at the highest point with a thick bed of green spongy moss. The rock is very dark in hue, blacker than usual, whence the name of the peak. We had not much time to admire the view, as the sun had just set behind the black battlements, though we hoped to have twilight to last us to the bottom of the corrie on the other side. It did suffice to light us to the 'first floor', but no more, and that we found no joke. The descent was tremendously blocked with huge stones, and the tarn at the bottom of the corrie is surrounded with them. About half-way down we came to a place where the invaluable plaid came into use. My companion, being the lighter man, stood above with his heels well set in the rock, holding the plaid, by which I let myself down the chasm. Having got footing, I rested my back against the rock, down which my lighter friend let himself slide till he rested on my shoulders. This little piece of gymnastics we had to practise several times before we got to the bottom of the glen above Coruisk. But there were, I think, two or three distinct floors between the first and the last.

From eight to half-past ten we descended, in almost total darkness, for though the moon rose, about nine, and we could see her mild glory in the depths below, we were all the way down in the deep shadow of the peak behind us. Most of the way was among shelving ledges of rock, and in one place it seemed to me that there was no going further, for there was no apparent outlet from the environment of rocks except down a dark gully, over which a stream descended in a small cascade. The thought of passing the night there was not pleasant, and we tried in all directions before we ventured on the experiment of wriggling down the wet rock, in a perfectly vermicular manner, and scrambled round the edge of the waterfall on to something that could be called *terra firma*. I certainly never in the same space of time went through so much severe bodily exercise as in that descent from Sgurr Dubh to Coruisk. My very finger tops were skinned from contact with the rough-grained rock. But the difficulties of the descent were compensated for when we got, with thankful hearts, into the full flood of the moonlight on the last floor, the valley above Coruisk.

A slight moistening in the eyes
MacIain Mor

This account of a visit to Skye some time in the late nineteenth century appeared in the *Celtic Monthly* in 1901. It's not possible to deduce exactly when this Arcadian episode occurred but it makes a contrast to some of the accounts of famine and want which figure in this anthology, and Angus MacLeod of Creachban has, for me at least, become a kind of Prospero figure as he appears in this vivid account recalled by MacIain Mor:

Having arrived in Portree on a lovely summer's evening , my two friends and I resolved on the following day to visit that grandest and most desolate of Scottish mountain lochs, Loch Coruisk. Carrying our lunch in our pockets we took coach to Sligachan hotel. Scorning the services of the guides we at once set out on foot with only a hand map to show the way. After an exhausting tramp we at length struck Loch Coruisk quite by chance. After lunch and a rest we started on our return. By six o'clock there were still no signs of civilisation, and at eight the awful truth that we were lost on the Cuillin hills burst upon us. Half an hour later, however, just as we had resigned ourselves to a night on the moor, our thoughts were startled by the barking of a dog in the distance, and on our running toward the direction of the sound, our hearts were gladdened at the sight of a man, probably a shepherd, walking swiftly to the entrance of the glen in which we stood.

When we came up with him we hailed him in English but he shook his head and pointing in the direction in which he was going he made signs for us to follow. Within half an hour we reached the seashore and on turning a sharp corner of rock, came on a cluster of three highland cottages or sheilings. Following our strange guide we entered the central house, and immediately found ourselves in the presence of an old man who must have been over ninety years of age. Our guide spoke some words to him in Gaelic, and then the old man interrupted him by asking us who we were, and where we had come from. On hearing our sad plight he at once offered us beds, and made us welcome to all that his house contained.

After partaking of his hospitality we ascended a ladder after our old friend and found ourselves in a loft or garret. The beds, seven in number, seemed like long boxes filled with the soft tips of the heather plant, Worn out as we were, we immediately wrapped ourselves in the plaids provided by our host, and were soon in the land of dreams.

Next morning when we descended the ladder, the only occupant of the kitchen was an elderly woman who kindly provided us with the best hospitality of the house, and in answer to our questions told us that the place was known as the 'Creachban' on the south coast of Skye and that it had been in possession of the family for over two hundred years. The old man who received us, the head of the family, was ninety-eight years of age and was grandson to one Donald MacLeod who fought as a youth for Prince Charlie at Culloden. Having finished our meal we went out on to the beach where we found old Angus MacLeod surrounded by eight stalwart men, who he introduced to us as his sons. Two of them wore the uniform of a Highland regiment and were on furlough, two more wore kilts of the MacLeod tartan, being in the service of their chief at Dunvegan. The others were fishers and crofters and with their wives and children occupied the other houses we had noticed.

We now informed old Angus that we would like to return to Portree, but this he would not hear of insisting that we should stay for a day or two. It appeared that once a year all his family who could do so repaired to his home and for a week high holiday was kept. We willingly assented and one of the sons told the

weekly carrier to notify the hotel folks at Portree of our where-
abouts. Thereafter we spent the day in a neighbouring haugh,
the whole family competing in such sports as putting the stone,
tossing the caber, running, leaping and wrestling. In the evening
we had dancing to the strains of the bagpipes played by Old
Angus who had been taught by the MacCrimmons when a lad.

On the following day we were shown the family treasures
which were kept in a sort of strong room with heavily barred
windows. These were chiefly old Highland weapons, but silver
and gold crooks, *sgian dubhs* and brooches testified that the
present family were not lacking in accomplishments, these
trophies having been won at various Celtic gatherings. The most
prized of all, however, was a Lochaber axe carried by their
ancestor in the "Forty-five' and an armchair and clay pipe used
by the young prince when he visited their hut in his wanderings.
These relics were in good preservation and Ranald, the younger
son, told me that seven years ago his father threw a curio dealer
bodily into the loch who had come all the way from London to
purchase them at any price. It was after this event that his father
had the iron bars placed across the windows. The following day
we spent fishing, while between searching for sea birds' nests,
shinty, hill climbing and sketching, the hours sped swiftly away.
Each of us made a watercolour sketch of the rustic cottages and
when we presented a copy to the head of each household, their
delight knew no bounds. In return they gave each of us a beautifully carved snuff mill. Mine is before me as I write and I have
no more valued possession. The Gaelic words carved on it mean
'A friend in the wilderness', and I never look at it but I think of
those Celtic friends of ours in their lonely Highland home. On
the following Monday we took our departure from Creachban.
The soldier sons, Angus and Donald, were going to join their
regiment at Edinburgh so we had their company all the way
south. Having said goodbye to the old patriarch and his family,
we were escorted as far as Sligachan by two of his sons with
their bagpipes. And then with many assurances of goodwill and
friendship we parted.

Late that evening the lofty peaks of Skye were but clouds
on the horizon and as we sat on deck looking towards them I
could not but notice a slight moistening in the eyes of Donald,
the youngest of the soldier brothers, whose home and loved

relations were now far behind and whose hopes in the future were to be shattered by his untimely and noble death on the rugged slopes of Dargai.

In capital trim for dinner
Malcolm Ferguson

In great contrast to the poetic traveller Robert Buchanan is Malcolm Ferguson, or Calum Macfhearhais as he always signed his photograph. These featured him, in his mid-sixties with a long flowing white beard, leaning on a Harry Lauder stick, a thumb in the ticket pocket of his tweed waistcoat, fully kilted and glengarried, besporraned and very much the Highlander. First published in the columns of the *Ayr Observer*, Ferguson's *Rambles in Skye* (which took place in the summer of 1882) are the sort of account that might have been written by an army officer on manoeuvres. His visit to the Quiraing was made of course, long before the days of the Staffin Road. The trip was laborious and almost obligatory for every tourist who visited the island.

The following morning (Monday) we started immediately after breakfast for the Quiraing. It was a beautiful, bright bracing morning. We got a very creditable turn-out, including a most intelligent and respectable-looking driver, a pair of good horses and waggonette. Our party consisted of half-a-dozen, two married couples – one of the couples enjoying their honeymoon – another gentleman and myself. Some four miles from Portree the Uig road forks off from the Dunvegan road to the right, at the head of Loch Snizort and winds along, overlooking the Loch all the way, passing the parish church and the manse of Snizort.

After a very pleasant drive of about 15 miles, we arrived at the Uig hotel – Mr. Urquart proprietor – where we had lunch, and a fresh team of horses for the rest of the journey. On leaving the hotel the road winds down a long steep brae, and is thence carried across a deep ravine, through which a considerable mountain stream comes tumbling down over a series of waterfalls. At the mouth of the deep indented gully stood for long the last resting-place of the hamlet's dead, but during a most memorable spate or flood which occurred on the 14th

October 1876, nearly the whole of the ancient churchyard was swept clean away and carried out to sea. Only one small corner, with a very few graves, was left. For several weeks afterwards, the beach along either side of the bay was thickly strewn with coffins and human bones etc. The summer residence of Major Fraser – proprietor of the district – which stood on a fine level lawn lower down, close to the beach, was also suddenly swept away. A large number of bridges were carried away, rivers broke through their old channels, and a vast amount of damage was done to roads etc. No such destructive spate has ever been witnessed by any of the oldest inhabitants now living in the locality.

After a drive of over seven or eight miles, we reached the point where the footpath for Quiraing strikes off the carriage road, and there were found a regiment of guides in waiting, and a more rustic, arab-looking squad we had rarely ever seen anywhere before, of various age and sizes from the barefooted, bonnetless, kilted laddie, to the weather-beaten, wrinkled, hard-featured old man of three score or more, none of whom could speak a syllable of English. The only words they seemed to have mastered so far, was "Twa shillans, twa shillans'. The oldest man, when he observed one of our party making a halt to gaze around one of the most striking scenes of the kind to be seen in the three kingdoms, had always the same stereotyped phrase, 'Fery pretty whatever'. We had been repeatedly advised not to engage them, as they were usually considered regular pests, so we refused to engage any of them. However, the whole squad joined our party, probably guessing that before we proceeded very far their services and assistance might be gladly accepted, which turned out to be quite correct.

As we proceeded the rough and rather indistinct path goes along the face of a very steep declivity, with overhanging precipices on our left and at some parts we had to pick our way over a *débris* of stones which had toppled down from the lofty cliffs above. We won't soon forget the singularly unique picture presented by our party, numbering in all rather more than a score, as we marched cautiously and slowly in single file, the guides pretty well mixed amongst us, a few of the kilted laddies taking the lead.

About a mile and a half more or less from the start, we

reached the most critical and dangerous part of the climb, where the path takes an abrupt bend to the left, and goes up through a very steep, slippery, narrow pass or gateway to the famous 'Quiraing Table'. On either side a perpendicular face of rugged precipices of huge columns of basalt and massive fragments of fluted rock rise sheer up in lofty inaccessible peaks, guarded at the entrance by a colossal, hoary sentinel in the shape of an isolated spiral column of finely tapered bare rock, 130 feet high, called the 'Needle'. On gaining the summit of the narrow gap, we landed on a beautiful green, grassy knoll. The singular and remarkable picture presented to our gaze is not very easily described.

It consists of a spacious circular opening, with an elevated verdant platform in the centre, several hundred yards in circumference (about 300 by 200 feet), covered with a close spongy sward, and surrounded on every side by lofty pinnacled cliffs. After crossing a deep moat or gully, we soon gained the top of the 'Table', from which, through a series of openings or gaps in the encircling towering bare peaks, a wide and interesting view is obtained of the outline of a long stretch of the Ross and Sutherland mountains, away towards Cape Wrath, the Lewis, Harris, etc., across the Minch, and looking almost sheer down on the bare-rockbound little island of Rona, Raasay etc. The secluded, out-of-the-way little hamlet of Steinschol, is seen close to the sea-beach, a couple of miles or so immediately below. There is a fine spring well gushing out from the face of the rock, a few steps from the edge of the 'Table', a draught of which we relished exceedingly after our long toilsome climb.

During the visit of the ex-Empress of the French and her son, the late Prince Imperial, to Skye in 1872, they both accomplished the climb to the Quiraing, without, I have been told, much difficulty or apparent fatigue. We got back to the Uig Hotel in capital trim for dinner, and found an excellent spread prepared for us and laid with as much taste as we could expect to see in the very best hotels in Scotland. We got back to Portree at 11 p.m.

The eagles are not numerous
Temple Bar

This unsigned account of the Cuillins in winter is datelined

Sligachan, 8 January 1883 and appeared the following June in the *Temple Bar*. What the author was doing there, apart from having a rest, he doesn't say:

I took advantage of the weather by borrowing a stout stick from Mr. Butters this morning, and setting out for the summit of Bruch-na-Frea, accompanied by two dogs which always attach themselves to visitors, a Skye and a spaniel, whose names as far as I can make out seem to be Funach and Chunach. Funach, however, not seeming equal to a long walk, had to be ordered home, but Chunach insisted on ascending to the summit, and frightening me by the most reckless behaviour on the frozen slopes of snow. These frozen slopes render Scuir-na-Gillean, which is easy enough for a good climber in summer, almost inaccessible in winter; but the view from its neighbour peak is quite as fine as its own. I started by the path leading past the gamekeeper's cottage towards Glen Brittle, and reached the top of the pass without much toil. The exhilaration of the keen air of January is in strong contrast with that of August, and the loneliness was more complete. Indeed, when I was last here in the August of 1881, the place could hardly be called lonely at all. The congress of doctors had taken place in London, and after that event most of the doctors seemed to have come to Skye. At any rate, I had left an English doctor with a sprained foot at the Inn; I met a lady student from Paris in the Glen; and I encountered a German doctor at the very top of Scuir-na-Gillean, devouring a sandwich. Now, however, I reflected that if I sprained my own ankle, there would be no doctor available nearer than Portree. From the top of the pass I proceeded to climb along the ridge towards the summit looking down on the right into Corrie-na-Crich and the Thunderer Corrie, over which I had in summer seen the glorious arch of a rainbow spanning its iron sides of plated mail. A few miles on in that direction stands the lonely house of the gentleman who 'farms' the whole range of the Cuchullins, who told me that the winter in Skye was often a weary time, when patience was the only resource for the farmer. He has himself shot more than thirty eagles on the hills, and when I remonstrated with him on the slaughter, he declared that a pair of eagles took one of his lambs every day, and he could not afford them the tribute any longer. The result is that eagles are not numerous, and one cannot often see a sight which I saw at Easter four years ago on the hills round Coruisk. For there I was lucky enough to see a battle-royal between a pair of eagles and a regular mob of ravens, which by repeated attacks and buffetings fairly succeeded in driving the eagles off the field. These ravens are quite as great a nuisance to the farmers. They make their nests among the Cuchullins, and make descents upon the surrounding country, even flying over to the Isle of Rum, there to peck the eyes from the unprotected lambs. But to-day there were no eagles to be seen, and hardly even a raven. The solitude was complete, and I was glad of the company of Chunach the spaniel. I reached the top, and looked down into Lota Corrie at my feet, and Harta Corrie lower down. In this latter corrie I remembered the occurrence of a misadventure to an English clergyman who was as keen as Kingsley in the pursuit of fish. He had obtained leave to fish in the stream which flows from Harta Corrie, but had been warned that there were no fish to be found higher than four miles up the stream. Mistaking his directions he plodded past all the fish for four miles through the long heather, and then began to whip the stream. The results of this process were nil, but he persevered almost to the source of the burn, and then fell into it himself; but luckily the water was not deep, and he returned disconsolate to the Sligachan Inn.

Rejoicing in the stillness
Mrs. Gordon Cumming

In the heyday of unrestricted private enterprise the rich would often spend a few summer weeks cruising in the Hebrides, seeing the sights and distributing largesse to the poor. Their yachts were like a glittering commercial for the benefits of Self-help. When one day in September 1885 the three-masted schooner owned by the railway entrepreneur Thomas Brassey sailed into Portree Bay a man who went on board was almost overcome by its opulence. Over 30 crew members and assorted servants waited on Mr. Brassey and his friends. This 530 tons of shimmering brass, dazzling pipeclay and varnish was no unusual sight. Mrs. Gordon Cumming, who herself spent several months yachting in the isles, described how on one occasion a yacht entered Portree bay so huge that it required an attendant steam-tug to service it. As late as the 'thirties some opulent privately owned yachts continued to cruise among the Hebrides, but today those that survive are owned not by wealthy individuals but by international corporations, and are more likely to be cruising the Mediterranean than the Minch.

The lavishly appointed fishing lodges staffed by willing hands, the steam-yacht at anchor in the bay, were seen by the Victorians to be naturally acceptable and naturally desirable, Poverty and destitution existing side by side with profligate wealth, was also a part of the natural scene. If it was the duty of the rich on occasion to relieve the more advanced suffering of the poor it was equally their duty to resist any attempt at disturbing the very pleasant *status quo*. So that a writer like Mrs. Gordon Cumming, although she might comment sympathetically on the poverty which she couldn't help seeing in Skye, was not able to detect any causal relationship between her feather-bedded life in yacht and lodge and the misery which bolstered up her comfort.

Her book, *In the Hebrides*, may be seen as a product of that gracious leisure which the society of her time conferred on the very few at the expense of the many:

To those who make their home in the Isles the possession of a yacht becomes almost a necessity. In the first place, all beauty lies along the sea-board and the visit to a neighbour even on the same island, which may entail a wearisome land journey through dreary country, is often a short and beautiful sail.

So it came to pass that the little fairy *Gannet* flapped her white wings one sunny afternoon, and bade us sail with her over the merry green waves to the opposite coast of Grieshernish, one of the few sheltered nooks where the plantations have actually struggled up to treehood.

Here we found our chief amusement in a wonderful music-room wherein every conceivable variety of musical instrument had its appointed place. It was a quaint fancy of one who had spent his best years on Indian plains, and who had devised this method of shutting out sight and sound of the wild storms and tempests that so often raved round his western home.

We returned to Uig in the evening so well pleased with the

swift, lovely little yacht, that we determined to start at once for a cruise round the coast – a cruise so delightful, that I am utterly at a loss whether to award the palm of real enjoyment to yachting in the Hebrides, or camping in the Himalayas.

Each day we sailed just so far as might seem pleasant, gliding silently over the water, rejoicing in the stillness of our noiseless progress; no jarring sound of wheels; no straining engines, or whirring steam; only the plash of wavelets when we anchored for the night, in some quiet natural harbour, under the lee of some bluff headland, whence we could row close in shore, among all the beautiful cliffs and caves, landing on the small islands, to the astonishment of every species of sea-fowl, and of colonies of rabbits, which last proved a very welcome addition to our larder. One favourite anchorage was just below Duntulm Castle in a clear, green bay, with a pleasant island on one side, where multitudes of large, white-winged gannets make their home, and gathered wonderingly round their namesake. They were sorely puzzled by our intrusion into this, their sanctum; and often as we sat on the brink of the cliff where they had built their nests, they would swoop past us again and again, flapping their great wings within a foot of us, with wild angry cries, as if to drive us away again.

Very pleasant it was in the early morning to land on this little island; and though the smooth grassy slope was drenched with heavy dew, to clamber up to the top, and find oneself overlooking a precipitous rockface, down into the clearest green depths of emerald-tinted waters, only disturbed by the ripple where the top of some broken basalt pillar rises above the surface.

The sleepers in the yacht are now all astir, and as we look down on the picturesque sailors in their blue jerseys and long scarlet knitted caps, all so busy, unfurling the white sails, we know that there is a chance of a move before long. So we hail the wee boat, that has been fetching the morning supply of milk, and practise rowing, till a tune on the pipes announces that breakfast is ready.

Warships in the bay
James Cameron

It is claimed that between 1840 and 1883 the number of families evicted in Skye was 6,940, or taking each family at five, and families were large in those days, a total of 34,700 men, women and children. It was this sort of disregard for the indigenous population that caused John Stuart Blackie in a white heat of fury to write:

> Now o'er the rugged Peasants' cot,
> Once bright with Highland cheer,
> A London brewer shoots the grouse,
> A lordling stalks the deer.
>
> What were your sins, ye simple men,
> That banished from your home,
> You left to deer your fathers' glen,
> And ploughed the salt-sea foam?
>
> Your fault was this, that you were poor,
> And meekly took the wrong,
> While Law, that still should help the weak,
> Gave spurs to aid the strong.

Not everyone was meek. In Glendale feelings ran high when the crofters were forced to pay rents which they couldn't afford. For the first time for 138 years hostile troops were dispatched to Skye. In 1745 they were hunting down and shooting Skyemen who had fought at Culloden; in 1884 no one was hurt and the expedition achieved little beyond exciting indignation in liberal breasts. James Cameron in his *The Old and New Highlands and Hebrides* published in 1912 described how H.M.S. *Assistance* arrived in Portree Bay at noon on Sunday, 17 November.

The appearance of warships in the bay of Portree did not visibly disturb the good people of the town. They looked upon the expedition from the purely commercial point of view, but it was a failure in this respect. The military invasion of Skye was full of promise to the newspapers and a little army of correspondents turned up at Portree. On the Sunday night when the *Assistance* anchored in the bay there were sixteen pressmen from Scotch and English dailies and two artists from illustrated London weeklies putting up in the Portree hotel.

Early on Monday morning the pressmen drove in two waggonettes from Portree to Uig to witness the arrival there of the warships. From Portree to Uig the distance by sea is some 35 miles, and the vessels taking a northeasterly course doubled the extreme northerly point of the island, till Uig bay was reached. Few residents in Uig seemed to be aware that the much-talked-of expedition was approaching. Occasionally an old man or woman came to the door of their small cottar houses, and shielding their eyes with their hands to avert the rays of the bright sun that was shining, gazed with apparent astonishment towards the formidable looking fleet, and retired after a moment into the interior.

Half an hour later a steam launch put off from the *Lochiel* with a boat in tow in which were seated six constables . . .

After some delay a detachment of Marines in full marching order was landed and they made arrangements to spend the night in the Uig schoolhouse:

The late autumn evening closed with the posting of sentries round the village schoolhouse and the gossip of the crofters as to the probable events of the succeeding day. Nothing could have been more striking than the extreme quietude which reigned in Uig throughout the day. The straggling hamlet might be compared to 'The Deserted Village'. The humble cabins of the crofters ensconced upon the hillsides were basking in the warmth of the sun. No sound was to be heard save the rattling of an over-laden cart treading its way over the high road across the hill. The beautiful bay reflected an azure sky spreading itself out into the Atlantic, its surface unruffled by the slightest breeze. Occasionally the clanging of a bell on board ship proclaimed the changing of the watch, and the passing of small boats between the ships told of the bustle on board the fleet. But on shore matters seemed to have fallen into a state of suspended animation, and the beetling cliffs surrounding the bay and rising sheer out of the sea, looked down upon the scene as if in mute wonder at what it all meant.

Next day the expedition went to Staffin, where the agitation broke out so early as 1879. From first to last the most rigorous discipline was observed, and if we had been in the Soudan or had been marching through an Afghan pass no greater caution could have been adopted. Proceeding the main body at a distance of 50 yards was an advance guard of twenty Marine military. Next came the police and higher criminal officials, then the main body of Marine Artillery and Marines. Mounted on a shaggy Skye pony, procured at the inn, rode Lieut.-Colonel Munro, the object of much quiet chaff amongst the men and the few bystanders that lined the thouroughfare at the point of starting.

As we started the gunboat *Forester* and the steamer *Lochiel* weighed anchor and steamed out of the bay northwards on the way to Staffin, there to wait the arrival of the troops proceeding overland. The day was cold and blustering and in the sharp hill breeze the Union Jack floated from the house of Macleod, the local 'Gladstone' and gave rise to comment and speculation.

The expedition covered a great deal of ground, but the prescence of the journalists was an acute annoyance to those in charge:

It was always a mystery to the Sheriff and the little group of satellites revolving round him nightly at the Royal Hotel how the newspaper men were able daily to locate the destination of the flotilla of gunboats, because the start was usually made from Portree Bay under cover of darkness. His lordship always maintained the greatest secrecy concerning those rapid sea movements of his, and laboured under the delusion 'that this time he had baffled the correspondents', but the delusion was always dispelled when he saw them seated on the shore smoking their pipes, waiting patiently for his arrival. It will not injure anyone now to disclose the mystery how the newspaper men procured the information which enabled them never to miss but once the disembarkation of the troops at whatever hour they landed in any part of the island. One of the Sheriff's closest friends who put up with him in the same hotel was bought over with hard cash by two of the correspondents.

This individual came nightly, Nicodemus-like, to the Portree hotel, and disclosed without a twinge of conscience next day's programme of the expeditionary forces. The one night on which he failed was on the occasion of the notorious raid on the township of Herbista. The raid took place at midnight and every house was entered without legal warrant and ruthlessly searched, even to the beds and underneath them. All the men of the village had been warned, and when the police entered the houses they found only women and children asleep. Some of the women fainted, but still the raid proceeded until every house (except one, I believe) was ransacked. News reached the boycotted pressmen before the raiders got back to Portree Bay. They drove to the terror-stricken village and interviewed the heads of every household. The publicity of the brutal details of the raid excited, not only at home but in Canada and Australia, feelings of disgust against a government that could permit such unholy things being done in its name.

Poverty, hunger and misery
J. and E. Pennell

In the late 'eighties Joseph and Elizabeth Pennell, two Americans, published a series of articles about the Hebrides in *Harper's Magazine*. They appeared in book form in 1890 under the title *Our Journey to the Hebrides*. It was, the authors claimed, the most miserable journey they had ever undertaken. Vast areas of land were being converted to deer forests and many crofters were living exclusively on potatoes with occasional fish and, if they were lucky, 'a boll of meal from the destitution fund'. The Pennells, who were profoundly depressed by what they saw, claimed that the people of the islands were 'the most down-trodden on Gods's earth'. It was the sort of generalization which *The Scotsman* dismissed as 'sentimental nonsense . . . culpable misrepresentation . . . amazing impertinence'. Although the articles were highly emotional and painted a scene of almost totally unrelieved gloom, they only echoed much of the evidence which had already been presented to the Napier Commission.

The Pennells saw Skye in terms of almost Marxian simplicity. It was an island where the deer-stalking landowners with

their fancy yachts and shooting lodges had condemned the inhabitants to poverty and starvation:

The real evil is that the Islanders have been ground down and tyrannized over simply to gratify the amusements of their masters . . . one cannot help saying that it is nothing less than infamous that a mere handful of landlords should have controlled the destiny of, and extracted every penny from, the population of these Islands – the people whom they have kept for generations in poverty, not that they might improve the land, but that they might pass their own time in useless idleness and cruel sport.

If perhaps these words sound too strong one might set alongside them the words of Alfred Russell Wallace the distinguished botanist who was working towards a theory of natural selection, independently of, but at the same time as, the even more celebrated Charles Darwin. In 1882 Wallace published *Land*

Nationalisation and his condemnation of the way in which he alleged many owners behaved was absolute:

For a parallel to this monstrous power of the landowner, under which life and property are entirely at his mercy, we must go back to medieval times, or to the days when, serfdom not having been abolished, the Russian noble was armed with despotic authority, while the more pitiful results of this landlord tyranny, the wide devastation of cultivated lands, the heartless burning of houses, the reckless creation of pauperism and misery out of well-being and contentment, could only be expected under the rule of Turkish sultans or greedy and cruel pashas.

The Pennells came to Skye by way of Harris on board the *Dunara Castle* which dropped anchor early one summer morning in Uig Bay. They set off in pouring rain on the long walk to Duntulm, she in her bustle skirt, he in his floppy artist's clothes, both heavily haversacked.

Near Duntulm Castle was a shooting-lodge; on the water a steam-yacht lay at anchor. The slave-driver is found for at least six weeks in the midst of his slaves.

We arrived at the inn about three in the afternoon, drenched and weary. A room was ready for us, a bright fire burning on the hearth. They always expected people to come home wet, the landlord's daughter said. She carried off our wet clothes; she lent me a dress; she brought us hot whiskey and water. One must be thoroughly tired to know what comfort means.

We had our tea with two English maiden ladies of the species one meets in Swiss and Italian pensions. We sat in a well-warmed room at a well-spread table. In the black, smoky huts half-starved men, women, and children were eating dry oatmeal; a few, perhaps, drinking tea with it. This is the extravagance with which the crofters have been reproached. They buy, or rather go into debt for, tea and sugar as well as meal, and therefore their landlords think them prosperous. They have never been so well off before, the Commissioners were told; once they lived on shell-fish throughout the summer. Yes, it was true, a minister of Snizort admitted, they did drink tea. But the people have no milk, now pasture-land has been taken from them. The landlord needed it for his large sheep farms and deer forests. I suppose they should go back to the shell-fish of old. If they have food to eat, why complain of its quality? If this be so, if crofters of to-day, compared to their ancestors, live in luxury, then has the time indeed come when something should be done for them. Who will call them lazy or indifferent who has considered what the life of the Islander has been for generations? The wonder is that he has energy enough to keep on living.

We went the next day to Dunvegan.

The road lay over long miles of moors, with now and then beautiful distant views of the mountains of Harris, but pale blue shadows on the western horizon, and of the high peaks of the Cuchullins, dark and sombre above the moorland.

Here and there at long intervals we came to the wretched groups of cottages we had begun to know so well. Old witch-like women and young girls passed, bent double under loads of peat or seaweed, so heavy that were the same thing seen in Italy, English people would long since have filled columns of *The Times* with their sympathy. As it is, these burdens are accepted as a matter of course, or some times even as but one of the many picturesque elements of Highland life. From one writer one hears of the Skye lassies, half hidden under bundles of heather, stopping to laugh and chatter; from another of Lewis women knitting contentedly as they walked along with creels, bearing burdens that would have appalled a railway porter of the south, strapped to their backs. We saw no smiles, no signs of contentment. On the faces of the strongest women there was a look of weariness and of pain. But perhaps the most pathetic faces in this land of sorrow were those of the children, already pinched and care-worn. I know others who have felt this even as we did. An Englishman who last summer spent a week in Skye has since told us how day after day he and his wife went upon their excursions lunchless, because in the first village to which they came they emptied their luncheon-basket among the half-naked, half-starved children they found there. They could not bear the sight of the hungry little faces.

Dunvegan and the overgrown graves of the Macleod burial ground provided food for further depressing thought; there was the long walk over the moors to Struan and disappointment of arriving at Sligachan:

There was not a room to be had in the inn. It was full of immaculately dressed young ladies and young Oxford men, all with their knickerbockers at the same degree of bagginess, their stockings turned down at the same angle. We might have thought that the landlady objected to tramps when the company was so elegant, had she not offered to put us up in the drawing-room and found places for us at the table-d'hôte luncheon. The talk was all of hotels and lochs and glens and travels. How long have you been in Skye? Is this your first visit? Did you come by Loch Maree? At what hotel did you stay in Oban? but there was not a word about cottages; for there is nothing in Sligachan, or near it, as far as we could see, but this swell hotel, which seemed very good.

Beds in the drawing-room meant to be at the mercy of the

company. We did not hesitate. And still the moors stretched out before us. No one who has not tramped in Skye can imagine its dreariness. In Portree, a miniature Oban, we lost all courage. We might have gone back to Loch Coruisk. We might have tramped to take a nearer view of the Old Man of Storr, which we had already seen in the distance. We might have walked to Armadale, or steamed to Strome Ferry. There were, in fact, many things we could and should have done; but we had seen enough of the miserable life in the islands – those great deserts, with but here and there a lovely oasis for the man of wealth. Our walks had been long; we were tired physically and sick mentally.

And so, early one morning, we took the boat at Portree and steamed back to the main-land; past Raasay, where Dr. Johnson stayed, and where there was a big house with beautiful green lawn and fine woods; past Glenelg, where we should have landed to follow the Doctor's route, but the prospect of a thirty miles' walk to reach the nearest inn made cowards of us; past Armadale, now as when Pennant saw it, 'a seat, beautifully wooded, gracing most unexpectedly this almost treeless tract'; past one island of hills after another; and thus into the sound of Mull, to get a glimpse of Tobermory in sunshine. It was a lovely day; sea and sky and far islands blue, the water like glass; though, before it had come to an end, we had twice fled to the cabin from heavy showers. There were many sight-seers on board, and we could but wonder why. The women read novels, the men went to sleep. But they had done their duty – they had been to Scotland for the holidays; they had probably seen the Quiraing and Dunvegan. But they had not gone our way. The coach roads are those from which the least misery is visible.

There is always something new
Norman Collie

Norman Collie first came to Skye in 1886 to fish, but the fever of climbing quickly took possession of him and from then on every free moment that he could snatch from his university (he was a Professor of Organic Chemistry) was spent amid the Cuillins. He died in Skye during the second world war. This tribute to the hills he loved appeared in the Scottish Mountaineering Club *Journal* in May 1897:

Those who have seen the Coolin from the moors above
Talisker in the twilight; or have watched them on a summer's
evening from Kyle Akin, rising in deep purple velvet, broi-
dered with gold, out of the 'wandering fields of barren foam',
whilst

The charmed sunset linger'd low adown
In the red west;

or lazed away a whole day on the sand beaches of Arisaig point
gazing towards Rum and Skye, lying light blue on the horizon,
and across a sea brilliant in colour as the Mediterranean
amongst the Ionian Islands; or lingered at the head of Loch
Coruisk till the last pale light has faded out of the heavens
behind Sgurr Alasdair, and only the murmur of the streams
breaks the stillness of the night air – those who have thus seen
the Coolin will know that they are beautiful. But to the climber
who wanders in the heart of this marvellous mountain land the
Coolin has more pleasures to offer. He can spend hour after
hour exploring the corries or threading the intricacies of the
broken and narrow rock edges that form so large a part of the
sky-line. From the summits he can watch the mists sweeping up
from below and hurrying over the *bealachs* in tumbled masses of
vapour, or he can dreamily follow the white sails of the boats,
far out to sea, as they lazily make for the outer islands; then
clambering down the precipitous faces he can repose in some
sheltered nook, and listen to the sound of a burn perhaps a

thousand feet below echoed across from the sheer walls of rock
on the other side of the corrie; there is always something new to
interest him, it may be a gully that requires the utmost of his
skill as a mountaineer, or it may be a view of hill, moor, and
loch backed by the Atlantic and the far-off isles of the western
sea. Nowhere in the British Islands are there any rock climbs to
be compared with those in Skye, measure them by what standard you will, length, variety, or difficulty. Should anyone doubt
this, let him some fine morning walk up from the foot of
Coruisk to the rocky slabs at the foot of Sgurr a' Ghreadaidh.
There he will see the bare grey rocks rising out from the heather
not 500 feet above the level of the loch, and these walls, ridges,
and towers of weather-worn gabbro stretch with hardly a break
to the summit of the mountain, 2,800 ft. above him. Measured
on the map it is but half a mile, but that half-mile will tax his
muscles; he must climb up gullies that the mountain torrents
have worn out of the precipices, and over slabs of rock sloping
down into space at an angle that make hand-hold necessary as
well as foot-hold; he must creep out round edges on the faces of
perpendicular cliffs, only to find that after all the perpendicular
cliff itself must be scaled before he can win back again to the
ridge that is to lead him to the topmost peak.

The individuality of the Coolin is not seen in their
summits, which are often almost ugly, but in the colour of the
rocks, the atmospheric effects, the relative largeness and
harmony of the details compared with the actual size of the
mountains, and most of all in the mountain mystery that wraps
them round: not the mystery of clearness, such as is seen in the
Alps and Himalayas, where range after range recedes into the
infinite distance till the white snow peaks cannot be distinguished from the clouds, but in the obscure and secret beauty
born of the mists, the rain, and the sunshine in a quiet and
untroubled land, no longer vexed by the more rude and violent
manifestations of the active powers of nature. Once there was a
time when these peaks were the centre of a great cataclysm;
they are the shattered remains of a vast volcano that ages since
poured its lavas in mighty flood far and wide over the land;
since then the glaciers in prehistoric time have polished and
worn down the corries and the valley floors, leaving scars and
wounds everywhere as a testimony of their power; but now the

fire age and the ice age are past, the still clear waters of Coruisk ripple in the breeze, by the loch-side lie the fallen masses of the hills, and the shattered debris left by the ice, these harbour the dwarf hazel, the purple heather, and the wild flowers, whilst corrie, glen, and mountain-side bask in the summer sunlight.

But when the wild Atlantic storms sweep across the mountains; when the streams gather in volume, and the bare rock faces are streaked with the foam of a thousand waterfalls; when the wind shrieks amongst the rock pinnacles, and sky, loch, and hill-side is one dull grey, the Coolin can be savage and dreary indeed; perhaps though the clouds towards the evening may break, then the torn masses of vapour, tearing in mad hunt along the ridges, will be lit up by the rays of the sun slowly descending into the western sea, 'robing the gloom with a vesture of divers colours, of which the threads are purple and scarlet, and the embroideries flame'; and as the light flashes from the black rocks, and the shadows deepen in the corries, the superb beauty, the melancholy, the mystery of these mountains of the Isle of Mist will be revealed. But the golden glory of the sunset will melt from off the mountains, the light that silvered the great slabs will slowly fail, from out the corries darkness heralding the black night will creep with stealthy tread hiding all in gloom; and last of all, behind the darkly luminous, jagged, and fantastic outline of the Coolins the glittering stars will flash out from the clear sky, no wind will stir the great quiet, only the far-off sound, born of the rhythmic murmur of the sea waves beating on the rock-bound shore of lonely Scavaig, remains as a memory of the storm.

A calm, cold, snow-dazzling morning
D.T. Holmes

In the whole of this anthology there is hardly a mention of winter in Skye. The guide-book writers, the mountaineers, the author-travellers confined their visits to the summer. But one who visited the island in all weathers was a man called Holmes. D. T. Holmes (B.A.) journeyed round the Hebrides for many years lecturing and looking after libraries. His *Literary Tours in the Highlands and Islands of Scotland* is an off-the-beaten-track, out-of-season account of Edwardian life in the Hebrides. On 22

December 1904 Holmes was on his way to Portree:

The summer tourist knows Skye very imperfectly, for he goes there in a commodious steamer and traverses the island at a season when the days are long and the weather benign. No one should vaunt of knowing Skye unless he has seen it in winter also. It is the small *Lochiel* that, in the dark days of December, bears the passengers along the chilly Sound of Sleat, and through the narrows of Raasay, into the haven of Portree. At such a time there is something fearsome and weird in the aspect of the coast, as seen from the cabin window of the brave little boat as she battles and plunges along in the teeth of the north-eastern gale. Her progress is slow, for when passengers are few, Macbrayne wisely economises his coal. The long-stretching hills of Raasay are white from head to foot, and gleam through the darkness of the afternoon vivid and ghostly. As Raasay House, with its lamp-lit windows shining in a snowy recess, is approached, the engines slow down, and through the howl of the wind can be heard the plashing of oars. The broad waves swirl and seethe cruelly around the ferry-boat and toss it about at all angles, up and down, on crest and in trough, till you fear it will end its struggles keel upwards, and send the mailbags down among the mackerel. But the boatmen know their trade, and so do the dripping top-booted seamen of the *Lochiel*.

Amid much running and shuffling and casting of ropes and animated bandying of (I fear) strong expressions in Gaelic sung out upon the night, the ship's ladder is cast down and the boat tied thereto. In a few minutes the transfer of mails is over, the ladder up, and the small boat leaping back to land. A new passenger has come on board and is seen to descend the cabin stairs to unfreeze his fingers over the tiny stove. Half-an-hour's heaving still remains before Portree. A lady who has been on the border-line of squeamishness for the last half hour hurriedly leaves the cabin, probably to see if her luggage is all right. Good news at last for all! Portree is visible, and its lights are twinkling on the height. The moon comes graciously out, silvering the snowy shoulders of Essie Hill. What a contrast is this moonlit haven with its background of terraced lights, to the rough surges outside. Glad indeed is everyone to set foot on the pier and trudge through disregarded slush to the warmth of home or hotel. We are told by our island friends that all Skye is under snow and that the roads are impassable. No mail coach has ventured to Dunvegan for two days and in other directions, the postmen, turned cavaliers, have gone off on horseback with their letters. (Let me say in passing, that a red-bearded Highland postman, clad in post-office livery and seated on a sheltie, is a sight which any artist would go a hundred miles to see). Winter sailing may at times be as pleasant as a cruise in June. At 8 a.m. in the snug cabin the breakfast table, with its tea, ham, eggs, and sausages, is a welcome piece of scenery, and the genial talk of the captain and his colleagues is far better than pepsin as a digestive. After breakfast, a pipe on deck is a necessity. Who that has once seen Ben-na-Caillich all white to the feet and softly veiled with airy mists, but wishes he were a Turner to paint, or a Shelley to sing. The sail from Broadford to Kyle on a calm, cold, snow-dazzling morning is (if one is wrapped and coated well) absolutely majestic. The sun pours, if not warmth, at least light and heat on the hundred bens of the mainland and, the breeze aiding, wakens a multitudinous smile on the glittering face of the cold waters.

Books Worth Reading

Abraham, Ashley, *Rock-climbing in Skye,* Longmans, 1908.
Anderson, G. & P., *Guide to the Highlands and Islands,* Inverness, 1834.
Anderson, I. F., *To Introduce the Hebrides,* Herbert Jenkins, 1933.
Barnett, T. R., *Autumns in Skye, Ross and Sutherland,* John Grant, 1930.
Bond, Charles, *The Hebrides and West Highlands,* James Biggs, 1852.
Bone, Stephen, *The West Coast of Scotland, Skye to Oban,* Faber & Faber, 1952.
Boswell, James, *Journal of a Tour to the Hebrides,* 1785.
Buchanan, Robert, *The Hebrid Islands,* Chatto & Windus, 1873.
Cairncross, A. K., *The Scottish Economy,* Cambridge University Press, 1954.
Cameron, Alexander, *History and Traditions of the Isle of Skye,* 1871.
Cameron, James, *The Old and New Highlands and Hebrides,* Kirkcaldy, 1912.
Campbell, J. G., *Superstitions of the Highlands and Islands,* James Maclehose,
      1900.
   Witchcraft and Second Sight in the Highlands and Islands, James Maclehose,
      1902.
Campbell, J. L. & Hall, T. H., *Strange Things,* Routledge & Kegan Paul, 1968.
Cockburn, Lord, *Circuit Journeys,* 1842.
Collier, Adam, *The Crofting Problem,* Cambridge University Press, 1953.
Darling, Fraser (Ed.), *West Highland Survey,* Oxford University Press, 1955.
Darling, Fraser & Boyd J. M., *The Highlands and Islands,* Collins, 1964.
Dendy, W. C., *The Wild Hebrides,* 1859.
Donaldson, M. E. M., *Wanderings in the Western Highlands and Islands,*
   Alexander Gardner, 1920.
Duckworth, C. & Langmuir G., *West Highland Steamers,* T. Stephenson, 1935.
Ferguson, Malcolm, *Rambles in Skye,* 1885.
Forbes, A. R., *Place-Names of Skye,* Alexander Gardner, 1923.
Forbes, Rev. Robert, *The Lyon in Mourning,* 1746.
Gardner, Arthur, *The Western Highlands,* The Moray Press, 1924.
   The Peaks, Lochs and Coasts of the Western Isles, Witherby, 1924.
Garnett, T., *Tour Through the Highlands and Western Islands,* 1811.
Geikie, Sir Archibald, *Scottish Reminiscences,* James Maclehose, 1904.
Gordon Cumming, C. F., *In the Hebrides,* Chatto & Windus, 1886.
Gordon, Seton, *The Charm of Skye,* Cassell, 1929, etc.
   Highways and Byways, The West Highlands, Birlinn Limited, 1995.

Gregory, Donald, *History of the Western Highlands and Isles,* W. Tait, 1836.

Grierson, Thomas, *Autumnal Rambles among the Scottish Mountains,* 1850.

Haldane, A. R. B., *The Drove Roads of Scotland,* Edinburgh University Press, 1952.

Harvey, W., *The Causes of Distress in the Western Highlands,* 1862.

Harvie-Brown, J. A. & MacPherson, Rev. H. A., *A Fauna of the North-West Highlands and Skye,* Edinburgh, David Douglas, 1904.

Hill, Dr. Birkbeck, *In the Footsteps of Dr. Johnson,* Sampson Low, 1890.

Holmes, D. T., *Literary Tours in the Highlands and Islands of Scotland,* Alexander Gardner, 1909.

Hope-Moncrieff, A. R., *Highlands and Islands of Scotland,* A. & C. Black, 1906.

Humble, B. H., *Tramping in Skye,* Maclellan, 1933.

  The Songs of Skye, Eneas Mackay, 1934.

  The Cuillin of Skye, Robert Hale, 1952.

Hume, P., *Early Travellers in Scotland,* 1891.

Insh, G. C., *Colonists from Scotland,* Oxford University Press, 1956.

Jameson, Robert, *Mineralogy of the Scottish Isles,* 1800.

Johnson, Samuel, *A Journey to the Western Islands of Scotland,* 1774.

Kennedy-Fraser, Marjorie, *The Road to the Isles,* Robert Grant, 1927.

Knox, John, *A Tour Through the Highlands of Scotland,* 1787.

Lamont, Rev. D., *Strath: In Isle of Skye,* Archibald Sinclair, 1913.

Lang, Andrew, *Prince Charles Edward Stuart,* Longmans, 1903.

MacBain, A., *Place-Names in the Highlands and Islands,* Eneas Mackay, 1922.

MacCaskill, Lady, *Twelve Days in Skye,* London, 1852.

MacCulloch, John, *A Description of the Western Isles,* 1819.

MacCulloch, J. A., *The Misty Isle of Skye,* Oliphant, 1910.

McDiarmid, Hugh, *The Islands of Scotland,* Batsford, 1939.

MacDonald, L., *The Past and Present Condition of the Skye Crofters,* Bell and Bain, 1886.

MacGregor, Alasdair Alpin, *Behold the Hebrides,* Chambers, 1925.

  Over the Sea to Skye, Chambers, 1926.

  Skye and the Inner Hebrides, Robert Hale, 1953.

  The Enchanted Isles, Michael Joseph, 1967.

Macintyre, James, *Castles of Skye,* Northern Chronicle Office, Inverness, 1938.

Mackenzie, Alexander, *History of the Highland Clearances,* Alex. Maclaren, 1883.

  The Isle of Skye, A. & W. Mackenzie, 1883.

Mackenzie, Hector Rose, *Yachting and Electioneering,* 1886.

Mackenzie, William, *Skye: Ichodar-Trotternish,* Alex. Maclaren, 1930.

  Old Skye Tales, Alex. Maclaren, 1934.

Mackenzie, W. C., *A Short History of the Scottish Highlands,* Alexander Gardner, 1908.

Maclaren, Moray, *The Highland Jaunt,* Jarrolds, 1954.

Maclean, A. C., *The Islander,* Collins, 1962.

Maclean, Dr. Norman, *The Former Days,* Hodder & Stoughton, 1945.

  Set Free, Hodder & Stoughton, 1949.

MacLeod of MacLeod, Rev. Canon, R. C., *The MacLeods of Dunvegan,* Clan MacLeod Society, 1927.

MacLeod, Kenneth, *The Road to the Isles*, Robert Grant, 1927.

MacLeod, T. F., *Eilean a' Cheo – The Isle of Mist*, Edinburgh, 1917.

MacPherson, Duncan, *Gateway to Skye*, Eneas Mackay, 1946.
  Where I Belong, Eneas Mackay, 1964.

MacQueen, M. A., *Skye Pioneers*, Winnipeg, 1929.

Macrae, Norman, *Highland Second Sight*, George Souter, 1908.

Martin Martin (Gent), *A Description of the Western Islands*, Birlinn Limited, 1995.

Meadows, E. G., *The Skye Scene*, Oliver & Boyd, 1951.

Miller, Hugh, *The Cruise of the Betsey*, Edinburgh, 1858.

Mulock, Thomas, *The Western Highlands and Islands*, 1850.

Munro, R. W., *Monro's Western Isles of Scotland*, Oliver & Boyd, 1961.

Nicholas, Donald, *The Young Adventurer*, Batchworth Press, 1949.

Nicolson, Alexander, *History of Skye*, Alex. Maclaren, 1930.

O'Dell, A. C. & Walton, K., *The Highlands and Islands of Scotland*, Nelson, 1962.

Parker, Dr. Alfred, *The West Highlands and Hebrides*, Cambridge University Press, 1941.

Pennant, Thomas, *A Tour in Scotland and Voyage to the Hebrides*, 1774.

Pennell, J. and E. R., *Our Journey to the Hebrides*, Fisher Unwin, 1890.

Perry, Richard, *I went a-shepherding*, Lindsay Drummond, 1944.

Portree High School Pupils, *Skye '68*.

Prebble, John, *The Highland Clearances*, Secker & Warburg, 1963.

Read, J. T., *Art Rambles in the Highlands and Islands*, Routledge, 1878.

de Saussure, Necker, *A Voyage to the Hebrides*, 1822.

Scott-Moncrieff, George, *The Scottish Islands*, Batsford, 1952.

Simpson, E. Douglas, *Portrait of Skye and the Outer Hebrides*, Robert Hale, 1967.

Southey, Robert, *Journal of a Tour in Scotland in 1819*, John Murray.

Smith, Alexander, *A Summer in Skye*, Birlinn Limited, 1995.

Smith, C. L., *Journal of a Ramble in Scotland*, 1835.

Smith, S. Heckstall, *Isle, Ben and Loch*, Arnold, 1932.

Smout, T. C., *A History of the Scottish People 1560-1830*, Collins, 1969.

Sutherland, Halliday, *Hebridean Journey*, Geoffrey Bles, 1939.

Swire, Otta, *Skye: The Island and its Legends*, Blackie, 1961.
  The Inner Hebrides and their Legends, Collins, 1964.

Teignmouth, Lord, *Sketches of the Coasts and Islands*, 1836.

Thomson, D. C. & Grimble, I. (Ed.), *The Future of the Highlands*, Routledge & Kegan Paul, 1968.

Vallance, H. A., *The Highland Railway*, David & Charles, 1963.

Vining, E. G., *Flora MacDonald*, Geoffrey Bles, 1967.

Walker, John, *Economical History of the Hebrides*, 1808.

Weld, C. R., *Two Months in the Highlands, Orcadia and Skye*, Longmans, 1860.

Wilson, James, *A Voyage Round the Coasts of Scotland and the Isles*, A. & C. Black, 1842.

Wright, J. E. B., *Mountain Days in the Isle of Skye*, Moray Press, 1934.

Some Dates

319

A.D. 1601 Battle of Coire na Creich – MacLeods routed by Macdonalds at this, the last clan fight in Skye

1642 Presbytery of Skye mentioned for the first time. The Rev. Archibald MacQueen appointed minister of Snizort, an office which was to be handed down from father to son for the next 145 years

1654 Publication of Timothy Pont's map of 'The Yle of Skie'

1703 Publication of Martin Martin's *A Description of the Western Isles of Scotland*

1718 First mention of a crofting system in Skye

1722 Flora MacDonald born at Milton, South Uist

1726 Skye divided into seven parochial districts

1745 Prince Charles Edward Stuart occupies Edinburgh and marches south to Derby. Lady Grange dies at Trumpan

1746 The disaster of Culloden, the last time when the clans went into battle under their Chiefs. Prince Charles on the run

1748 The Disarming Act – the military potential of the clans destroyed and the wearing of Highland dress proscribed

1750 Potato introduced into Skye

1755 Population rises to 11,233

1770 Beginnings of emigration. The tacksmen on Lord MacDonald's estate buy 100,000 acres of land in South Carolina. The patriarchal system begins to bleed to death

1772 Thomas Pennant tours Skye with his artist Moses Griffiths

1773 2 September, Johnson and Boswell land at Armadale

1787 The British Fisheries Society builds the village of Stein

1790 Flora MacDonald dies at Peinduin, buried in Kilmuir churchyard. Population: 14,470

1798 Regiment of volunteers raised to defend Skye against a possible French invasion

1799 Surveyors mark out a highway from Kylerhea to Stein through Broadford, Sconser, Bracadale and Dunvegan

1800 Jail built in Portree. First shop in the island built at Kyleakin by Lord Macdonald

1801 Population: 16,000

A.D. 1811   K. Macleay, D.D. publishes an account of the Spar Cave. Road built from Dunvegan to Snizort

1812   Broadford-Ardvasar road completed

1813   Kylerhea-Ardvasar road completed

1814   Walter Scott visits Skye

1815   Armadale Castle designed by Gillespie Graham

1816   Sligachan-Portree road completed

1819   Publication of John MacCulloch's *Description of the Western Isles*. Portree-Uig road completed

1824   Loch Chalum Chille drained in Kilmuir

1827   Alexander (Sheriff) Nicolson born at Husabost

1831   Turner paints Loch Corriskin

1836   Professor J. D. Forbes ascends Sgurr nan Gillean

1837   450 Skye people shipped to Australia

1838   Uig emigrants set sail from Culnacnoc

1840   Borve cleared of crofters

1841   600 shipped from Portree parish to Australia and America. Population: 23,000

1843   The Disruption – Free Church of Scotland formed

1851   £7,200 raised by Sheriff Fraser of Portree to ship 200 emigrants from Skye

1853   Lord Macdonald's factor, Ballingall, extends the deer forest of Sconser and enforces more clearances

1861   Population: 19,000

1865   Publication of the most successful book on Skye ever written, Alexander Smith's *A Summer in Skye*. Common grazing of Ben Lee let to a tenant, an event which was to culminate in the Battle of Braes

1873   Sheriff Nicolson is the first to ascend Sgurr Alasdair

1877   Cloudburst damages large area of Uig

1881   Population: 17,700

1882   Battle of Braes, warships sent to the lochs of Skye

1883   Gladstone appoints a Royal Commission

1886   Crofters' Holdings Act

1894   King Edward Pier built at Uig for £9,000

1900   Population: 13,800

Isle of Skye Mileage Chart

61	63	36	45	25	22	50	32	60	17	ARMADALE
44	46	19	28	11	8	33	15	43	BROADFORD
30	39	24	22	54	51	27	58	DUNVEGAN
59	61	34	43	26	23	48	ELGOL
39	41	14	23	44	41	GLENBRITTLE
52	54	27	36	11	KYLEAKIN
55	57	30	39	KYLERHEA
16	18	9	PORTREE
25	27	SLIGACHAN
9	STAFFIN
UIG

Courtesy of the Automibile Association

MAP OF SKYE

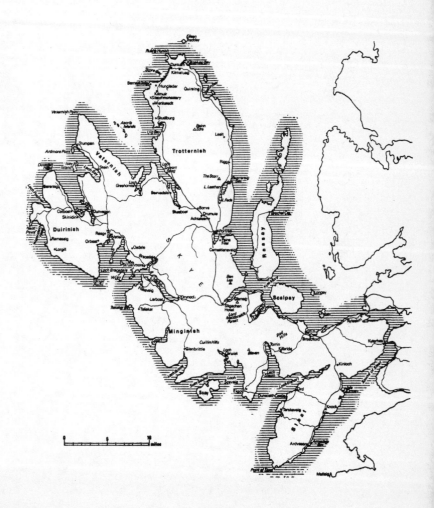